D1429782

Street Addressing and the Management of Cities

Catherine Farvacque-Vitkovic, Lucien Godin, Hugues Leroux, Florence Verdet, and Roberto Chavez

WORLD BANK
Washington, D.C.

© 2005 The International Bank for Reconstruction and Development / The World Bank
1818 H Street, NW
Washington, DC 20433
Telephone 202-473-1000
Internet www.worldbank.org
E-mail feedback@worldbank.org

All rights reserved.

1 2 3 4 08 07 06 05

The findings, interpretations, and conclusions expressed herein are those of the author(s) and do not necessarily reflect the views of the Board of Executive Directors of the World Bank or the governments they represent.

The World Bank does not guarantee the accuracy of the data included in this work. The boundaries, colors, denominations, and other information shown on any map in this work do not imply any judgment on the part of the World Bank concerning the legal status of any territory or the endorsement or acceptance of such boundaries.

Rights and Permissions
The material in this work is copyrighted. Copying and/or transmitting portions or all of this work without permission may be a violation of applicable law. The World Bank encourages dissemination of its work and will normally grant permission promptly.

For permission to photocopy or reprint any part of this work, please send a request with complete information to the Copyright Clearance Center, Inc., 222 Rosewood Drive, Danvers, MA 01923, USA, telephone 978-750-8400, fax 978-750-4470, www.copyright.com.

All other queries on rights and licenses, including subsidiary rights, should be addressed to the Office of the Publisher, World Bank, 1818 H Street NW, Washington, DC 20433, USA, fax 202-522-2422, e-mail pubrights@worldbank.org.

Photo credits:
Cover: ©Austrian Archives/CORBIS
Page 10: V. Mihailovic. Pages 19, 127: D. Diallo, Cellule Guinée. Pages 40, 121, 128, 133, 173, 182, 198: T. Lahlou, Cellule nationale du Mozambique. Others: Groupe Huit.

Drawings:
Page 198 : B. Gnoumou, Cellule Burkina Faso. Others: Groupe Huit.

On the cover, an astrolabe, one of the first tools of referencing, and an addressing map.

ISBN 0-8213-5814-4   e-ISBN 0-8213-5816-2

Library of Congress Cataloging-in-Publication Data has been applied for.

Contents

Boxes
Chapter 1
Chapter 2

Foreword

The most spectacular change in sub-Saharan Africa over the last few decades has been the dramatic demographic shift from rural areas to cities. Over 80% rural at independence, the region will soon be nearly 50% urbanized.

As cities in the developing world have confronted this demographic explosion, urban management has become all the more challenging amid the current trend toward decentralization. With little experience in urban management, local governments have often been unable to develop the resources they need to deal with urban growth.

Against this backdrop, systems for identifying streets, buildings, and plots have simply been unable to keep up with the pace of urbanization. As a result, 50% or more of the city streets in these countries have no names or addresses, and the problem is particularly acute in the poorest neighborhoods.

This creates a worrisome predicament for urban services. With no system of street coordinates and no baseline information, how do you find your way around a constantly growing city? How do you dispatch ambulances, firemen, and law enforcement personnel quickly? How do you send mail and messages to private homes? How do you locate urban facilities and infrastructure ? How do you pinpoint breakdowns in water, electricity, and telephone systems? How do you improve on-site collection of water and electricity bills? How do you set up an efficient local tax system?

Makeshift solutions to these problems exist, but the delivery of urban services according to these methods is generally problematic or ineffective. Over the past two decades, several projects aimed at improving urban information systems in developing countries were launched. Most of these projects had a limited impact because the proposed approach involved techniques that exceeded available local resources. The lack of available local resources stimulated the search for a simpler, more progressive approach to urban information systems. Street addressing requires few resources and a short implementation time frame, and it is intended to provide municipal authorities with an efficient system of baseline information on the city, allowing them to apply high-performance management tools. The broad range of experiences resulting from these projects demonstrates that municipal involvement is one key factor in guaranteeing the system's sustainability. Municipalities should gradually broaden the scope of the intervention beyond the unit

implementing the street addressing initiative to encompass the establishment of a municipal unit that will collect and analyze data and provide
city authorities with the information they need to make decisions.

The challenge is to move gradually forward by teaching local leaders a
step-by-step approach to managing information about their cities
through: mapping the city, codifying streets, conducting census surveys,
setting up a simple computerized system, and developing applied
management tools. Street addressing goes beyond mere urban management. Assigning individuals an identifiable location in the city provides
both a physical and a symbolic connecting point for all citizens within the
community. Street addressing is thus an essential avenue of recognition
for the civic rights of all citizens.

Since the mid-1980s, the World Bank (International Development
Association) and France (Ministry of Foreign Affairs) have provided
financing for street addressing initiatives in several sub-Saharan African
countries. More than 15 countries have applied this concept and its
specific tools to their capital cities. In light of the positive results achieved,
they have pursued the same strategy in secondary cities. Moreover,
beginning in 1999, meetings to promote an international exchange of
ideas have been organized, fostering a deeper understanding of how to
make street addressing initiatives more effective.

At the joint initiative of France's Ministry of Foreign Affairs and the
World Bank, an international Street Addressing Workshop held in Paris in
April 1999 hosted almost all of the African countries involved in this issue.
In May 2001, the World Bank Infrastructure Forum, which each year
brings together government and private sector professionals with World
Bank project officers and decisionmakers, helped to broaden awareness of
this idea through the dissemination of the first draft of a simple technical
manual on street addressing. In April 2002, during the World Bank's
Urban Forum, African officials responsible for street addressing initiatives gave an update on the current situation in cities in their respective
countries.

A 1997 World Bank publication, *The Future of African Cities: Challenges
and Priorities for Urban Development*, mapped out the key issues raised by
Africa's increasing urbanization and identified addressing as one of the
key tools for urban management. This manual, *Street Addressing and the
Management of Cities*, is the logical successor to the "toolbox" introduced
in 1997. It reviews the role of street addressing within the array of urban
management tools, outlines current and future applications, highlights
practices in several countries, and offers a methodological guide for
implementing street addressing initiatives. It will be produced in four
languages (French, English, Spanish, and Portuguese). Plans are also
under way to make it available over the Internet.

This publication is the result of a fruitful partnership between the World Bank and France's Ministry of Foreign Affairs. We hope it will make a substantial contribution toward improving urban management and encouraging a broader recognition of the civic rights of all citizens.

Michel Wormser   *Claude Blanchemaison*
Sector Director   *Executive Director*
Finance, Private Sector, Infrastructure   *International Cooperation*
Africa Region   *and Development Department*
World Bank   *French Ministry of Foreign Affairs*

Acknowledgments

This book was based on the experience gained from numerous street addressing projects in sub-Saharan Africa financed by the World Bank and France's Ministry of Foreign Affairs since 1980. The players involved in implementing these projects have benefited from exchanging ideas at various meetings, including the Street Addressing Workshop in Paris (April 1999) and the World Bank's Urban Forum (November 2002). The publication also benefited from the wise advice of many practitioners of street addressing, particularly in Benin, Burkina Faso, Cameroon, Chad, Congo, Côte d'Ivoire, Djibouti, Guinea, Mali, Mozambique, Niger, Rwanda, Senegal, and Togo.

The authors wish first to thank the "practitioners": D. Belemsagha, D. Domboué, B. Gnoumou, E. Kiendrebeogo, F. Ouedraogo, P. Ouedraogo C. Paré, G. Sankara, P.F. Titinga, Y. Traoré (Burkina Faso); M.A. Kiniffo, B. Oloundé, R. Perrier (Benin); E.R. Ateba, A. Essaka-Moussoumbo, G. Mandeng, M. Manyinga, D. Tchouamou, J.Yango (Cameroon); A. Ahmat, M. Abbazen, A. Atadet, Y. Dago, P. Martin, M. Traoré (Chad); D. Bantsimba (Congo); C. Nado, P. Rakotomalala (Côte d'Ivoire); A.C. Barkad, T. de Comarmond, A.A. Hemed, M.A. Houssein, I. Moumine (Djibouti); D. Diallo, J.L. Doumbouya, S. Kouyaté, M. Sylla, G. Tchidimbo (Guinea); G. Doublier, O. Konaté, M. Keita, B. Koné, J. Massein, I. N'diaye, M. Ouane, A. Traore (Mali); M. Athié, M. Ould Babetta, M. Ben Cheikroun, M. Brahim, E. Charvet, A.M. Ould El Kory, A. Ould Horma, C.A. Ould Houebib, A. Lebigot, M. Macina (Mauritania); M. Chiconela, T. Chissequere, J. Cuna., T. Lahlou, T. Vales, B. Nhachengo (Mozambique); A. Souley, C. Hontoundji, A.I. Barkiré (Niger); J.P. Galland (Rwanda); I. Barry, C. Diop, I. Ly, P.M. N'diaye (Senegal); C. Badabon, P. Karma, T. Kwassi, B. Wa'aloum (Togo).

The authors also wish to acknowledge representatives of the donors that supported the street addressing projects: I. Andersen, S. Debomy, C.Diou, R. Ludwick, R. Maurer, E. Ouayoro, F. Péchon, C. Reliquet, N. Ridolfi, B. Veuthey, D. Vaudaine, P. Watson (World Bank); J.L. Armand, J. Couillandeau, X. Crépin, N. Frelot, A. Harnist, B. Hoarau, G. Pourret (French Cooperation Agency); M. Bouillot, M.H. Chambrun, V. Daön (Decentralized Cooperation); C. Barrier C., A. Chetaille A., F. Filippi, R. de la Rochefoucauld, J.L.Venard (AFD); J.M. Renno (AIMF).

Thanks go also to G. Antier, P. Billot, C. Pinchon, B. Haurie, V. Chomentowski, J.P. Lestang, C. Bouchaud, F. Damette, I. El Amrani, G. Josse, B. Michelon, M. Popesco, A. Sinet, J. White (Groupe Huit), A. Caroll, D. M. Schraft, A. Tirane, and F. Ortiz.

About the Authors

Lucien Godin
An urban planner, architect DPLG (Paris), and co-founder of Groupe Huit (1967), Lucien Godin has worked on urban development projects, many financed by the World Bank, in a variety of countries, especially in the Maghreb, Africa, and Asia. He has also contributed to various publications (*Préparation des Projets Urbains d'Aménagement*, *Préparer un Projet Municipal*, and *The Future of African Cities*).

Hugues Leroux
An engineer with degrees from the Paris Ecole Polytechnique and the Centre des Hautes Etudes de la Construction, Hugues Leroux co-founded Groupe Huit (1967) and is a specialist in urban planning for developing countries. He has headed numerous feasibility studies and has worked in 27 countries, including Tunisia, Morocco, Mali, Burundi, and China. He has also contributed to a number of World Bank and United Nations publications and taught courses in several universities and schools of engineering.

Florence Verdet
Florence Verdet holds a DESS in Urban Planning and Urban Management and has been a member of Groupe Huit since 2000. A specialist in computer mapping, geographic information systems, and database processing, she supervises several addressing projects in Niger and Mozambique and provides local units with technical support and training for all operational tasks.

Roberto Chavez
An architect and urban planner (Arch., University of Morelos, Mexico '74; M.Arch.A.S., MIT, USA '76), Roberto Chavez has over 25 years of experience in urban upgrading, low-income housing, municipal development, and cultural heritage projects and studies in Africa, Latin America, and North Africa. Upon returning from four years as the Bank's Resident Representative in Mozambique in 1997, he helped launch the Bank's Knowledge Management program, focusing on communities of practice and on indigenous knowledge. With the exception of his tenure as Nicaragua's National Director of Urban Development from 1983 to 1985, he has worked in the World Bank since 1977. He is co-author of *Simple Computer Imaging and Mapping*.

Catherine Farvacque-Vitkovic
An urban planner and urban development specialist with degrees from the Université des Sciences Sociales in Grenoble, France, and the School of Government and Business Administration, The George Washington University, USA, Catherine Farvacque-Vitkovic has 20 years of World Bank experience in Africa, the Middle East, and the Maghreb. She has worked extensively on the preparation and implementation of urban development and municipal management projects and is the author or co-author of several books (*Crest 1650-1789: La Ville et son evolution*; *Politiques Foncières des Villes en Développement* [Reforming Urban Land Policies and Administration in Developing Countries]; and *The Future of African Cities, Challenges and Opportunities for Urban Development*).

Abbreviations and Acronyms

ADM	Agence de Développement Municipal (Municipal Development Agency, Senegal)
ADM	Agua de Moçambique (Mozambican Water Authority)
AFD	Agence Française de Développement (French Development Agency)
AGETIP	Agence d'Exécution de Travaux d'Intérêt Public pour l'Emploi (Public Works and Employment Executing Agency, Senegal)
AGETUR	Agence d'Exécution de Travaux Urbains (Benin; Togo)
AIMF	Association Internationale des Maires Francophones (International Association of Francophone Mayors)
APUR	Atelier Parisien d'Urbanisme (Urban Planning Agency of Paris)
BDE	Banque de Données Economiques (Economic database)
BDU	Banque de Données Urbaines (Urban data bank)
BTP	Bâtiment Travaux Publics (Public Works)
Carpol	Cartographie Polyvalente (Multi-purpose cartography unit, Mali)
CCC	Compte de Crédit Communal (Municipal Credit Fund, Senegal)
CCIA	Chambre de Commerce, d'Industrie et d'Artisanat (Chamber of Commerce, Industry and Handicrafts)
CFPB	Contribution Foncière sur les Propriétés Bâties (property tax)
CNA	Cellule Nationale d'Adressage (National Street Addressing Unit, Mozambique)
CNSS	Caisse Nationale de Sécurité Sociale (National Social Security Office)
CSDU	Cellule Spéciale de Développement Urbain (Special Urban Development Unit)
CTAC	Cellule Technique d'Appui aux Communes (Technical Committee to Support the Municipalities of Bamako District, Mali)
CUN	Communauté Urbaine de Niamey/de Nouakchott (Metropolitan government of Niamey/Nouakchott)

DAT	Addressing and Toponymy Directorate
DCL	Direction des Collectivités Locales (Department of Local Governments)
DGF	Dotation Globale de Fonctionnement (Global operating grant, Côte d'Ivoire)
DGI	Direction Générale des Impôts (National Tax Authority)
DIU	Projet de Décentralisation des Infrastructures Urbaines (Urban Infrastructure Decentralization Project, Mauritania)
EDM	Energie du Mali (Mali's Electric Company)
EU	European Union
FAC	Fonds d'Aide et de Coopération (Aid and Cooperation Fund, France)
FECL	Fonds d'Equipement des Collectivités Locales (Municipal Services Fund, Senegal)
FEICOM	Fonds d'Equipement et d'Investissement des Communes (Municipal Services and Investment Fund, Cameroon)
FIG	Fédération Internationale des Géomètres (International Federation of Surveyors)
FPCL	Fonds de Prêts aux Collectivités Locales (Municipal Loan Fund, Côte d'Ivoire)
FSD	Fonds Spécial de Développement (Special Development Fund)
GDP	Gross domestic product
GIE	Groupement d'Intérêt Economique (Local Business Initiatives Group)
GIS	Geographic Information System
IDA	International Development Association (World Bank)
IGN	Institut Géographique National (National Geography Institute)
INSEE	Institut National de la Statistique et des Etudes Economiques (National Institute of Statistics and Economic Studies)
IPIE	Inventaire pour la Programmation des Infrastructures et Equipements (Infrastructure and Services Programming Inventory)
MAE	Ministère des Affaires Etrangères (Ministry of Foreign Affairs, France)
MOD	Maître d'Ouvrage Délégué (Delegated Contract Manager)
MSF	Médecins Sans Frontières (Doctors Without Borders)
NGO	Nongovernmental organization

OED   Département d'Évaluation des Opérations
                     (Operations Evaluation Department)
OM   Ordures ménagères (Household waste)
ONEA   Office National d'Eau et d'Assainissement
                     (National Office of Water and Sanitation, Burkina Faso)
PAC   Programme d'Appui aux Communes Sénégalaises
                     (Urban Development and Decentralization Program,
                     Senegal)
PACUM   Projet d'Appui aux Communes Urbaines du Mali
                     (Municipal Support Project, Mali)
PACVU   Projet d'Amélioration des Conditions de Vie Urbaine
                     (Urban Environmental Project, Burkina Faso)
PDCC   Projet de Développement des Communes Côtières
                     (Coastal Towns Development Project, Côte d'Ivoire)
PDM   Programme de Développement Municipal
                     (Municipal Development Project)
PDUD   Projet de Développement Urbain et de Décentralisation
                     (Urban Development and Decentralization Project, Mali)
PIGU   Programme d'infrastructures et de Gestion Urbaine
                     (Infrastructure and Urban Management Project,
                     Rwanda)
PIP   Programme d'Interventions Prioritaires (Priority
                     Investments Program)
PLIC   Programme Léger d'Initiative Communale
                     (Municipal Initiatives Program, Guinea)
PROP   Programme de Réhabilitation et d'Ouverture Prioritaires
                     (Priority Rehabilitation and Road Opening Program,
                     Guinea)
PUH   Permis Urbain d'Habiter (Occupancy Permit)
PUR   Plan Urbain de Référence (Urban Reference Plan)
RAF   Réforme Agraire et Foncière
                     (Agrarian and Land Reform, Burkina Faso)
RFU   Registre Foncier Urbain (Urban Land Register, Benin)
SCAC   Service de Coopération et d'Action Culturelle
                     (French Cooperation and Cultural Outreach Service)
SMEs   Small and medium-scale enterprises
SONABEL   Société Nationale Burkinabè d'Electricité
                     (National Electric Power Company, Burkina Faso)
SPTD   Service Public de Transfert des Déchets
                     (Public Solid Waste Transfer Department, Guinea)
SSA   Sub-Saharan Africa
TOR   Terms of Reference

TF	Titre Foncier (Land Ownership Title)
TOM	Taxe pour l'enlèvement des ordures ménagères (Household waste tax)
UDP	Urban Development Project
UP	Unité de Projet (Project Unit)
UPSU	Unité Pilote des Services Urbains (Pilot Unit for Urban Services)
VAT	Value added tax
VRD	Voirie et Réseaux Divers (Roads and Utilities)
WHO	World Health Organization

One U.S. dollar equals about 590 CFA francs (2004).

1
What Is Street Addressing and Why Is It Necessary?

In recent decades, many cities in the developing world have experienced extremely rapid growth. This growth has created many underserviced neighborhoods. The street identification systems initially used in old neighborhoods in the city centers have rarely been extended to new ones. Inadequate identification systems have created a worrisome predicament for urban services. With no system of street coordinates, how do you find your way around a constantly growing city? How do you dispatch ambulances, firemen, or law enforcement personnel quickly? How do you send mail and messages to private homes? How can municipal services be provided? How do you pinpoint breakdowns in water, electricity, and telephone systems? How do you set up an efficient tax collection system?

As the pace of urbanization accelerated, many governments in the early 1990s were also embracing decentralization. The abrupt emergence of local governments made capacity building of municipal government teams a priority. Municipal governments were unequipped to meet the challenges of such a broad array of problems: substantial new investments and maintenance work were required while few resources were available to do so, owing to almost nonexistent tax revenues.

The first street addressing initiatives in sub-Saharan Africa were implemented against this backdrop in the early 1990s. At the time, they appeared to be an alternative to costly and ineffective cadastral projects. Street addressing makes it possible to begin at the beginning: to lay out the city using a simple approach that can be put in place by local governments as they strengthen their urban management expertise in the following four priority areas: (a) collecting information on their cities and facilitating the updating of simplified urban planning documents, (b) planning investments, (c) maintaining facilities and infrastructure, and (d) mobilizing local resources more effectively.

What is street addressing?

Street addressing is an exercise that makes it possible to identify the location of a plot or dwelling on the ground, that is, to "assign an address" using a system of maps and signs that give the numbers or names of streets and buildings. This concept may be extended to urban networks and services: in addition to buildings, other types of urban fixtures, such as public standpipes, streetlamps, and taxi stands also get addresses.

Designating a home address is a big problem—indeed, it is one of the most difficult to resolve in urban life, although it may not seem so. The problem is significant because individuals are as defined by their place of residence as they are by their height or the color of their hair or eyes. Today, one's home address is an integral part of personal identification data: it is found on voter identification and social security cards. This problem is so difficult to resolve that it has taken a lot of time to find a solution, and yet, the solution is continually being modified."[1]

Houses need a distinctive marker that is easily recognizable, but the system chosen most of the time, which defines the address using the street number of the house on the street, and the city, was adopted only after much trial and error. In fact, the "street-house" idea was not immediately obvious. It was sometimes supplanted by the idea of a block of houses, as in 18th century Mannheim, Germany, which was considered the prototype of American cities in the 19th century (chapter 4).

More than just a simple street identifying operation, street addressing provides an opportunity to (a) create a map of the city that can be used by different municipal units, (b) conduct a systematic survey that collects a significant amount of information about the city and its population, and (c) set up a database on the built environment, a rich source of urban information that is too often unavailable. Information gathered is associated with an address, thus making it easily locatable. This database (which can take the form of a GIS [geographical information system] at a later stage) is the major innovation of street addressing initiatives, particularly in countries with rapidly growing urban areas where local authorities have lost control of the urbanization process. The real advantage lies in the potential of the urban information database, which, in conjunction with a street addressing plan and a street index, can be used for various applications and benefit the population as a whole, local governments, and the private sector.

Why is street addressing necessary?

Street addressing has several objectives:
(a) For the public, it makes the city more "user-friendly" by
  - Improving the system of street coordinates to enable people to get around the city more easily,
  - Facilitating the delivery of emergency health, fire, and police services, and
  - Locating urban facilities.
(b) For local governments: it increases municipal revenues and improves urban management through the use of:
  - Tools for planning and managing municipal services by technical departments: the identification of public assets (street system, facilities, their length, number, and condition) allows a monitoring system to be put in place to assist with urban planning and programming of investments;
  - Tools to improve local tax collection: using information gathered by street addressing initiatives, it is possible to locate and compile a

register of taxable individuals or businesses and thereby more accurately determine the tax base.

(c) For the private sector: it enables utility concessionaires to manage their networks more effectively. In fact, street addressing helps water, electricity, and telecommunications concessionaires to maintain their networks and collect fees.

Historical perspective and street addressing across countries

Using the "street-house" idea to determine an address involves adopting a system to identify streets and houses. A brief historical overview and examples from different countries will make clear that this task is not as easy as it might appear at first glance.

IDENTIFYING STREETS

The story begins with references to local placenames and shop signs ("the inn at Côte Chaude"). The most conspicuous or popular sign lent its name to the street. In France, until the 17th century, cities had very few streets,[2] and the issue of what to call them arose only with efforts to restructure urban areas (Louis XIV). At this time, new streets were created to replace the walls of the city or to extend old streets. The next task was to make the chosen street name visible: although it appeared to be a simple undertaking, more than two centuries were required to draw up and establish procedures to do so (box 1.1).

Circumstances over the course of history often lead to changes in a street's name. The way these changes occur and how citizens can become involved in effecting the changes, which often come about through a long process, both need to be articulated. The merging of cities in the old metropolitan area of Quebec provides a good example of the mechanisms, participants, and selection criteria (box 1.2). Although precautions may be taken, citizens often react in unexpected ways, as in the case of residents of Gatineau (Canada), who were troubled by the Toponymy Commission's decisions, which did not provide the history lesson expected in the new street naming process (box 1.3). Another example of name changes is that of Belgrade (Serbia/Montenegro), where the signs reflect the changing street names rewritten by the vicissitudes of history (box 1.4).

During the feverish urbanization of recent decades, the main issue has been not so much changing the names of streets as assigning them names at all; in rapidly growing cities, the majority of streets go nameless for a long period of time because attributing a name is usually controversial. All manner of experiences underscore the impossibility of broadly assigning street names right from the outset. Street naming causes too much controversy to implement quickly. Resorting to legal measures is often insufficient, as demonstrated by the case of Cameroon, where a presidential decree on street naming has remained unheeded for years (annex 3).

The only recourse therefore is to adopt a more neutral street numbering system.[3] It can be implemented quickly and serves as a springboard to the subsequent decision on a street name. Although this numbering system adapts well to a regular street layout (cities in the United States, old colonial cities in Latin America or West Africa), it is obviously more difficult to implement when the layout is less uniform.

A few references to Asia will conclude this section: the transcendent role of the compass in Chinese philosophy and its influence on China's street addressing system (box 1.5) and the helplessness of the tourist (and the average citizen) in search of an address in Japan (box 1.6).

Box 1.1. Inscribing the names of streets in Paris

Before 1728, no street names were indicated in Paris,[4] except in very rare cases, such as "Rue Saint-Dominique, formerly des Vaches" (1643). The systematic inscription of street names goes back to 1728, when the police stipulated that street names[5] be posted in large black letters on tin metal sheets, but owing to its fragility, this system was replaced by a system of stone tablets in 1729. The owner of the house at the end of a street then became responsible for inscribing the street name; thereafter, an 1806 decree stipulated that the municipality would be responsible for new oil-based inscriptions. After several decades, they became illegible and had to be redone in 1847. The new signs were made of porcelain fired at high temperatures, and a 1938 decree provided the technical specifications: width of between 70 and 100 centimeters and height between 35 and 50 centimeters; white letters and numbers; sky blue background; bronze green frame measuring 3.5 cm wide, with a shadow effect created by white and black thin lines.

The right to assign a name to a street was granted to the municipal council, which had to seek the opinion of the local district council and submit the proposed name to the commission charged with evaluating proposed street names. Paris' street naming system is considered historic "because the old street names preserve the memory of the people that chose them and the names given to the new streets will help to perpetuate the memory of great men and their grand gestures of which the nation may be proud." The system also conforms to the following rules:

(Box continues on the following page.)

Box 1.1. (*continued*)

- Simple names: "For a name to be chosen, not only must it be worthy, it must also meet a variety of practical requirements: easy to spell, pronounce, describe and memorize.
- The biggest streets shall have grandiose names that are publicly recognized.
- Streets that run alongside churches shall preferably be designated by the names of saints, prelates or famous preachers.
- Areas around the railways and neighborhoods where industrial sites are located shall bear the names of famous engineers, inventors and men of industry; the names of doctors shall be found on streets close to hospitals; astronomers and scholars shall be near the Observatory or the schools."[6]

Box 1.2. Changes to street names in Quebec

In 2004, "Quebec" will designate the territory covered by 13 cities merged into the old metropolitan area of Quebec. All 4,825 street names in the territory will be standardized in order to eliminate identical names and thereby ensure public safety while facilitating the delivery of mail and listing in the telephone directory.

A working group has been charged with inventorying streets with identical names and drawing up selection criteria for designating streets that require a name change. Streets that require a name change will be submitted to the Toponymy Committee of the City of Quebec, which will suggest new names. The public may also suggest names, thereby adding to the bank of names available for naming city streets. All citizens affected by the change in a street name will be consulted about their preference for a new street name.

Selection Criteria
- conform to the norms of the Toponymy Commission
- age or historic value
- number of residential addresses
- number of private businesses, organizations or institutions
- impact on the naming system in place (example: flower names given to many streets)
- importance of the transportation route
- logic of the name in relation to its surroundings
- whether or not the street has already had its name changed in the last decade.

Box 1.2. (*continued*)

Based on the bank of names and suggestions provided by all citizens, historical societies and local district leaders, names will be chosen and submitted to members of the Toponymy Commission who will review them and choose a name for each street at issue. Each proposed new street name will be submitted to all citizens affected by the change. They may give their opinions on the proposed names or make other suggestions. The Toponymy Commission will make its final recommendations to the municipal council, which will rule on the new names.

Box 1.3. Disgruntled residents and the Toponymy Commission (Canada)

"Overall, the Transition Committee did a good job. We are nonetheless flabbergasted to find the English names of trees on the list of recommendations for the Aylmer sector: Chestnut, Hickory, Aspen. This is acceptable for the names of people who played some historical role in this area then, but English tree names, that's beyond the pale. The public document distributed by the City of Gatineau says that 'for those who don't have time to read, street names are a history lesson that is much easier to learn because it's always right under their noses.' A history lesson indeed! If these street names are to be chosen, people will always have right under their noses proof that the Transition Committee and the City of Gatineau preferred to anglicize the identity of the residents on these streets. We completely disapprove of this choice! This is some bizarre history lesson!"

Box 1.4. Belgrade: History is written on the walls

In Belgrade, changes to street names are frequent, but a sign often recalls the history behind the change. Belgrade's main avenue, which links the Place Slavija to the Place Terazije, has changed names several times, and each change has reflected momentous changes in the country's history. First called King Milan Avenue, it was then renamed Marshall Tito Avenue, followed by Avenue of the Serbian Monarchs, only to be returned recently to its original name, King Milan Avenue, after the first Serbian king following the Ottoman occupation. In a similar fashion, the Boulevard of the Revolution was recently renamed Boulevard of King Alexander (Kralj Alexander), one of the country's last kings, assassinated in Marseille at the outbreak of the Second World War.

Box 1.5. China: Compass-based street addressing

Street names and the street numbering system in China are two features of the country that capture the immediate attention of every tourist that travels there. They may also be a source of great confusion if one does not understand either the logic or the basis of the system itself. Indeed, a street name may change as many as sixteen times within a large city, and the numbering will begin again with each new name. This superficial complexity, however, has a profoundly logical basis.

In fact, among the characteristics[7] of classical Chinese philosophy that persist to the present day is the transcendent role played by the four cardinal points of the compass and its central point. This organizational principle is reflected at the national level, in the name China itself (country of the center), which makes reference to this principle, and in the name of the capitals, Beijing (capital of the North) and Nanjing (capital of the South). Names of the provinces are also strongly influenced by these references to geographical direction.

Within cities themselves, long streets are divided into east and west (or north and south, depending on the street's orientation), and the street numbers start over on each part of the street. This is the reason that the famous "Nanjing Street" in Shanghai is divided into "Nanjing dong lu" or the western part of Nankin Street. Other particularly long streets are divided up into three parts : dong lu, zhong lu, xi lu (east, central, and west part). This division into parts can occur in more or less arbitrary fashion, but it often references ancient outer walls that circled the city.

When these street names, which already include directional information, appear on a street sign (or sign giving directions at the exit from the metro, for example), the cardinal direction is also indicated by additional information given at the bottom of each side of the sign: south or north, east or west. At every moment, then, citizens are oriented within the city itself and also with respect to the cardinal points, as if a compass had been placed everywhere: not surprising in the country that invented it!

IDENTIFYING BUILDINGS

The need to identify buildings arose with the growth of cities in Europe and China in the 18th century. Addresses consisted of a street indication where the house was located as well as additional information on the approximate location. Here is a Paris address from 1778 : "from Sahuguet d'Espagnac, rue Meslé, the fourth door on the right entering from the rue du Temple."

The building numbering system adopted in France in the 15th century was not systematically adopted until the 18th century for several reasons: "The population wasn't big enough for the need to be felt. The fear of tax

---

Box 1.6. Japan: Helpless citizens

Aside from a few main thoroughfares, streets in Japan do not have names. In fact, the city districts (ku) are divided into neighborhoods (chome) that group together several dozen houses and thus form a block. Houses are numbered according to the block to which they belong and not as a function of the street.[8] The house numbering system is based on their construction date. Thus, two houses located next to each other can be numbered out of sequence.[9] As a result, it is very difficult to find a specific place based on an address. The simplest approach is to go to the nearest police station, as the Japanese themselves do.

In contrast to Tokyo, however, Kyoto is easier to get around, since the city is regularly laid out, at least in terms of the main streets. Nine main thoroughfares cut across the city from east to west, beginning with Ichijo (1st street) to Kyujo (9th street), which are traversed by several avenues.

---

authorities, adherence to old habits, the fairly legitimate desire not to become a mere number—all of these factors contributed to things being left as they were."[10] The numbering of buildings addressed several different concerns:

- In the 15th century, the numbering system for houses near Notre-Dame in Paris reflected the city's concerns with the management of its assets and properties.
- Beginning in the 16th century, the main concern was controlling illegal housing construction in the inner suburbs,[11] where "carriage houses," whose construction was forbidden, were given numbers.
- Beginning in 1768, security became an important concern and was reflected in efforts to number houses "in all the cities, towns and villages where troops are housed" (box 1.7).
- In 1779, street addressing was part of the "citizen project" set up by a private citizen named Marin Kreenfelt, who proposed assigning exact and convenient addresses in order to promote good relationships between citizens (box 1.8).
- With the Revolution, broadly implemented street addressing initiatives reflected a fiscal concern: surveying property owners subject to a new tax, the property tax. However, street numbering by section, which was put into place with little planning or method, produced results of dubious utility.
- In 1805, the Empire lay the groundwork for the modern system, the principles of which are still in force today. The system is recognized because

---

Box 1.7. Numbering of houses in Crest (France) in 1766

The first mention of house numbering is found as early as 1766. Two years later, in 1768, a government order made the process official. Numbering houses met a real need, and the great majority of cities in the Dauphiné region hastened to conform to the order. The numbering system put in place by two artisans in Crest, Jean Fréau, a glazier, and Pascal Giri, was initiated on December 23, 1766, and completed on January 3 of the following year. The system consisted of a single series of numbers beginning at the town hall.

Box 1.8. A "citizen project"

Marin Kreenfeldt, chief deputy to the Elector of Cologne and author of the Paris Almanac, added an identification number to the addresses already listed in his publication by street. He requested the assigning of numbers to all doorways and, through his own efforts and at his own cost, provided the first examples, when he obtained authorization from the chief of police to number houses in the Opera district. This operation was sometimes perceived as preparing the way for some new tax law and was therefore performed in part at night. Numbering began on the left with the number 1 and continued to the end of the street, continuing on the right side of the street so that the first and last numbers were opposite each other.

---

of its "usefulness for all administrative purposes, in particular for facilitating tax payments," but also as "a measure of order and security."[12] Municipal authorities and especially private individuals have made many innovations and proposals with respect to the system.[13]

Street addressing guidelines

HOW SHOULD STREETS BE IDENTIFIED? The manner in which a city or neighborhood develops often dictates the framework for street identification.

• *Naming streets.* This is the most vivid way of identifying streets, and the most commonly used because of its suitability for any street layout. Name selection, however, can pose many problems that unduly lengthen the implementation process. This solution works well when a city evolves

Figure 1.1. History is written on the walls of Belgrade . . . the inscriptions change in the streets in Paris

slowly enough to allow municipal authorities to devote some time to naming decisions.

- *Numbering streets in cities with a "checkerboard" or grid layout.* This is a more "neutral" system that is easier for people to understand because the streets are arranged in numerical or alphabetical order. Chapter 4 offers examples of this solution as applied in Puebla, Mannheim, and Washington. Additional examples can be found in neighborhoods of African cities including Dakar, Djibouti, and Abidjan.
- *Numbering streets in cities with an irregular layout.* This system is often used in anticipation of gradual street naming. One way to simplify the process of establishing street coordinates is to group the streets into neighborhoods or zones, which can then be assigned a sequential number with a prefix that designates the neighborhood or zone. Most of the street addressing initiatives referred to in this publication have adopted such a system.
- *Unidentified streets.* Developing cities are not the only setting where street addressing initiatives aim to remedy the problem of unidentified streets. High-density housing projects and other residential developments also contribute to the information gap when they ignore surrounding street layouts, add private streets, and identify buildings by numbers or letters rather than by street coordinates.

HOW SHOULD BUILDINGS BE IDENTIFIED? The practice of continuous numbering (1, 2, 3, 4, 5 and so on) along a street or in a neighborhood should be abandoned. This solution was adopted in Paris during the Revolution and resulted in great confusion. Regardless of the type of solution adopted, a system of alternate numbering—even numbers on one side of the street, odd numbers on the other—should be used.[14]

- *Sequential numbering.* Odd (1, 3, 5 and so on) and even (2, 4, 6, and so forth) numbers are assigned sequentially to buildings on opposite sides of the street. Structures that are built between existing buildings after numbers have been assigned will use the suffix *bis* or *ter* (5, 5 bis, 5 ter).
- *Metric numbering.* Structures are assigned even or odd numbers corresponding to the distance between the building entrance and the beginning of the street.
- *Decametric numbering.* Even and odd numbers are assigned sequentially as in the first two solutions, but according to ten-meter-long sections of street. This compromise between the first two solutions offers the dual advantage of simplicity and estimated-distance numbering (chapter 4).

DEVELOPING CITIES AND SUB-SAHARAN CITIES. Prior to independence, colonial authorities generally assigned names to streets in the city center but were content to number the streets in the so-called "indigenous" neighborhoods that featured a systematic layout, such as Abidjan-Treichville and Dakar-Médina. In the wake of independence, cities experienced rapid, largely unplanned growth. In the succeeding years, there has been little attempt to retain the once-prevalent system of street identification and doorway numbering, which has led to the present situation.

Cities must contend with a twofold problem: How can the street addressing system be updated in the city center, where the layout is often regular? How should irregular settlements and peri-urban areas be treated?

In the old city centers, the colonial authorities generally introduced a sequential numbering system.[15] Such a system was well-suited to a slow, controlled urban growth process. The urban population explosion of the postindependence era resulted in a profusion of unnamed streets and unnumbered buildings. Some streets did receive new names after independence, but increasing densification in city centers led to inconsistent numbering of buildings. As city officials contemplate a street addressing initiative, they need to decide whether or not to update the system used in the old city center. If the answer is yes, should they retain the sequential system or replace it with a metric (or decametric) numbering system for the entire city? If the old city center has retained its original uniform numbering system, it might be simpler to update it and adopt a metric system for peri-urban areas.

Recently urbanized areas have either been configured into subdivisions with a regular street layout, or they have developed as so-called squatter settlements or informal settlements with little or no organized layout. In either case, the streets usually go unidentified and buildings lack a consecutive numbering system.[16] The desire to avoid the major complications involved in hasty street naming (owing to the need for consensus-building) has led city authorities to introduce a numbering system that allows for both rapid identification and time to name streets gradually.

Recent street addressing projects undertaken in sub-Saharan Africa have adopted a system that identifies each street in a neighborhood or zone by a sequential number with a prefix that designates the neighborhood. The municipality of Matam in Conakry (Guinea) has been assigned the prefix "MA," so the twelfth street in that neighborhood is called "MA.12 Street." In Burkina Faso, the city of Ouagadougou is divided into sectors, and street names consist of the sector number followed by the street number. The city of N'djaména in Chad uses a prefix pertaining to the district number. In Senegal, Niger, and Togo, the prefix refers to the name of the neighborhood.

Dwellings have generally been assigned a metric numbering system for two reasons: it takes account of distances, and it is well suited to a gradual urbanization process because numbers can be assigned at any time as new buildings appear.

The choice of a system for squatter settlements depends entirely on the attitude of the authorities. They may decide not to implement a street addressing system because of the illegal status of the settlements, or conversely, they may choose to begin incorporating the settlement into the overall urban plan. For a poorly defined network of streets, the best option is to identify the major routes and then institute an addressing system. This type of operation can be undertaken as part of an upgrading initiative.

Early street addressing systems in sub-Saharan Africa

The earliest urban projects financed by the World Bank did not tackle the problem of street addressing. Some initial experience was gained, however, during the first Urban Project for Mali (1980), when street signs were posted to supplement the existing signs in the neighborhoods of downtown Bamako. In the 1980s and 1990s, the government and donors were more preoccupied with introducing cadastres for tax purposes, which were expected to significantly bolster municipal finances. The difficulty of identifying the tax base figures prominently among the many impediments that led to at least a temporary rejection of such cadastres. Although a cadastral system does establish a reference point for a specific plot, it does not create a visible manifestation on the public roadway, so even a tax collector will be unable to find that plot on the street as he would with an address. Tax collection notices could be sent to post office boxes, but many ploys can be used to return the notice to the sender.

Under these circumstances, the tax collection goal at the core of cadastral projects could well be jeopardized unless priority is given to establishing a system that identifies streets and buildings. Beset with the same problem, water and electric utility concessionaires are often forced to create their own systems, sometimes using painted numbers on building facades or organizing a system of "rounds" for presenting bills.

Street addressing as an urban information and management tool is a key element of the municipal capacity-building strategy adopted by most governments and donors. The idea is to build a knowledge base and use simple applications to benefit local governments. The failure of cadastral projects and the institution of tax reforms (residence tax, single land tax) have helped spur the development of street addressing initiatives.

All of these methods were developed in Burkina Faso in 1985 in connection with the second urban project (UDP 2) financed by the World Bank, but the first implementation occurred in Chad under a project headed by the French Cooperation Agency. Acting on the momentum and general support provided by these two donors, fifteen countries adopted and tailored street addressing techniques to their own diverse circumstances, as summarized below.

- Chad (1991) was the first country to carry out a street addressing initiative (N'djaména), with assistance from the French Cooperation Agency and the city of Paris.
- Burkina Faso (1991) established an initial baseline for street addressing in Ouagadougou and Bobo-Dioulasso with World Bank financing. The most noteworthy application was the linking of the street addressing system to a new "residence tax."
- Cameroon (1993) designed its street addressing project with World Bank assistance and received implementation support from the French Cooperation Agency. Operations on the ground were supervised in part by NGOs.
- Guinea (1993) received World Bank support to launch a street addressing initiative in Conakry, which was tirelessly implemented by a highly motivated municipal street addressing unit. The most significant applications created under this initiative were the organization of a solid waste collection system and support for secondary street maintenance.
- Mali (1993) conducted a street addressing initiative in six cities including Bamako, with assistance from the World Bank and the French Cooperation Agency. Local artisans crafted street signs that continue to serve as a benchmark despite a few shortcomings.
- Togo (1996) concurrently launched a street addressing initiative and a residence tax in Lomé.
- Mozambique (1996) was the only non-Francophone country to conduct this type of operation, for which the French Cooperation Agency pro-

vided support and technical assistance over several years. Six cities including Maputo have implemented street addressing systems and developed a variety of applications.

- Mauritania (1997) implemented street addressing in twelve cities including Nouakchott, with assistance from the World Bank, the French Cooperation Agency, and the French Development Agency (AFD). The initiative was combined with a fiscal application.
- Djibouti (1998) and Congo (1999) conducted street addressing studies but did not implement them.
- Senegal (1999) carried out a street addressing initiative in twelve cities. This operation, conducted under the Urban Development and Decentralization Program financed by the World Bank and the AFD, is one of the strengthening measures that city authorities decided to use in their "municipal contract."
- Niger (2001) instituted a remarkably effective street addressing system in Niamey with support from the International Association of Francophone Mayors (AIMF). The French Cooperation Agency is currently providing support for an addressing initiative in Maradi (2003).
- Benin initially adopted a block addressing system (neighborhood, block, plot), which was later replaced by a "street-house" system under the 1990 Urban Land Register project initiated in 1990 Cotonou and Parakou with financing from the French Cooperation Agency. A similar project was also undertaken in Rwanda; a new program, PIGU (Infrastructure and Urban Management Project), is planned to assign addresses to informal settlements in Kigali (2005).
- Côte d'Ivoire limited its street addressing project to the installation of street signs in Abidjan, Abengourou, and San Pedro. Financing for San Pedro came from the national government and the European Union under the Coastal Towns Development Project (PDCC).

Several countries can be cited for exemplary results, including Burkina Faso for its early achievements and fiscal applications, Cameroon for its implementation methods, Guinea for the creation and rapid implementation of a street addressing system in squatter settlements, and Mozambique for its diverse, high-quality applications.

The role of street addressing in municipal development

Street addressing plays a key supporting role in municipal development, for which we can cite five main features or trends:

- An increasing focus on providing priority services: as a result of demographic pressure and limited resources, cities now tend to target prior-

ity needs in terms of basic services and infrastructure and pay special attention to squatter settlements.
- A significant municipal dimension: local governments and municipal managers have become the partners of choice. This trend supports the decentralization process, which has been initiated fairly effectively by every country in the region, and rallies the donor community already deeply committed to democratization.
- A two-pronged approach: finance and urban planning must be addressed concurrently. This is the underlying objective of the financial and urban audits implemented in some countries (Senegal, Guinea, Mauritania, Niger, Madagascar, Rwanda, and Cameroon, for example), in which priorities are ranked and scaled according to each municipality's financial resources.
- Financing shared with a mandatory local counterpart. Even though local counterpart funding is relatively limited, it has become an indisputable rule of the game and a sign of the beneficiaries' adherence to the principle of cofinancing.
- An institutional and financial arrangement intended to place responsibility on the various partners: a contractual approach. Senegal provides the strongest example of this mechanism through its municipal contracts, which outline both the content of the Priority Investment Programs and the obligations of the municipalities under their Municipal Adjustment Programs.

Notes

1. P. Lavedan (preface from *Les numérotages des maisons de Paris du XV ^{e} siècle à nos jours* [House Numbering in Paris from the 15th Century to the Present Day] by J. Pronteau.

2. Paris had about 300 streets in 1300, 650 in 1700, 1100 in 1800, 4300 in 1900, and 5200 in 1960.

3. Numbering and number assignment: see glossary.

4. The first street names in Paris most often arose from customary usage reflecting a crossing point, a notable figure, proximity to a building (rue du Temple) or center where an occupation or craft was practiced (rue de la Verrerie [glasswork]), a special characteristic (rue de l'Abreuvoir [watering hole]) or, in particular, a shop sign (rue de la Huchette [bin]).There were no signs displaying street names. And since there were no street maps, it was often necessary to walk a considerable distance before finding the street at issue.

5. Official names were given to some streets beginning in the 17th century in homage to the royal family or notable figures (Colbert). Later, street names appeared honoring merchants, aldermen, or municipal employees, and in 1782, famous people who had died (Molière). During the Revolution, street names

commemorated the grand ideas and great men of the time. Many streets were renamed: rue de la Raison [reason] (formerly rue Notre-Dame), place de la Liberté [freedom] (de l'Oratoire [oratory]). The Empire celebrated its victories. Since then, streets have almost always borne names of people. See J. Hillairet; op.cit.

6. Marc Voelckel (2002). L'inscription des noms de rues à Paris [Inscription of Street Names in Paris]. Ruavista

7. Marcel Granet (1929). La civilisation chinoise [Chinese Civilization]. Albin michel.

8. Example of an address: "Teramachi 3-2-97," or "temple district," third section, building 2-97.

9. This peculiarity may be the result of a deeper underlying principle, that of traditional board games like "go" or "shôgi," which are played by placing pieces not on the squares themselves but rather on the intersections of the squares on the board.

10. J. Pronteau. 1966. Les numérotages des maisons de Paris du XV° siécle à nos jours [House Numbering in Paris from the 15th Century to the Present Day].

11. After 1548, the monarchy was concerned about limiting the growth of Paris and its inner suburbs. In 1724, no "carriage houses" could be built in the inner suburbs, and in 1726, to facilitate surveying of these houses, a number was carved on one side of the door frame. Beginning in 1778, a proposal was made to extend the system to houses in the city.

12. This operation generated so much interest that the prefect of the Seine region and the chief of police vied for its implementation.

13. Leblond, inventor of the meter, conceived a metric numbering system that would also indicate the length of the street (1800). Huvé proposed a decametric numbering system (1801). Garros was the first to have the idea of an alternating numbering system, with even numbers on one side of the street and uneven on the other (1799). Mathieu and Belu suggested "combining the street lighting system with the house numbering system" (1802); Choderlos de Laclos came up with an unusual street addressing project for the city of Paris in which the direction the numbers would go was determined by the street's orientation to the Seine. Indeed, the craziest project was related to the revolutionary idea of numbering streets by sections.

14. Merruau Report, 1862.

15. This alternative numbering proposal was introduced by an individual named Garros in 1799, but it was initially rejected by the police chief as "of little use, and in itself quite perverse and very awkward to use . . . ."

16. Note that a decametric numbering system was introduced in a neighborhood of Bobo-Dioulasso during the colonization period.

17. Numbers are often painted on walls by utility concessionaires or census workers, but such inconsistent markers are useful only for those who have inscribed them.

2
Street Addressing Applications

Street addressing has many potential applications. The first and most general application involves the connection between street addressing and civic identity. Other more practical applications explore links between street addressing and urban information systems, support for municipal services, tax systems, the land tenure issue, upgrading of informal neighborhoods, support for concessionary services, and economic development.

Street addressing and civic identity

The notion of a city embraces the complementary concepts of the urban and the civic, which stem from the traditional Roman distinction between *urbs* and *civitas*. *Urban* describes a "physical space for habitation, creation, exchange," which is continually developing and changing. It presents complex managerial and administrative problems that become all the more formidable in the more impoverished countries, where resources are scarce and even the most basic tools are often lacking. The idea of *civic* refers to the community life in which citizens participate. This metaphorical space requires a system in which resources and responsibilities are distributed fairly, and where the local level is recognized as important for handling problems that directly concern the local population. The local level also needs to have individuals capable of assuming such authority in a thorough, competent manner. The local government, however, is often no more than an administrative unit with severely limited resources, thus leaving no opportunity for civic institutions to take root. The development of the municipal level, therefore, must be viewed as a decisively strategic step that is essential for the effective management of urban problems.

Early urban projects came almost entirely under the *urbs* umbrella in view of their technical and economic focus. The results achieved by such projects were not insignificant, but they suffered from certain limitations, which can be overcome not by refining methods and procedures, but rather by embracing the notion of *civitas*—in other words, introducing the idea of civic involvement to address problem areas and design intervention methods.

In the cities of the developing countries, and particularly in sub-Saharan Africa, the urbanization process often takes place informally, resulting in unnamed streets and unnumbered houses. Some will say that things are fine as they are and that people can find one another. This is true if one assumes that "find" is understood in terms of traditional relationships in the context of extended families, neighbors living in close proximity, family lineage, and long-standing business relationships. The lack of urban street coordinates goes hand in hand with a certain type and level of social relationship. In a traditional milieu, both family and business relationships share the commonality of being "non-urban" in the sense that they perpetuate the social systems that existed before the birth of the city. Although a city without a system of street coordinates comprises a physical urban space on some level, it cannot transform into a civic community without such a system in place. A citizen is not an anonymous entity lost in the urban jungle and known only by his relatives and co-workers; he has an established identity. He can reach and be reached by associations and government agencies, and he can interface with fellow citizens outside the traditional networks, all by dint of residence in the same city. An individual without an address has no civic identity; a citizen, however, can communicate with fellow citizens. Having an address is essential for this exchange to occur.

Street addressing is therefore the foundation on which civic identity can develop, and a prerequisite for the development of civic institutions. Although addressing will surely not in and of itself produce institutions, which are in essence a sociopolitical phenomenon, it is a technical requirement for transforming a city from an informal urban space to a civic community.

Street addressing is a necessity, but it can also serve as a reference tool for streamlining the technical and financial aspects of city management. City managers are directly affected by these street addressing applications. In areas with limited resources, the implementation of urban management tools based on street addressing systems enables gradual progress and ensures technical expertise at the local level.

A gradual pace is a prerequisite for the success of any operation of this nature. Too often in the past, sophisticated projects that use state-of-the-art methods and the latest software have been introduced, but they are operational only with outside assistance. Street addressing needs to be less a technological feat than a tool that local players can use to progressively improve the way municipal business is conducted.

Street addressing generally involves three dimensions:

- relations between citizens, which are at the core of any system and can exist only with a street addressing system;
- relations between citizens and government authorities, which implies that each individual and economic activity can be located for both fiscal and political purposes;
- control of urban space, for which street addressing is the first in a series of applications intended to ensure the gradual development of management tools.

The distinctive feature of street addressing is that it creates a common ground on which the concepts of urban space and civic community/identity can come together. It is a prerequisite for undertaking a new approach that will create a lasting connection between *urbs* and *civitas*. A city is, first and foremost, a means for coexistence, exchange, communication, and integration. Street addressing is just one of the many requirements that will help a city achieve social integration. Although it is one tool among many rather than a panacea, it merits special attention because of its crucial role.

Street addressing and urban information

Through its surveys and spatial identification of locations, street addressing offers an exceptional opportunity to gather baseline information on a city. The database and maps created through such an initiative make it possible to evolve into a simplified geographic information system that can be coordinated with other urban management tools. The process of maintaining this reference tool provides an opportunity for progressive updates as new information becomes available.

Address management

In order to make optimal use of the database created through addressing surveys, it is advisable to obtain or write a special address management software that incorporates the standard functions of a database (search, criteria-based retrieval, cross-search) and the functions designed to handle the spatial dimension of the data (search, retrieval, and cross-reference by territory, and so forth). This software will facilitate the following activities:

(a) Access the database by subject:
  - according to type of occupancy, retrieve data individually or by group for dwelling or type of dwelling, economic use or type of economic use, facilities, urban fixtures (public standpipes, streetlamps, and the like); data should be retrievable by street or neighborhood, or for the entire city;
  - according to address, retrieve data associated with the address or with a street, a neighborhood, or a zone to be identified;
  - drawing on cross-referenced data, show features such as pharmacies or physicians in a specific neighborhood, and so forth;
(b) Store in memory all changes in occupancy for purposes of creating history files that will make it possible to observe trends;
(c) Easily change or retrieve a new address at any time;
(d) Add open parameters (data associated with the address) at any time and in unlimited quantity;

Box 2.1. Monitoring of epidemics (Maputo, Mozambique)

The primary objective of this monitoring effort was to locate individuals who were sick. Computerized mapping makes it possible to identify areas where a disease concentrates and develops, but owing to privacy concerns, the health centers do not always release very specific information. Pinpointing the location of affected individuals, however, can reveal at-risk neighborhoods and thereby facilitate the work of physicians and focus municipal efforts (drinking water supply, sanitation and drainage, waste collection, welfare measures, and so forth).

Maputo provides a revealing example of such an effort. From mid-August of 1997 to late April 1998, the city suffered a major cholera outbreak of 15,000 declared cases in 53 neighborhoods. The Ministry of Health, WHO, and Doctors Without Borders (MSF) asked Maputo's municipal street addressing unit for its maps and database. With the assistance of that entity, the Ministry conducted epidemiological research beginning in November 1997. The work, carried out in real time over several weeks, helped to determine the factors responsible for transmitting the disease and shed light on the principal causes that trigger and spread the disease (sources of contamination, inadequate drainage, poor access to health centers, and other factors). The most affected neighborhoods were then made aware of hygiene issues. A set of maps was prepared in order to:

- help MSF anticipate the number of equipped beds to be set up in each neighborhood;
- monitor the evolution of the epidemic;
- report the status to the various donors;
- identify neighborhoods that are most vulnerable for priority intervention;
- organize the distribution of bleach and waste collection campaigns;
- analyze water quality in wells and public standpipes in specific neighborhoods.

(e) Define "territories" (groups of addresses) upon request and as needed;
(f) Take into account the distinction between even and odd numbers on doorways for opposite sides of the street;
(g) Easily import and export data from/to other applications (street system, facilities, tax system) or another database;
(h) Print data retrieved and/or all data.

EVOLUTION TOWARD A GEOGRAPHIC INFORMATION SYSTEM. Address management software was effectively used in all of the addressing operations discussed in this manual. The software program was sometimes coordinated with related applications (inventory of streets and/or facilities, for example)[1] or it evolved into a Geographic Information System (GIS) (Yaoundé, Douala, Nouakchott). It is usually preferable not to plan to move over to a GIS until later, after the teams responsible for number-coded mapping and the computerized database have become completely familiarized with their tools. When operational, a GIS is quite compelling as a powerful yet complex tool that combines mapping with a relational database, each of these elements requiring several years of experience to master.

Street addressing and support to municipal services

As illustrated in the preceding section, street addressing moves beyond a simple identification task to play a key role in the development of munici-pal management tools. It can be instrumental in consolidating municipal expertise according to priority subject areas, such as street system manage-ment, maintenance of facilities and infrastructure, household waste collec-tion, urban property identification, investment planning, and so on.

Street system management

Street identification is a clear necessity for any intervention program, but in the absence of specific identifying information, only a rough approxi-mation can be achieved. Locating and recording street information is not an easy task, yet a street system constitutes a primary asset for municipal governments, requiring significant capital investment and annual mainte-nance expenditures. Consequently, street identification deserves priority attention and rigorous monitoring by municipal authorities and technical experts.

The first stage in the proper management of such an asset begins with an identification process. Each street is given a name or number and a defined location with beginning and end points, and this initial informa-tion is then represented on a map. Without this preliminary step, it would be impossible to organize maintenance work, street rehabilitation, and waste collection. The second stage calls for recording the features of each street, beginning with those most heavily used (classification, traffic, dimensions and condition of pavement, sidewalks, and shoulders; nearby public works and facilities; degree of deterioration; and so on). The data are usually gathered in part during an initial street addressing operation and subsequently completed during specific periodic surveys intended to identify "trouble spots" and emergency repair work.

The municipal unit in charge of the street addressing initiative provides support to the technical departments, and the municipality gains awareness of an area often ignored despite significant allocation of resources. More specifically, the streets are divided into sections or blocks between two crossroads, which are then identified with a number that links them to the street number.[2] Various software programs[3] analyze the data and give expenditure forecasts for street maintenance and rehabilitation according to the amount and type of work to be done (for example, Douala and Yaoundé). Street addressing data have been used in Conakry to implement annual maintenance programs for secondary streets and bring neighborhoods out of isolation.

This street addressing application thus transcends mere address management. The tasks of the municipal unit in charge of such initiatives can encompass not only recognition of streets but also gathering data on street features and determining work to be done.

Household waste collection

Another application of street addressing is waste collection, for which Conakry, Guinea, provides an especially eloquent example. The local authorities, with the support of the World Bank–financed Third Urban Project beginning in 1999, decided to tackle an extremely troublesome situation in which garbage littered the streets and sidewalks (Box 2.2).

This type of application could be incorporated into the broader notion of municipal services and encompass other operations such as street cleaning or public transportation.

Inventory of municipal built assets

Few municipalities have an awareness of the extent of their assets, or at the very least the property over which they have domain, if not possession. Their infrastructure, buildings, and land tend to be poorly identified. An initial inventory can be conducted during the first street addressing survey. The survey identifies the general layout of national and municipal streets, records street distances as buildings are given a metric numbering system, and notes the use category of each plot (residential, business, utilities, empty lot, or other use). If the addressing survey is then supplemented through the identification of urban fixtures (public standpipes, bus shelters, telephone booths, and the like) or specific surveys of street systems or utilities, simple utilization of the address directory will provide the basis for an inventory of assets. Other information can be added to the inventory, such as the ownership status of the facility or land, property appraisals, and estimated cost of upkeep.

The value of these assets can be estimated on the basis of unit cost of investment (floor area, for example), and the annual cost of upkeep can be

---

Box 2.2. Household waste, Conakry, Guinea

Household waste management in Conakry in the late 1990s was initially the sole responsibility of municipal authorities. Unsanitary conditions in that city led to efforts to clarify and assign the tasks of solid waste collection, transfer, and treatment. The responsibility for waste collection was turned over to SMEs (small and medium-scale enterprises), which could then bill the users directly. This system called for a precise delineation of each entity's coverage area and the establishment of waste transfer points. The task of transferring waste to the existing landfill was handled by the city's Public Solid Waste Transfer Department (SPTD).

The Second Urban Project (UDP 2), financed by the World Bank, had just completed its first street addressing project and had published a street map, which at the time was one of the few such documents that were up-to-date. The neighborhood boundaries shown on the map served as a guide for the delineation and distribution of collection zones among the various SMEs. The installation of street signs simplified this process and made it easier to delineate collection zone boundaries and routes and to set up transfer points. The street addressing system thus played a highly positive role in launching an operation that indisputably owed its success to the concentrated efforts of several authorities, operators, and donors focused on a radical transformation of the city's image.

---

calculated as a percentage of the investment amount. Additional information on the degree of deterioration of public works will provide the basis for a more accurate assessment of residual values of assets and more exact estimation of upkeep costs. These simple calculations can be done by the street addressing unit and/or the municipality's technical departments. This type of calculation has been done by local consultants in the context of urban audits (box 2.3).

An aid to investment planning

Local governments need to have information about their city for purposes of investment planning. Decision-making about financing priorities requires knowledge of existing conditions based on a needs assessment. An address directory can provide information on the population, infrastructure, and facilities in each neighborhood, thus making it a useful tool for the implementation of the Infrastructure and Services Programming Inventory (IPIE). This tool is a decisionmaking aid intended to guide urban interventions and identify priorities. By drawing on indicators and scores, the tool can be easily applied to show the extent of access to public services and to

---

Box 2.3. Inventory and valuation of built assets (Senegal and Guinea)

Under the Senegal Urban Development and Decentralization Program (PAC) co-financed by the World Bank and the AFD, urban audits were developed for each local government. The goal was to conduct a needs-based evaluation of the city and use the results to decide on a priority action program to be financed by the PAC. The audits consist of a brief evaluation of all municipal properties for which the municipality has responsibility for upkeep, such as streets and drainage, administrative and recreational facilities, markets, and the like. A simple property census and assessment of condition can provide an important guideline for scheduling future rehabilitation and maintenance work, and it also complements the Infrastructure and Services Programming Inventory (IPIE) drawn up during the audits. This type of research was carried out in Senegal, as well as in Guinea during UDP 3, and in Mauritania, Niger, Cameroon, Rwanda, and other countries. In each case, the audits were prepared by local consultants, who performed with overall success.

---

establish a classification system so that neighborhoods can be ranked according to priority of intervention and type of service[4] (box 2.3).

Street addressing and tax systems

Street addressing projects usually state among their objectives a "contribution to improved mobilization of fiscal resources." The discussion below focuses on ways in which such projects can help improve the performance of the existing tax system and reform the property tax system.

Improving the performance of the existing tax system

One of the primary benefits of using the address directory is the ability to obtain a list of economic activities that is usually more complete than the one used by the tax department and reveals the size of the population not listed on the tax rolls. The key challenge is the reconciliation of address data with tax department data.

The World Bank–financed Urban Development and Decentralization Program offers a revealing lesson learned in Senegal (Thiès and Kaolack) with tax registers (box 2.4). The process, managed by the Tax Department, involves reconciling the address directory with the taxpayer rolls in order to create a tax register that includes both taxpayer rolls and address information[5] (box 2.5).

Using such a reconciliation approach, tax departments can evaluate the results of tax enrollment and tax collection efforts. At the same time, the documents and street identification make it easier to locate potential taxpayers. This is usually accomplished through the use of cadastral maps and subdivision plans that are often imprecise, and it requires the involvement of specialized staff. The main problem derives from the lack of spatial identification. Streets may not be identified, and plot references may not correspond to the address or appear on building façades. The use of street addressing information with tax registers therefore constitutes an important step toward determining the tax base and increasing tax revenues (see annex 1, Terms of Reference).

Problems encountered and lessons learned

These types of solutions for improving the performance of tax systems are difficult to implement, however, owing to:

- logistical problems: tax departments do not have enough resources, leaving them ill-prepared to work with a broader population segment;
- lack of agreement on methods and procedures: central governments—often backed by the IMF—prefer to focus primarily on potentially major taxpayers and exhibit little interest in local taxation compared to national taxation.
- legal and institutional issues: difficulty of fostering the cooperation between central tax departments and local governments needed to implement a tax register.

Street addressing is nevertheless an undeniably useful tool for tax departments, although it is advisable to conduct a prior assessment of the potential for technical coordination with their procedural framework. Municipalities need to establish a stronger connection with the tax departments in order to anticipate the applications that will be needed, even well into the future. This type of planning will make it possible:

- to strengthen the dialogue with a central government that usually has little contact with the municipality, thereby creating a climate of trust between the two partners (most street addressing initiatives have set up a technical steering committee, which usually serves as an administrative connection between the tax and treasury departments); and
- to identify the necessary components for inclusion in the street addressing surveys so that the tax rolls can more easily be reconciled with the

---

Box 2.4. Development of tax registers (Senegal)

The Senegal program set three objectives:

- to determine the number of people not listed on the tax rolls by comparing them with address directories;
- to include address information on tax rolls and assessment notices as data to identify potential taxpayers and establish the tax base;
- to provide support to the taxation and collection services for data-gathering on groups not yet listed on the tax rolls and for developing strategies to bring the taxation system into line with economic realities such as urban poverty.

More specifically, the project is broken down into several steps:

(a) Assess the performance of tax enrollment and collection operations for business taxes and license fees and for property tax (list of names of taxpayers surveyed, amounts assessed, and so forth);
(b) Close the information gap between the address directory and the existing tax rolls for commercial licenses and fees and/or property tax (assuming that the two can be compared quickly, either through the use of cadastral or other references used in drawing up the subdivision plans, or by randomly adding names already on the tax rolls to the address directory);
(c) Include address information on tax rolls and assessment notices;
(d) Locate addresses not surveyed (businesses, dwellings, mixed-use properties);
(e) Conduct additional field surveys;
(f) Create a register of all potential taxpayers;
(g) Determine tax amounts and create rolls or registers for collection of advance payment.

---

address directory. It would be a waste of resources to conduct another tax survey after the street addressing initiative in order to find taxpayers' addresses. Such an undertaking is best accomplished by cadastral staff during an addressing operation.[6]

Street addressing and property tax reform

A number of urban development projects in Francophone Africa that include a street addressing component provide an opportunity to re-examine the municipal taxation system, and in particular the property tax system, so that it can be adapted to the local context. The property tax

---

Box 2.5. Tax department involvement in street addressing surveys (Niger)

The city of Niamey, which spearheaded a street addressing initiative using AIMF (International Association of Francophone Mayors) financing, established several mixed teams consisting of municipal agents, a representative of the water company (SEEN), a representative of the electric company (NIGELEC), and a cadastral agent.

The cadastral agent travels around with maps of the area to be assigned addresses. Each street and door number is penciled in on the cadastral map on paper. The team leader fills in each door number on the survey forms according to the cadastral reference for the plot. In this way, the two directories are reconciled with one another in real time.

When the area being assigned addresses has not yet been surveyed and entered in the cadastre, the subdivision plan also held by the cadastral and municipal agents is often used. This type of dual codification system for street-addressing and cadastral purposes makes it possible to reconcile the address directory with the other directories kept by the government and utility concessionaires.

"Business activities" data from street addressing operations shared with tax and treasury departments (Burkina Faso)

The tax departments have implemented street addressing software and have developed a data import-export module to simplify municipal technical department updates. The information is sent to the various departments, which tailor the parameters of their software to serve their own needs (additional information associated with each address, for example).

The tax departments have indicated an interest in identifying business activities along public roadways, with an eye to using the same door addressing system to locate these types of facilities.

---

generally produces little revenue for several reasons: there is no real political will to enforce it, central tax departments have little incentive to collect a tax that devolves to the municipal level, tax laws dating back to the colonial era are inadequate, and tax exemptions have been an overriding policy. Under these projects, some cities have been able to move away from an ownership-based property tax system that relies on a complex process involving rental values (taxes on "improved land," that is, land with buildings, and on unimproved land, which are poorly gauged to the socioeconomic circumstances of the taxpayers and the administrative capacity of the tax departments).

- Two factors create a gap between the objectives of a traditional property taxation system and the socioeconomic circumstances of the taxpayers. First, it is difficult to use ownership as the basis for direct property taxation when titles are issued only sparingly and most people have no land title. This type of taxation system is poorly understood, and it is often difficult to distinguish between owner, renter, and occupant. And secondly, owing to the taxpayers' usual inability to pay and the objectively low value of the properties, tax levies have been limited to amounts that are often too low to make traditional property valuation and tax collection operation financially viable.
- The management of a direct property taxation system is hampered by the complex procedure for assessing rental or commercial values when there is no formal real estate market, and sometimes by the lack of administrative resources such as information systems and site visits.

Such a system creates dysfunctions including unreliable tax assessments, frequent tax avoidance, a weak effective tax base, and perpetuation of procedural complexities from the assessment to the collection stage.

In order to overcome these problems, municipalities have sought to simplify procedures and move away from reliance on a tax based on property valuation. Basing the property taxation system on occupancy rather than on ownership delinks the tax from the tenure status of the property, on the notion that every resident—whether he owns or rents his home—consumes urban services and therefore should help defray the related municipal costs. Rather than struggle under a cumbersome and complex taxation system based on antiquated, largely unenforceable tax laws, municipalities are moving toward simplification of the tax laws and adopting a property taxation approach more closely aligned with existing capacities and resources.

Although this trend toward a new taxation system has not been widespread in Francophone Africa, examples can be cited in Burkina Faso, Togo, and Mali, where property taxation reform has been coupled with street addressing projects conducted under the auspices of World Bank–financed urban development projects. The cities of Ouagadougou, Bobo-Dioulasso, and Lomé carried out street addressing initiatives in conjunction with the implementation of a local tax on all types of residences, using a simplified basis more in accordance with household capacity to pay. This type of residence tax was inspired in part by the urban tax in Morocco and the old Tunisian rent tax.

On the whole, the assessment of taxes on a simplified basis and the use of an address directory have reduced some of the procedural complication. The issue of payment and collection is still largely unresolved, for these same simplified assessment procedures and street addressing initiatives have significantly swelled the tax rolls and necessitated more collection efforts.

Street addressing and the land tenure issue

The cadastral projects financed by the World Bank in Africa during the 1980s were not as successful as anticipated. These projects, which called for a long-term effort, were abandoned as a result of factors including the complexity and scope of the problem to be solved, the extensive resources to be mobilized, the need for day-to-day monitoring, and inadequate local expertise. In other respects, such an approach might be regarded as questionable, in view of the fact that one of the main obstacles to effective property tax management (which the cadastre itself helped to create) was the absence of addresses. The customary use of post office boxes for receiving mail has led to a system that is unreliable if, for example, the addressee is to sign an acknowledgement of receipt of an official letter, particularly in the case of a tax assessment notice. Under these circumstances, then, it was understandable that considerable importance would be placed on street addressing projects, which would "begin at the beginning," produce rapid and noticeable results, be managed by city authorities, and easily draw on local expertise, all for a cost nowhere near that of a cadastral project.

The great enthusiasm demonstrated for such projects sometimes creates the impression that there has been "competition" between cadastres and street addressing, when the more appropriate term would be "complementarity" between the two tools. To clear up any possible confusion, we will briefly summarize below the unique characteristics of each tool and then suggest ways in which they can be used.

CADASTRE AND STREET ADDRESSING
Owing to the many types of cadastres and the wide range of experiences with street addressing operations, only a few simple comparisons are outlined in table 2.1. Both of these tools offer illustrative documentation in the form of cadastral maps or addressing maps, and written documentation in the form of registers or directories.

Street addressing is a method for identifying streets and buildings that makes it possible to locate structures through the use of identifying markers such as street signs and entrance numbers, the planimetric representation of blocks of houses, and an address directory.

A cadastre is a comprehensive and perpetual inventory that describes and assesses the value of landholdings. It consists of a set of documents in which are recorded the breakdown of landholdings and the name of the owner of each plot. This definition gives rise to two possible applications or interpretations: (a) a *fiscal cadastre*, which seeks to describe the property tax base and serve as the basis for property valuation; or (b) a *legal cadastre*, intended to define the ownership rights attached to each plot. The recorded data accurately define the property boundaries and also serve to ensure ownership and property tax levies.[7]

The cadastre and land ownership in Francophone Africa

In most Francophone African countries,[8] the primary function of the cadastre is to recognize and define land boundaries for the purpose of removing lands from the public domain and allocating them to private owners. "The people have no rights over the land except as granted by the state." Rather than property rights being produced "from the bottom up" under a prescription system (whereby de facto occupancy becomes legal ownership after a certain prescription period that also requires proof of a date of purchase from a former owner who has already acquired ownership through prescription), property rights are produced "from the top down." In other words, the state declares itself the original owner of the land and exercises its sovereign power to grant titles of ownership, thereby removing lands from its domain." The state assigns title only after a long process that is cumbersome, costly, nontransparent, and inefficient. As a result, only about a hundred clear titles are issued each year, during which time thousands of buildings, erected without construction permits, fall outside the legal property ownership system and enjoy absolutely no legal protection.

Under these circumstances, a cadastre has only limited impact, and therefore city authorities would be well advised to seek ways to improve the situation by applying street addressing techniques. Four solutions are discussed here: reform the existing cadastre; supplement it with street addressing data; review the property taxation system; and undertake new street addressing initiatives in slum neighborhoods.[9]

Options for improvement

REFORM THE CADASTRE

In order to come to grips with the situation described above, the reform of the land tenure system would seem to be a prerequisite for achieving cadastral reform. Under one possible approach,[10] property rights would no longer be allocated as a reward for perseverance over a long obstacle course, but rather through a swift transformation from de facto ownership to legal status. Land

Figure 2.1. Cadastre and street addressing

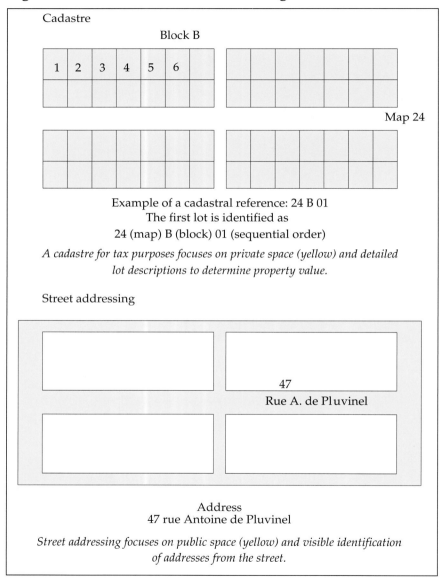

Cadastre

Block B

| 1 | 2 | 3 | 4 | 5 | 6 |

Map 24

Example of a cadastral reference: 24 B 01
The first lot is identified as
24 (map) B (block) 01 (sequential order)

A cadastre for tax purposes focuses on private space (yellow) and detailed lot descriptions to determine property value.

Street addressing

47
Rue A. de Pluvinel

Address
47 rue Antoine de Pluvinel

Street addressing focuses on public space (yellow) and visible identification of addresses from the street.

tenure would then bestow on the owner not only a right but also a responsibility to pay an annual property tax,[11] and this would enable city authorities to keep an up-to-date list of property owners. Such a change would justify a radical simplification of the procedure for recognizing property rights, which

Table 2.1. Cadastre and street addressing: a comparison

	Cadastre	Street addressing
Definition	"A general inventory of improved and unimproved land in a municipal territory, with an individual listing of their physical composition, using a planimetric plot representation, their economic use (yield), and their ownership, to provide the government with a sufficiently precise estimate to equitably apportion taxes on the landholding."	A method for public identification of streets (and related urban fixtures) and properties that makes it possible to locate buildings in a city through the use of identifying markers, the planimetric representation of blocks of houses, and an address directory.
System of coordinates		
Streets/public space *Plots*	A cadastre focuses on identifying properties (private space) rather than streets (public space). All plots are identified by a number ("cadastral reference") and their specific location is shown on a cadastral map (surface area).	Street addressing specifies an address according to street name, and therefore all streets and other public spaces are identified. Street addressing identifies doorways rather than plots.
Urban fixtures	A cadastre does not identify the location of urban fixtures (public standpipes, for example).	Street addressing identifies the location of urban fixtures and assigns them an address. This task is not carried out systematically during the initial intervention phase.
Representation in map form		
Type of map	A cadastre includes a set of maps on a scale of 1:500 to 1:2000 that represent improved land, plot boundaries, and cadastral references (which cannot be used for location purposes since they do not indicate external markers, unless the maps are geometric). This document is not publicly distributed.	Street addressing establishes a city map on a scale of 1:10,000 that shows street names and/or numbers; numbers of doorways of some buildings; subdivisions; utilities. This document is widely distributed to government offices and the general public.
Representation on the ground		
	A cadastre does not deal with street signs or building numbers and may or may not use the address if it is available.	Street addressing identifies street names or numbers and buildings through the use of signs and doorway numbers.
Directory/ register		
	A record of occupants, lot description and the associated land rights, drawn up in conjunction with the map.	An address directory contains a limited amount of information, including street identification, building number, economic use (residential or business activity), and perhaps cadastral reference and water and electric meter numbers.

(Table continues on the following page.)

Table 2.1. Cadastre and street addressing: a comparison (*continued*)

	Cadastre	Street addressing
Registration of ownership	A cadastre does not systematically guarantee ownership rights (for example, a fiscal cadastre).	Street addressing does not specify anything about ownership rights. It can help confirm occupancy rights in slum neighborhoods.
Information provided about lots and buildings		
Economic use	A cadastre does not indicate economic use, though it provides information that could help determine the property value.	Street addressing provides information on economic use when applicable to a particular property.
Physical composition	A cadastre provides exact descriptions, such as surface area, apartment number, and property value.	An address directory often indicates how the plot or building looks from the street.
Ownership	A cadastre indicates the name(s) of the owner(s) and/or rightful claimants.	An address directory does not confirm the occupants' or owners' names. It does not necessarily list names of occupants.
Implementation	A cadastre takes years to implement. It is updated regularly, primarily for changes of ownership. (France's cadastre has been redone three times.)	A street addressing operation usually takes about a year. Updates are usually done at the initiative of an ad hoc municipal agency.
Tax application	A cadastre does not necessarily result in a tax application, but in most cases it is useful for that purpose.	Street addressing has no direct tax application, but the address directory is generally useful for tax levying purposes because it enables tax assessment notices to be sent.
Cost	The cost of implementing a nationwide cadastre is difficult to estimate, but some World Bank projects indicate a cost of about $100 million.	A street addressing operation in a large city costs approximately $200,000.
Staff	A large and highly qualified staff is needed to implement and maintain a cadastre on a long-term basis.	Implementation and upkeep requires only one or two qualified professionals.

henceforth would be accomplished in a single stage, eliminating the requirement of improvements to the land (site improvement or *mise en valeur*). Land would be allocated immediately with full ownership rights conveyed and would be recorded in the land register;[12] the owner would immediately acquire the obligation to pay the tax and the right to sell the property without encumbrance. A street addressing operation undertaken in conjunction with the reform would simplify the issuance of the tax assessment notice.[13]

This type of reform will surely not be implemented without some difficulty. If carried out as part of a project that is externally financed, the donor will likely prefer a fundamental change in the notion of property rights over simple technical solutions. Moreover, the relevant government agencies, aware of the actual or potential benefit to be gained from a lengthy property transaction process, may resist any change in the status quo.

SUPPLEMENT THE CADASTRE WITH STREET ADDRESSING DATA
In the event that such a reform proves to be overly ambitious, a less sweeping program can be adopted by using street addressing data to supplement the data recorded by the cadastral unit. If field workers experienced with maps have no problem identifying individual properties, the same will hold true for tax or treasury agents responsible for tax auditing and collection, as mentioned above in regard to the tax registers. This type of intervention would take a two-pronged approach: (a) incorporate the addresses into the cadastral data; and (b) establish a correspondence between addresses and cadastral references for plots that are so identified.

REVIEW THE PROPERTY TAXATION SYSTEM
As discussed in the preceding section, cadastral documentation that is inadequate or nearly nonexistent and often out of date does not preclude the implementation of innovative property taxation systems, for which street addressing initiatives can play a fundamental role, as in the case of the residence tax[14] in Burkina Faso. The innovation lies partly in requiring citizens to participate in the costs of the city (rather than taxing property that is often unregistered), and partly in seeking simple solutions.[15] Innovative solutions, of course, cannot solve every problem.

Street addressing and slum upgrading

In the context described above, cadastral registration generally covers less than 10% of the population while urban areas continue to grow in an essentially informal way. Efforts to regularize land tenure (by issuing titles to land), which were at the heart of a large number of upgrading programs for underserviced neighborhoods, have been largely fruitless in the face of such an extensive problem.

Street addressing initiatives in "slums" or informal settlements are an option although they are difficult to implement in practice for the following reasons:

- the neighborhoods are often known to be illegal, and the authorities fear that street addressing is a pretext for their de facto regularization;
- the street layout is often indistinct or even nonexistent;
- street addressing in formal neighborhoods is always viewed as a priority; under these circumstances, informal settlements are often overlooked.

This hesitation to deal with the slums, as understandable as it may be, must be overcome because it contributes to prolonged exclusion of slum populations from society. Of course it is true that street addressing alone will not significantly change their living conditions, but it may help these settlements to better integrate into the city by strengthening their place in the larger community. Street addressing can thus lead to a kind of collective regularization of the slum which, even if limited in scope, often bears fruit much sooner than difficult and slow-moving land tenure regularization projects.

The specific goal is to gather evidence that the slum population permanently resides in the neighborhood while setting out a way for them to move from their precarious and unrecognized status to occupancy rights. The results of this research should not be confined to the address directory; they should be reported in government records to bolster their legitimacy. The idea is not to include them in the cadastre, which would surely be an almost insurmountable obstacle, but rather to create a possible parallel register accessible to eligible persons and located in a decentralized department.

Two possible scenarios emerge as to whether the initiative is a component of an upgrading program or is integrated into a city-wide street addressing project. Whatever the circumstances, street addressing is an alternative to the formal regularization of property rights, which has largely failed to achieve results in Africa.

COMPONENT OF AN UPGRADING PROGRAM. Under this scenario, the slum is targeted for improvement or upgrading projects, and street addressing should support and round out the intervention, thereby helping the neighborhood to take its place in the larger community. If street addressing proves difficult to implement, it may be limited initially to the simple installation of street signs on upgraded streets; the initiative will be completed at a later time.

INTEGRATION INTO A CITY-WIDE STREET ADDRESSING PROGRAM. Under this scenario, no upgrading work is scheduled for the neighborhood, but a street addressing project is prepared for the city. The initiative consists of including the neighborhood among those targeted by the street addressing project, even if it means adjusting the actions to be taken:

- If the neighborhood streets are regularly laid out or if the right-of-way for the main routes permits automobile traffic, signs are installed on at least the main access streets;
- If neighborhood streets are not regularly laid out and main routes are poorly defined, the following steps are taken: (a) in conjunction with residents, define the main routes by dividing the neighborhood into 5- to 10-hectare zones with adequate right-of-way to accommodate service delivery networks and vehicles (carts, ambulances); (b) install signs on the main routes.

WHERE IS INNOVATION NEEDED? No matter which scenario is used, residents must take ownership of the street addressing initiative, which is achieved by their participation in naming the streets. As limited as these interventions may seem, their impact should not be underestimated. They help to relieve the isolation of neighborhoods that are usually neglected and gradually integrate them into the city.

Some innovation will no doubt be required in the implementation of the usual street addressing techniques for residents to feel secure in their land tenure status while evidence that they are permanent residents of the neighborhood is gathered:

- GPS use should make it possible to identify the main routes and dwellings in an unorganized urban milieu;
- Contents of the address directory should be adapted; paradoxically, more information must be collected than would be required for an organized neighborhood: household names, information establishing the presence of a household (electricity bill, receipt for tax payment) or numbers placed on residences by census workers or utility concessionaires, and the like.
- Information gathering may also lead to innovation. For example, if emphasizing the vulnerability of certain especially disadvantaged groups appears to be important, it may be more useful to document their situation as a group rather than in terms of individual households considered separately.

Street addressing and concessionary services

It is increasingly common to use street addressing for concessionary and neighborhood services (box 2.6).

Figure 2.2. Street addressing in informal settlements

Box 2.6. Street addressing and concessionary services (Mozambique)

The Mozambican Water Authority (ADM) monitored the work being done to implement a street addressing initiative in Maputo and four other cities. As a result, it was able to update the ADM address directory and inventory its own networks (a very positive result for Maputo). ADM benefited in several ways from this collaboration:

- It now has a unique account identifier for its subscribers—their address.
- It can now update its own address directory and manage it more effectively.
- It now has tools to facilitate its own interventions on the network (repairs, extensions), allowing it to regularize poorly identified connections.
- It completed its cartographic database using graphic street address information (location of public standpipes, for example), which facilitates future implementation of a GIS.

Finally, an information exchange agreement between the municipality and ADM was prepared to define the areas where street addressing and the concessionaire's business management system may overlap.

Concessionary services

When utility concessionaires in urban areas (water and electricity) take part in street addressing, the results are often very positive:

- Concessionaire representatives frequently monitor the conducting of surveys and numbering of buildings: at this time, they establish a table in which the address and meter number are matched up (Chad, Mozambique).
- Concessionaires require that future subscribers give an address (Burkina Faso, where the publication of the street addressing map was an important step forward in the process).
- A truly cooperative relationship is established between the municipal unit set up to manage the addressing process and water companies, whose directories have used the address as a key account identifier (Mozambique).

- Concessionaires have sometimes "addressed" their equipment (poles, transformers, public standpipes) to facilitate locating and maintaining them.

However, concessionaires may also have concerns:

- They have already set up their own reference system and mapped networks and subscribers (sometimes on GIS); they have worked out a system of "rounds" for paying visits to subscribers, and they consider the introduction of street addressing to be superfluous.
- They want street addressing initiatives but are sometimes disappointed when the project is completed and is not extended to new neighborhoods. On their own initiative, they sometimes extend street addressing efforts but do so based on an approach that differs from the existing system (Bamako).

Any street addressing initiative should be launched only after prior consultation with concessionaires so that they are aware of issues and challenges that may be of concern to them.

Improving neighborhood services and the case of the post office

Emergency services such as fire, police, and ambulances are usually cited as direct applications of street addressing, since an address map, its index, and directory reduce the emergency response time. But there are also direct applications for several other types of neighborhood services such as taxis, deliveries, and mail service, for example. It is quite surprising, however, that mail delivery was not identified as one of the areas where street addressing could have the greatest impact, even though very little experience had been gathered in this area; when the first initiative was implemented, some people even referred to it as the "postal address initiative."

This hesitation is not without some basis. Emphasizing the link between street addressing and mail delivery suggested that once street addresses had been assigned, the postal service could distribute the mail to each address within no time. In fact, many countries operate with a postal box or general delivery system, which at first seems less efficient but more economical than a "door-to-door" system. The cost is in fact shared by the postal service, which gathers the mail at the post office, and the end-user, who comes to collect his or her mail.

This is the reason street addressing for mail routing has usually been adopted only with the agreement of postal officials. That being said, for the last several years, private express mail delivery services have sprung up, and the new demand for this service has led to a rethinking of this hesitation,[16] especially given that some countries, like Mozambique and Senegal, are trying to leverage their street addressing experience to improve mail delivery. An agreement was signed between the city and the *Correios de Moçambique* to set forth the terms and conditions of cooperation between the postal service and the municipal unit responsible for implementing the street addressing initiative. Moreover, private sector initiatives are beginning to appear: in Burkina Faso, the GIEs (Local Business Initiatives Groups), often established by unemployed young graduates of teaching programs, have offered their services to the post office and water and electricity concessionaires to ensure that bills and reminders of unpaid accounts were delivered.

Street addressing and economic development

Street address information concerns not only municipal managers but also the many actors that make up the social and economic fabric of a city. The information is found in maps and databases and makes them easier to use and understand, especially for public and private economic operators who have a particular interest in answering the following questions. What kinds of activities go on in the city? Where do they take place? How are households distributed? In other words, how is the city organized in spatial, economic, and social terms?

The address directory provides a very important piece of information: a list of existing formal and informal economic activities. The list is a good barometer of the city's economic potential and the nature and location of activities taking place there. In addition, by preserving the history of a location's changing uses, address management software provides a reliable indicator of the economic dynamics at work and can serve to document trends.

Private companies are usually interested in street address databases because they can use them to tailor their individual and joint business strategies. A database makes it easier to understand the competition and to prospect for business by dividing activities into sectors and economic categories and the potential clientele into households and companies. Mapping helps each type of business to identify its own location in the city as well as that of the competition; this leads to a better understanding of clients and potential markets and thus helps define a more effective and targeted business development strategy.

The municipality launches street addressing initiatives and thus plays a key role in making available the information they generate. Various experiences show that it can put this information to good use and thereby keep address systems up-to-date and in place. Indeed, different entities would like to adapt address mapping to their own uses (tourism, concessionaires, Chamber of Commerce), and the municipality may negotiate some of its rights to the information. For example, in Mozambique, each address map is copyrighted in the name of the municipality, and its use allows the municipal street addressing unit to earn some revenue. Along the same lines, reconciling economic data with data from the address directory makes it possible to set up an economic database (BDE). Maputo is an example of a BDE used by the city government (box 2.7), but this can also come about through the initiative of the private sector, professional groups, the Chamber of Commerce and Industry, or the trade council.

Possible action items

WEB SITE. The creation of a street addressing web site is one way to allow for public (local community site) or private (CCIA [Chamber of Commerce, Industry and Handicrafts], Yellow Pages, etc.) use of the information. This may be achieved with a simplified but precise and user-friendly map. One advantage of a web site is the hypertext function, which makes it possible to run the site with a great deal of flexibility (something like a GIS), especially in the area of marketing the information.

STREET ADDRESS TRAINING. It has been noted in cities where street address-ing initiatives have been conducted that certain occupations—such as taxi and ambulance drivers, fire fighters, and police—have difficulty using address systems. Motivating dispatchers to get training may complement efforts to make the data available to them. This training could be provided by the municipal unit in charge of the street addressing initiative; profes-sional associations; women's, youth, or neighborhood groups; NGOs, etc.

SPONSORSHIP AND ADVERTISING. Street addressing initiatives may be sponsored in different ways. One approach is to use signs or posts where the name or brand of the sponsor who provided financing for the initia-tive is inscribed. Another might make use of published documents, charts and maps, catalogues, or even Internet sites. Other avenues such as televi-sion are also available.

  In sum, street addressing initiatives can stimulate a more dynamic relationship between local government and the private sector. The information contained in street address directories often contrasts with that of traditional economic indicators because it reflects all activities, including those of the informal sector, thereby providing a comprehen-sive overview of economic activities in a city and including a frequently neglected segment of economic life.

Box 2.7. Economic database (Maputo)

To increase revenue and improve city management, the city of Maputo took steps to learn more about its economic fabric and fiscal potential. An economic database (BDE) was thus put in place, with two objectives:

- to facilitate management of licenses by the Department of Economic Activity (state deconcentrated services, integrated into city services);
- to ultimately increase revenue from local and national taxes on business activities (IRTB [tax on income category B for farmers], CI [industrial tax on small craftsmen without employees], value-added tax [VAT], local taxes) by setting up a directory of companies.

The BDE was expected to produce three secondary effects:

(a) to facilitate decisionmaking on the municipal level, by increasing awareness of the web of existing activities and the pace of their evolution;
(b) to allow BDE data to be reconciled with the directories of other entities (Tax Department), with a view toward eventually improving tax system performance;
(c) to upgrade the information given to economic operators in the city by making available to them updated data on economic activity.

DICT (Department of Industry, Commerce and Tourism) information existed in the form of a manually updated directory. This information was reconciled with the street address directory, creating the opportunity to develop a computerized database consisting of 9,000 companies and business activities. The street addressing initiative compiled 7,295 addresses for business purposes, and the DICT generated 8,912 licenses, which represents a gap of 20% owing to: (a) licenses granted for businesses without a business location, (b) the fact that several businesses had the same address, with no real distinction between them on the ground, and (c) cessation of business activities by several entities that did not so indicate.

The data retrieval is initiated by the unit in charge of the street addressing initiative, but the processing is being done at DICT, which has greater expertise with the formulas and procedures (the two departments signed a protocol to exchange information). DICT regularly transfers the list of new registered businesses to the DNS (Department of Statistics) and to two "tax districts" (Ministry of Finance) responsible for issuing tax rolls and collection, but whose main activities are focused on the 500 "largest" taxpayers.

This chapter has provided an overview of the various applications of street addressing. The next chapter provides examples of these applications as implemented in a number of countries.

Notes

1. Cityvia, Infrastructure and Services Programming Inventory

2. Example: Sections C.12-1, C.12-2 of street C.12.

3. Programs such as Cadix, Cityvia, Urbavia, and Viziroad.

4. *The Future of African Cities*, Chapter 5.

5. The taxation services use the notion of a "pre-roll that requires validation."

6. In Burkina Faso, the heads of the street addressing units in Ouagadougou and Bobo-Dioulasso established a connection between cadastral references and data in the address directory.

7. Countries that have a fiscal cadastre include Belgium, Spain, France, and Italy. Countries with a legal cadastre include South Africa, Germany, Hungary, Switzerland, and Turkey. The United Kingdom and Ireland have no cadastre.

8. J. Comby. "Quel cadastre, pour quoi faire? L'exemple du Gabon." [Using which cadastre to do what? Gabon case study.]

9. This solution is discussed in section 6.

10. According to J. Comby.

11. The formula for determining the annual tax would discourage beneficiaries from holding onto land of which they do not have use. At the present time, many properties, even if registered, quickly change hands informally. Levying a tax on allocated land each year creates an automatic update of the list of landowners. Anyone who is no longer a landowner will refuse to pay, and, conversely, payment of the tax quickly creates a legal presumption of ownership. (J.Comby)

12. Rather than occurring on a plot by plot basis at the request of the interested party, this procedure would be carried out sector by sector at the government's initiative.

13. Alternatively, the tax might also be payable at the revenue office.

14. Identical to the tax instituted in Togo.

15. In Burkina Faso, two criteria are used to determine the tax: neighborhood services and residential services (such as water and electricity consumption). In Côte d'Ivoire, the tax on improved land is also based on two simple criteria: neighborhood services and declared number of habitable rooms.

16. A similar hesitation is associated with tax departments: street addressing certainly improves tax collection, but this is probably not a very good advertising slogan.

3
Street Addressing Practices

This chapter describes the street addressing projects carried out during the 1990s in various cities in sub-Saharan Africa. The first part of the chapter presents an overview and comparison of the various efforts. The subsequent sections describe the individual projects in each country.

Overview of main experiences

The addressing activities undertaken between 1989 and 2004 include projects in 52 cities in 15 countries (Benin, Burkina Faso, Cameroon, Chad, Congo, Côte d'Ivoire, Djibouti, Guinea, Mali, Mauritania, Mozambique, Niger, Rwanda, Senegal, and Togo). A summary of the various operations compares several features taken from a sampling of 21 cities[1] that successfully completed virtually all of their street addressing tasks (table 3.1).

The sample represents 11.2 million people. The population in the cities represented ranges from 80,000 to 1,300,000 inhabitants. The overall budget for these operations totals US$6,800,000, for an average of US$325,000 per project. In all, 84,000 street signs were installed and 1,200,000 buildings were assigned an address, thus serving about 75% of all households.[2] The average cost is US$0.6 per capita[3] and US$5.7 per addressed doorway. Before street addressing projects were undertaken, only 8% of streets had names; in other words, 92% were unidentified. However, budgetary constraints necessitated the sparing use of street signs, resulting in an average of 1.2 signs per intersection. Thus, in some neighborhoods, only one in every two intersections received a street sign.

Various donors contributed to financing the addressing effort, including the World Bank, and the French Cooperation Agency represented by the Minstry of Foreign Affairs (MAE) and other departments (Decentralized Cooperation, AFD, and AIMF). These two donors have clearly worked closely together. In some instances, they divided their financing among cities for the same addressing project: PDUD (Urban Development and Decentralization Project) in Mali and PAC (Urban Development and Decentralization Program) in Senegal. In other cases, they helped to expand efforts launched by the other donors (Burkina Faso, Cameroon, and Niger).[4]

Actual project implementation differs by country (table 3.2):

- A country's addressing project may have involved one or several cities: (Mauritania, Senegal (11), Mali, Mozambique (6), Côte d'Ivoire, Benin (3), Burkina Faso, Cameroon, Niger (2), and Guinea (1);
- The operation was initiated either within the scope of a Project Unit (Burkina Faso, Cameroon, Mali, and Senegal) or within the Technical Department of the municipalities (Guinea, Mozambique, Niger, Chad, and Togo);

Table 3.1. Features of addressing operations based on a sampling of 21 cities

	Average	Total
Number of cities in the sample		21
Number of inhabitants (year 1 of addressing)	540,000	11,200,000
Surface area of cities (in ha)	4,200	88,000
Number of streets	2,000	42,000
Number of intersections	3,400	72,000
Number of street signs	4,000	84,000
Number of doorways addressed	57,000	1,200,000
Percentage of streets named	8%	
Cost of equipping addressing unit		US$35,000
Cost of operations	US$325,000	US$6,800,000
Annual municipal budget	US$2,600,000	US$54,000,000
Number of streets/ha	0.5	
Number of intersections/ha	0.8	
Number of signs/intersection	1.2	
Cost per doorway addressed	US$5.7	
Cost per capita	US$0.6	
Average municipal budget/capita	US$4.8	

- The efforts either received ongoing technical assistance (Cameroon, Mali, Mauritania, Mozambique, and Chad), or occasional support from technical missions (Burkina Faso, Guinea, Niger, and Senegal).

Addressing applications also vary by country (table 3.3). However, projects involving taxation were the most prevalent (residence tax in Burkina Faso and Togo, tax registers in Senegal, and municipal taxation in Mauritania). Other applications involve urban management (street system and household waste collection in Guinea, Cameroon, and Burkina Faso, an urban observatory in Cameroon).

Table 3.2. Execution and financing of addressing by country and city

Country and city addressed	Addressing year 1	Population (year 1)	Tasks							Financing					
			1 CS	2 SI	3 SN	4 AM	5 AL	6 SS	7 LF	8 WB	9 MAE	10 AFD	11 DC	12 EU	13 AI
Burkina Faso															
Ouagadougou	1992	600,000								■	■				
Bobo-Dioulasso	1993	300,000								■	■				
Benin															
Cotonou	1993										■				
Parakou	1993										■				
Porto-Novo	1993										■				
Cameroon															
Yaoundé	1992	800,000								■	■				
Douala	1992	1,100,000								■	■				
Congo															
Brazzaville											■				
Côte d'Ivoire															
Abidjan	2000														
Abengouro	2003								■						
San Pedro	2000													■	
Djibouti															
Djibouti	1997										■				
Guinea															
Conakry	1993	1,100,000								■					
Mali															
Bamako	1993	920,000								■					
Gao	1996	84,000								■					
Kayes	1996	53,000									■				

Mopti Sévaré	1996	100,000
Ségou	1996	110,000
Sikasso	1996	103,000
Mauritania		
Nouakchott	1997	700,000
Aleg	1999	6,600
Atar	2000	24,000
Bouttilimit	2001	17,000
Moudjeria	2002	3,500
Nouhadibou	1997	90,000
Rachid	2002	1,800
Rosso	2000	44,000
Tekane	2002	2,000
Tiguent	2001	3,500
Tidjika	2002	10,000
Mozambique		
Maputo	1995	1,300,000
Pemba	2000	90,000
Quelimane	2000	195,000
Nampula	2000	280,000
Beira	2000	410,000
Matola	2000	380,000
Niger		
Niamey	2001	800,000
Maradi	2003	
Rwanda		
Kigali	1993	270,000

(Table continues on the following page.)

Table 3.2. Execution and financing of addressing by country and city (continued)

Country and city addressed	Addressing year 1	Population (year 1)	Tasks						Financing						
			1 CS	2 SI	3 SN	4 AM	5 AL	6 SS	7 LF	8 WB	9 MAE	10 AFD	11 DC	12 EU	13 AI
Senegal															
Dakar	2003	820,000								■		■			
Guiédiawaye	2003	450,000								■					
Pikine	2003	470,000								■					
Rufisque	2003	140,000								■					
Diourbel	2000	100,000								■					
Kaolack	2000	200,000								■		■			
Louga	2000	70,000								■					
St. Louis	2000	140,000								■					
Tambacounda	2000	60,000													
Thiès	2000	230,000								■					
Ziguinchor	2000	170,000													
Chad															
N'Djaména	1989	600,000									■				
Togo															
Lomé	1996	850,000							■	■					

☐ task completed   ☐ in progress   ■ principal financing

Key

Completion of tasks
1. CS Codification study
2. SI Sign installation
3. SN Surveys, numbering of buildings
4. AM Creation of address map
5. AL Address list (spreadsheet)
6. SS Addresses in specialized software

Financing
7. LF Local financing
8. WB World Bank
9. MAE French Ministry of Foreign Affairs
10. AFD French Development Agency
11. DC Decentralized Cooperation
12. EU European Union
13. AI Intl. Assoc. of Francophone Mayors

Table 3.3. Addressing applications by country

	Burkina Faso	Benin	Cameroon	Guinea	Mali	Mauritania	Mozambique	Niger	Rwanda	Senegal	Togo
Civic identity											
Addresses	░	░	░	░	░	░	░	░	░	░	░
Elections						▒					
Urban information	░		■			░	░			░	
Municipal services											
Street system	░		■				░				
Inventory of municipal built assets	░									░	
Household waste collection			■								
Tax systems	■			▒	■		░			■	■
Land management	▒										
Slum upgrading				▒	▒			░			
Concessionary services											
Water & electricity	░						■				
Postal services	░						░		░		
Health services							■				
Economic development							■				

■ Major impact   ▒ Moderate impact   ░ In progress

Burkina Faso

Ouagadougou	
Number of inhabitants	600,000
Surface area of urbanized zone	10,750 ha
Number of streets	4,910
Number of intersections	12,400
Streets named	70 streets in 1997
	250 streets in 2002
Number of doorways addressed	100,000
Total cost of operation	US$491,000
Cost/addressed doorway	US$3.6
Addressing unit established	1992
Number assignment, surveys, sign installation	1994–1997
Creation of address directory	1996–1997
Bobo-Dioulasso	
Number of inhabitants (1993)	300,000
Surface area of urbanized zone (formal)	4,050 ha
Number of streets	1,700
Number of intersections	3,650
Streets named	95 (7%)
Number of doorways addressed	40,000
Total cost of operation	US$186,125
Estimated cost/addressed doorway	US$4.7
Addressing unit established	1993
Number assignment, surveys, sign installation	1994–1997
Creation of address directory	1996–1997

Background and objectives

The addressing system described in this document was originally developed in Burkina in 1987 as part of the UDP 2 (Second Urban Development Project). This project had two components: the mobilization of municipal resources and the strengthening of urban infrastructure. Mobilizing resources proved somewhat problematic since real estate property rights had been abolished in the Revolution, thereby eliminating property titles and their accompanying property taxes. To overcome these challenges, authorities instituted two simple, complementary tools: the residence tax and street addressing. Together, they helped to achieve the following objectives:

- To increase municipal resources through better collection of local taxes and fees;
- To improve management of urban services.

Financing and implementation

The addressing project received the following outside funding:

- As part of UDP 2, the World Bank financed an addressing system in Ouagadougou and Bobo-Dioulasso starting in 1992. The Bank provided additional financing in 2000 as part of the subsequent project (PACVU [Urban Environmental Project]) in order to complete street sign installation after the municipality had decided to name the main streets that had previously been numbered;
- In 2002, the French Cooperation Agency, which had financed a rewrite of the Urbadresse software as part of another project, financed the transfer of addressing data to this new software, and financed training on the software as well.
- Initially, the addressing unit (UDP 2) handled the project, and at the end of the effort, the municipalities' technical departments assumed responsibility for the work.

Technical features

- *Division.* Originally divided into neighborhoods, the city was subsequently divided into "sectors" at the time of the Revolution (President Sankara): 30 sectors in Ouagadougou and 23 in Bobo-Dioulasso. Addressing adhered to the sector division that had gained acceptance by both citizens and governments.
- *Street codification.* Streets are identified by a number composed of two elements. The first is the sector number followed by a sequential number (for example: street 5.14 is the 14th street in sector 5).
- *Numbering doorways.* Numbering is metric and alternating (even and odd on opposite sides of the street).
- *Street sign installation.* A local firm selected following an international bidding process supplied street signs. Small local companies handled sign installation.
- *Surveys and number assignment.* The UDP 2 addressing unit carried out initial efforts.
- *Survey data.* Include: the address, occupant's name, plot use category, and cadastral references.
- *Address directory.* A specialized software program (developed in Macintosh 4D) originally managed the data; in 2002 they were transferred to the Urbadresse software written for PC.

- *Address map.* For both cities, 3,000 copies of an address map and a street index were created and distributed.

Results

In neighborhoods where an addressing initiative was considered viable in both cities, the UDP 2 project numbered doorways, took surveys, and installed street signs. The project included the printing of 3,000 copies of a guide map with street index (2,000 copies for Ouagadougou and 1,000 copies for Bobo-Dioulasso). In each city, an address directory was created in a special software program.

At the end of UDP 2, the addressing units of both cities became part of the municipal technical departments (STM) that use addressing for at least three purposes:

- Collecting household waste in collective trash bins: bins and collection points are assigned addresses,
- Street cleaning (78 km in Ouagadougou and 24 streets in Bobo-Dioulasso are identified using the address system),
- "Door-to-door" collection of household waste (2,000 households in Ouagadougou); addressing is used to collect garbage and waste collection fees.

Over the past several years, addressing has continued with the following efforts:

- Matching addresses with cadastral references of the plots. The State Land Management Department assisted in this effort. However, maps or address directories have not yet been updated;
- Creation of a Toponymy Commission. This is a major initiative of the municipality of Ouagadougou. The commission produced a list of potential names to gradually replace the numbers assigned to streets. Remarkably well organized and documented (Annex 2), this list has enabled the municipality to name or rename 2,000 streets in Ouagadougou. For example, "Street 12.69" has become "Street K. Moryamba" and the "avenue de la Révolution" has been renamed "avenue de la Nation";
- Purchase and installation of 2,000 new street signs in Ouagadougou;
- The addressing unit of Ouagadougou has prepared and organized training sessions and awareness programs for national departments (tax and treasury departments), municipal departments, and other users (such as taxi drivers);
- Transfer of data, for both cities, to a new software program better suited to the country's IT environment;

- Training for technical and tax departments on how to use the new soft-ware. This training was designed to help various departments collabo-rate to facilitate future data sharing.

Burkina Faso proved quite innovative in three areas of its addressing initiatives. First, it set up a formal system of rules for addressing. At the same time, it implemented a new tax based on the address system. Finally, it created a compendium of place names that an ad hoc commission now uses to name streets. However, because of its impact, we will concentrate on the residence tax.

Specific application: residence tax

BACKGROUND. When the UDP 2 project began (1987), the country had a property tax paid by those persons with a furnished home. The tax was based on the home's rental value. The tax was calculated by applying a rate of 2% to the rental value after deducting a minimum rent. Two additional taxes supple-mented this main tax: a tax on the rental value of residential accommodations (1% of the rental value) and additional centimes (15% of the main tax).

One of UDP 2's goals was to increase resources because several obstacles interfered with the application of this property tax such as:

- No control over the tax base because potential taxpayers were not filing statements. When the business tax calculation was made, only a few merchants were actually taxed.
- Lack of consistency in calculating rental value.
- Few tax assessment notices issued, compared to potential tax revenue.
- High cost of managing the tax compared to actual yield.

In addition to these challenges, the government had abolished all land rights, which negated any application of the tax and, at the very least, the entire system needed to be reevaluated. Thus, the government instituted the residence tax, which subsequently underwent various adjustments as the effects of the revolutionary period gradually diminished.

CREATION OF AND ADJUSTMENTS TO THE RESIDENCE TAX
With land rights abolished, the residence tax no longer applied to land owners, but to "residents" who would be expected to help pay the city's expenses. The 1992 reform was designed to: (a) condense the tax assess-ment procedure by eliminating additional taxes, (b) simplify the method for determining the tax base by instituting a fixed scale, thereby promot-ing internal consistency, (c) increase the number of tax assessment notices issued, and (d) choose simple criteria for taxation.

Two criteria determined the residence tax amount: level of services in the neighborhood and quality of the home measured by water and electricity consumption. A survey of the same sample of homes simulated two different tax systems. The first was based on the criteria of the former property tax system, and the second was based on water and electricity consumption. There was such a strong correlation between the results that the country opted for the second system because it was much easier to implement, since it was based simply on obtaining readings from utility concessionaires on amounts of water and electricity consumed. These data determine the home's level of services without necessitating actual inspection of the premises. Neighborhood facilities and level of services were easy to assess. A scale system determined the level of taxes. Thus, a home without water or electricity, located in a neighborhood with few facilities, was taxed at about two dollars per year, but a home with high consumption rates (because of a pool or air conditioners) and located in a residential neighborhood with good facilities was taxed at a rate fifty times higher.

When the reform was adopted, the addition of two more criteria complicated the procedure: type of building (permanent, semi-permanent, or cob) and number of rooms. But the results obtained were inconclusive. The 1995 reform returned the system to the two criteria initially used, and their application was revised and enhanced through better management (automation), requirement to file, better investigation of taxpayers, and the application of financial or legal penalties for anyone not filing or not paying taxes. In 1999, a new reform again adjusted the tax so that it was more compatible with the standard of living of low-income populations.

The following measures further improved the system:

- An inventory made to create an address directory,
- The design of data entry and data processing software to process information from tax forms filed by taxpayers,
- The use of various directories to supplement the information found on tax forms filed by taxpayers (directories from SONABEL [National Electric Power Company], ONEA [National Office of Water and Sanitation], and CNSS [National Social Security Office]).

PROBLEMS ENCOUNTERED

- Using the directory from the electric company (SONABEL) led to a number of double taxation issues.
- Incorporating a processing department for a new tax within the National Tax Authority (DGI) proved more difficult than expected.

- The still-limited use of the address directory by utility concessionaires (water and electricity) has not helped taxpayers become accustomed to using the address system.

ISSUING NOTICES AND COLLECTING TAXES

Since monitoring began (in 1996), tax assessment notices have been issued erratically, stabilizing at around 350 million CFAF in Ouagadougou and 200 million CFAF in Bobo-Dioulasso. Yield was initially better in Bobo, with 36,000 potential taxpayers, compared with 40,000 in Ouagadougou, a city at least twice as large. However, Ouagadougou has improved its issuing of tax notices over the past few years (65,000 in 2000).

Collections remain below expectations. This is partially due to the procedure itself and due to local governments' lack of involvement. Results indicate that a system of tax withholding at the source for employees, monitoring during any formalities with financial or local administrations, and, finally, increased media coverage to increase citizens' awareness of how local resources are used (to improve local facilities and services) would improve the tax collection rate.

HOW THE RESIDENCE TAX CHAIN WORKS

Initially established to simplify procedures (system of wealth-related tax calculated by the taxpayer; entire urban population taxed), the residence tax is still weighed down by its cumbersome procedures. This is primarily because the operations are split between the tax department (issuing notices) and the treasury department (collections). Since the early 1990s, the operations of most other taxes are managed (issuing notices and collections) entirely by either one of these departments. The DGI has suggested the possibility of splitting the two residence tax units in Ouagadougou and Bobo-Dioulasso between the central tax departments of the financial administrations in both cities, but it has not offered any specific timetable or method for transfer at this time.

HOW THE TAX COMPARES TO OTHER RESOURCES

The residence tax remains a minor revenue for municipalities: less than 2% for Ouagadougou in 2001 and about 5% for Bobo-Dioulasso. However, it represents the only direct tax on households at the local level. A comparison with other household taxation systems throughout the region does not seem to indicate that any fundamental changes are needed to the system that was created in 1992. Several other countries have set up a property tax system based on the French system (Senegal, for example). An analysis of this tax system shows that the majority of the tax (over 85%) is collected on premises used for professional purposes, i.e., from companies. Thus, the tax on improved property is perceived as an additional taxation on economic activity.

Overall, the success of the residence tax will depend on how to reach a very large potential taxpaying population (70,000 in Ouagadougou and 40,000 in Bobo) and manage tax directories that have traditionally been managed by both the tax department and the treasury department. Thus, efforts must focus on effective tax collection techniques and management of the computerized taxpayer directory.

Figure 3.1. Ouagadougou: Divided into sectors

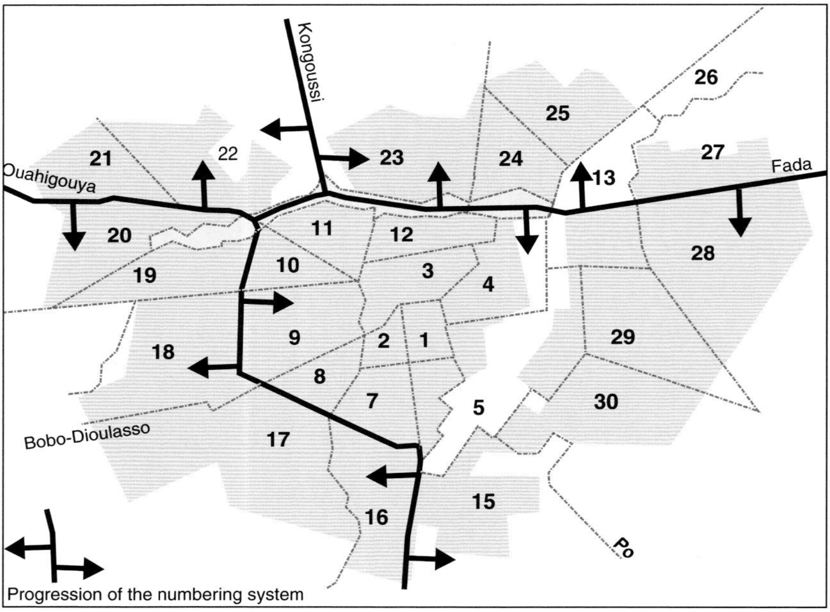

Cameroon

Yaoundé	
Number of inhabitants (1992)	780,000
Surface area of urbanized zone	5,040 ha
Number of streets	1,670
Number of intersections	2,400
Streets named	110 (6%)
Number of doorways addressed	130,000
Cost of signs and installation	US$135,000
Total cost of operation	US$280,000
Cost/addressed doorway	US$2
Addressing unit established	1992
Douala	
Number of inhabitants (1992)	1,100,000
Surface area of urbanized zone	8,750 ha
Number of streets	3,100
Number of intersections	4,870
Streets named	130
Number of doorways addressed	180,000
Cost of signs and installation	US$185,714
Total cost of operation	US$442,860
Cost/doorway addressed	US$2.4
Addressing unit established	1992

Background and objectives

The crisis that hit the Cameroonian economy in the late 1980s resulted in a drastic reduction in resources available to the government to finance facilities, infrastructure, and urban services. The second Urban Development Project (UDP 2), in preparation at the time, sought to identify new means for financing urban management. Various diagnostic studies revealed that the main problems stemmed from an inability to identify potential taxpayers and users of city services. Thus, establishing an address system in the cities of Yaoundé and Douala seemed to be one way to solve these problems quickly and easily. The main objectives were:

- To locate potential taxpayers to increase revenues,
- To identify users of public services as part of efforts to privatize concessionaires of commercial city services.

Governmental authorities in Cameroon had been interested in an addressing project for some time: in 1971 a presidential circular gave instructions regarding street names (annex 2). Some addressing measures had already been carried out in places like the city center of Douala, Biyem Assi, and Cité Verte in Yaoundé. However, these initiatives remained limited to just a few neighborhoods until 1992, when two addressing projects were launched in Yaoundé and Douala as part of UDP 2.

Financing and implementation

The addressing project received the following financing:

- As part of UDP 2, the World Bank financed the first addressing efforts in Yaoundé and Douala starting in 1992;
- Through the FSD (Special Development Fund), bilateral French assistance helped expand addressing in Douala in 1994–95 to include zones where addressing operations had originally been postponed.

Initially, the steering unit of UDP 2 (CSDU [Special Urban Development Unit]) carried out the project before handing over responsibility to technical departments of both metropolitan governments.

Technical features

- *Division*: The urban zone was divided into 6 major zones.
- *Street codification*: Streets are identified by a number composed of two figures. The first represents the sector number followed by a sequential number (for example: street 4.15 is the 15th street in zone 4).
- *Numbering doorways.* Numbering is metric and alternating (even and odd on opposite sides of the street).
- *Street sign installation.* A local firm selected following a bidding process manufactured and installed street signs.
- *Surveys and number assignment.* Teams composed of municipal employees and survey takers employed by a local NGO performed surveys and number assignments. The information gathered includes the address, occupant's name, plot use category, type of activity, and, when applicable, cadastral references.
- *Address directory.* In Douala, the addressing unit entered addresses to ensure confidentiality and use of data by municipal departments. The Douala Addressing Software (LAD) was developed locally (Windev).
- *Monitoring.* A supervisory committee was created. It included the Director of the metropolitan government, the director of technical departments, and representatives of utility concessionaires.

- *Address map*. In Yaoundé, an address map and street index were created and printed. There was no official printing of the map for Douala; but it was used to create a base map for the GIS prepared by municipal departments.

Results

Efforts undertaken in Yaoundé and Douala are comparable, and their sustainability over the past decade is remarkable. In particular, these efforts have resulted in a much more influential addressing unit, which has become an urban observatory within the Technical Departments Division. Also of note is Douala's determination to gradually complete its addressing project in spite of the difficulties of its situation:

- The city employed a "cumulative" process that began in the easiest areas to address and progressed to more difficult areas, and typically involved an update every two years.
- A systematic search for financing allowed Douala to take over from the World Bank, most notably by combining funds from the metropolitan government with funds from bilateral aid.

Specific applications[5]

CREATING AN URBAN OBSERVATORY. In response to a lack of information about the city, the metropolitan government developed an integrated information system with support from French bilateral aid and the IGN (National Geographic Institute). Douala created an urban observatory within the departments of its metropolitan government. The observatory is designed to gather, process, and distribute information. The computer graphics shop within the observatory takes part in all metropolitan government (CUN) projects and studies, and handles mapping. This represents a vast amount of work to map land use (MOS), neighborhood projects, bus lines, water distribution networks, major road projects financed by various donors, and household waste collection circuits. These data have been helpful in providing a great deal of information (through thematic maps and other data) about the city through:

- Development of addressing software (LAD),
- Use of a GIS for automated mapping (street system, hydrography, buildings, green spaces, etc.),
- Development of a street system management software program to assess the level of road deterioration and cost for road rehabilitation (Camvoirie).

The city organizes annual campaigns to collect urban data from a variety of networks including streets, public lighting, and urban fixtures. An urban documentation and information center was created and maintains the information gathered in the field through the addressing project. This center is part of the Secretariat of the metropolitan government and is open and accessible to the public, whereas only technical departments and other partners (network utility concessionaires and other institutional partners such as land developers and governmental departments) have access to the observatory.

STREET SYSTEM MANAGEMENT. The local government wishes to monitor road conditions and, based on a visual observation, estimate needs for regular and periodic maintenance. During the 1990s, the metropolitan government acquired a specific spreadsheet-based application that uses addressing codifications for streets (Urbavia, Camvoirie). Bilateral cooperation assisted in redeveloping this application on a more advanced system. It is especially designed to provide useful information for the "street maintenance account," set up by the metropolitan government in 2001. However, the particularly difficult period in the 1990s limited financing so drastically that all of the main streets have quickly become almost impassable. So the first priority at this time was no longer maintenance but a major rehabilitation required for all streets, which became a World Bank project in 2002.

UTILITY CONCESSIONAIRES AND POSTAL SERVICES. The address directory was sent to water and electric companies and to the postal services. The post office uses the addressing system to distribute invoices. As for water and electricity, they are participating in an initiative through which their consumer identification index will match the address system, thus becoming their primary tool for customer identification and resource mobilization.

Guinea

Conakry	
Number of inhabitants (1993)	1,100,000
Surface area of urbanized zone	4,500 ha
Number of streets	3,100
Number of intersections	6,000
Streets named	35
Number of doorways addressed	87,000
Total cost of operation	US$500,000
Estimated cost/addressed doorway	US$5
Addressing unit established	1993
Numbering and surveys	1994-1995
Sign installation	1996
Creation of address directory	1997
Address map printed	1997
Update	2003

Background and objectives

In Guinea, the end of the 1980s marked the end of a difficult planning period and signaled the institution of major reforms. Among these, the decentralization policy resulted in the creation of five municipalities in Conakry. However, these municipalities had few resources at their disposal and possessed little information about their territory. They also lacked experience. Potential tax revenue was poorly evaluated, and the resources to implement any taxation systems were sorely lacking, so that fewer than 40% of tax assessment notices issued resulted in collection of tax. To help these new municipalities deal with the difficulty and build their capacities, an addressing component was included in the second urban development project (UDP 2). The situation was particularly difficult, but due to the addressing unit's tenacity and rigorous approach, Conakry managed to reach its goals of:

- Establishing an updated city map,
- Defining a system to make it easier to locate places in a city where housing had developed in a totally disorganized fashion over previous decades,
- Helping to better identify the potential tax base.

Financing and implementation

As part of the UDP 2 project, the World Bank financed most of the operation. In 2003, the new project (UDP 3) financed the purchase of new street signs for peri-urban areas and an update of the address map. An addressing unit handled these efforts. That unit was part of the city's technical departments, but it also had a certain amount of autonomy that allowed it to successfully complete the operation within expected deadlines in a transparent manner that was verified by an auditor.

Technical features

- *Division*. The division corresponds to the city's five municipalities: Kaloum, Dixinn, Matam, Ratoma, and Matoto.
- *Street codification*. Each street number is preceded by a code representing the neighborhood initials (for example: KA.23 is the 23rd street of the Kaloum municipality).
- *Numbering doorways and surveys*. Numbering is metric and alternating (even and odd on opposite sides of the street). The addressing unit handled surveys and numbering. The survey gathered the following data: address, occupant's name, plot use category, water and electricity meter numbers.
- *Street signs*. A local company selected following a bidding process manufactured the signs. The addressing unit and municipal technical departments installed the signs.
- *Address directory*. Addresses entered by the addressing unit into a special software program (LAC) written for Mac were transferred to a new version of the software developed for PC (Urbadresse) in 2002.
- *Address map*. The addressing unit designed the address map on the computer and printed the map along with the street index. Both were made available for purchase at a local bookseller.

Results

Prior to the addressing project, information about the city was practically nonexistent, and even the technical departments occasionally had difficulties identifying a street. One of the most significant results of the addressing effort was the production of an overall city map. Over the years, the city had developed informally in a geographically constraining site. Only the Kaloum municipality, planned during colonization, possessed any kind of updated mapping.

Aerial photography, the compilation of various documents, and rigorous surveys all enabled the addressing unit to establish a computerized address map after some "on the job" training. This document included a huge amount of information about the city, gathered during addressing surveys. In particular, it provided information about streets. Its distribution and use by various technical departments made it possible to develop other applications.

The first expansion of the addressing project involved the Niger market, where numbering of squares and boutiques helped increase revenues. The second expansion, carried out during UDP 3, included addressing in growth areas. However, the most specific applications are targeting household waste collection[6] and neighborhood accessibility.

Specific applications

INCREASING NEIGHBORHOOD ACCESSIBILITY. Due to the area's physical constraints, some neighborhoods are quite isolated. This "finger jutting out into the sea" spreads out over 36 km and is cut crosswise by various thalwegs that limit access to some of the poorer neighborhoods. The situation is even more worrisome since the booming urbanization that had developed over the past three decades was chaotic and has not helped improve services to these areas at all.

To manage this situation and improve conditions for the populations living there, one component of UDP 3 involves opening up these neighborhoods. The project involves work on secondary roads ranging from maintenance to opening up roads. The goal is to ensure that underserved neighborhoods can gain access to community facilities (schools, dispensaries, police stations) in order to better channel the city's expansion.

To achieve these goals, two programs have been defined:

- The Municipal Initiatives Program (PLIC) for smaller, non-mechanized projects performed by small and medium-scale enterprises to improve use of secondary roads. This includes work on drainage canals, box drains, and pavement (potholes).
- The Priority Rehabilitation and Road Opening Program (PROP) involves larger projects designed to better organize access to very remote neighborhoods.

As part of these programs, the following addressing efforts have proven helpful:

- Scouting out and mapping the network of streets for which no such documentation existed previously;
- Installation of street signage to improve access to these neighborhoods and facilitate street navigation;

- Identification of features (length, rights-of-way, drainage, etc.) and condition of roads.

These efforts have made it possible to work on neighborhoods that had previously been considered inaccessible because their streets had not been identified and had not even been located by the technical departments. In addition, the PLIC and PROP programs used the information gathered in the addressing survey about street features and main problems of deterioration to define needs and perform project forecasting.

WASTE MANAGEMENT. Until 1995, Conakry was beset with distressing sanitation problems. Garbage could accumulate in the city over several weeks, completely blocking certain intersections. The situation, which was further aggravated by heavy rainfall, was the perfect breeding ground for cholera, which remained a latent disease even during the dry season. The Pilot Unit for Urban Services (UPSU), in charge of waste management, had only operated effectively for a few years while its rolling stock was operating properly. To make up for the lack of waste collection, the city used trucks and volunteers and sometimes resorted to "emergency" efforts.

The will of the national and municipal governments to radically alter the situation translated into a mobilization of resources under UDP 3 and the implementation of an innovative waste collection and transfer system. Small and medium-scale enterprises would now be in charge of collecting waste and taking it to various transfer points. Households would pay the cost directly. The SPTD (Public Solid Waste Transfer Department), which replaced the UPSU, would now transport waste from transfer points to the landfill.

The addressing system was particularly useful in preparing for waste collection. It helped to select the location of transfer sites, define zones that would be assigned to various small and medium-scale enterprises, and map collection routes. Addressing made it possible to estimate the number of homes in each zone. The competition for waste collection concessions was fierce, and having this information was essential for equitable awarding of concessions and ultimately for monitoring the service. The address map created, signage installed, and data gathered during the survey all facilitated cooperative discussion to determine zonal boundaries and helped ensure the program's smooth implementation.

Subsequently, the addressing unit helped to keep the system running smoothly by evaluating the service's rate of penetration in waste collection zones. The small and medium-scale enterprises that have been awarded concessions are evaluated according to these rates, and they are occasionally required to improve their performance to retain their service concession. It is therefore important to have an accurate count of the number of doorways in each zone and to be able to update this information regularly. The results so far have been positive:

- the rate of waste collection has increased from 20% to 80%,
- the penetration rate is 64%,
- 76% of bills are paid,
- an estimated 3,000 jobs have been created,
- the cost of collection, transfer, and dumping in the landfill for a ton of waste is moderate: US$15.

There has been a synergy created between the public and private sectors, and cholera has not been endemic here since 1997.

Figure 3.2. Conakry: Divided by "communes"

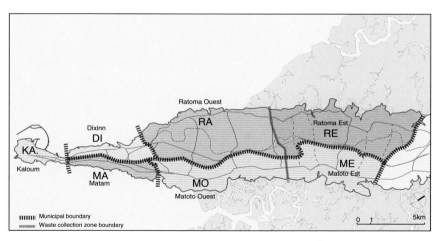

Mali

	Bamako	Sikasso	Kayes
Number of inhabitants	1,016,000	120,000	55,000
Year	1998	1999	2000
Surface area of urbanized zone	10,000 ha		
Number of streets	2,600	585	397
Number of intersections	2,400		
Streets named	150 (6%)	7 (1.2 %)	10 (2.5 %)
Number of doorways addressed	60,000	9,843	8,371
Cost of signs and installation		US$19,000	US$23,000
Total cost of operation	US$262,000	US$69,000	US$55,000
Estimated cost/doorway addressed	US$4.40	US$7.00	US$6.60
Addressing unit established	1993	1999	2000

	Ségou	Mopti Sévaré	Gao
Number of inhabitants (2001)	145,000	118,000	110,000
Number of streets	711	507	452
Streets named	9 (1.3%)	11 (2.2 %)	9 (2 %)
Number of doorways addressed	13,840	10,634	8,376
Cost of signs and installation	US$26,000	US$28,000	US$31,000
Total cost of operation	US$75,000	US$72,000	US$75,000
Estimated cost/doorway addressed	US$5.50	US$6.80	US$9.00
Addressing unit established	2001	2001	2001

Background and objectives

Since the 1980s Mali has instituted various reforms intended to strengthen its decentralized services. In 1982, the first urban project (PUM), financed by the World Bank, mobilized resources from the District of Bamako for the District's State Land Inspectorate, responsible for reorganizing all land documents, and for the Departmental Tax Inspectorate, responsible for creating and implementing a street system and waste collection tax (TVEOM). Mali launched its first addressing project as part of these efforts. Although limited to installing street signs in neighborhoods in the city center, especially to facilitate the identification of businesses, it also gave EDM (Mali's Electricity Company) the opportunity to use addresses to reference some of its transformer equipment based on the street numbering system.

The second urban project, financed by the World Bank (1986–1992), helped to set up a financial division in the District of Bamako and to create a multipurpose cartography unit (Carpol) for the future creation of a cadastre.

In 1992, the FAC[7] financed an addressing initiative as part of the Bamako District Support project (1992–1997). That project created an addressing unit within the district's technical unit using Carpol resources for the project. The operation involved 2,600 streets, 60,000 entrances, and 600 street signs.

Then, in 1999, the third urban project (PDUD), financed by the World Bank, led to the institution of an "urban fee," and addressing was expected to help identify the tax base. Five regional capitals implemented street addressing initiatives including Sikasso, Kayes, Ségou, Mopti, and Gao. In 2000, a new project, Municipal Support Project, Mali (PACUM), financed addressing in Kayes.

Financing and implementation

Various forms of financing have followed one another to support addressing efforts in Mali: the three urban projects financed by the World Bank, and in particular the Bamako District Assistance project,[8] financed by the French Cooperation Agency. The addressing unit, founded in 1993 as part of the district's technical support unit, which later became the Technical Committee to Support the Municipalities of Bamako District (CTAC),[9] has primarily been responsible for addressing. This committee, in charge of addressing in Bamako, led addressing efforts in regional capitals during the Third Urban Project.

Technical features

- *Divisions*: In Bamako, the urban area is divided into nine address zones: three in municipalities I, II, and III and 6 in municipalities IV, V, and VI.
- *Street Codification*: The street is identified by a number composed of a radical (address zone number) followed by a sequential number (for example: street 3.157 is the 157th street in zone 3). Numbering of streets running east-west is even, and numbers increase chronologically along opposite sides of the Niger River. Numbering of streets running north-south is odd, and numbering begins at the administrative borders of municipalities II, VI and III, V.
- *Numbering doorways*. Numbering is metric and alternating (even and odd on opposite sides of the street).
- *Street sign installation*. Signage presented an opportunity to develop innovative solutions using artisanal stenciling. The project was handled

within the CTAC with FAC project technical assistance. Various local business initiative groups performed the work.

- *Surveys and number assignment*. Teams made up of district employees and survey takers from local business initiative groups completed surveys and number assignments. The address directory was created in Dbase IV. Carpol handled the digital cartography.

Results

Some of the most significant results include:

- The remarkable synergy of various donors' contributions;
- The use of low-cost, artisanal stenciling techniques for signs;
- Creation of the region's first digital address map;
- The Bamako addressing unit's work in addressing regional capitals: Sikasso served as a test site, followed by Kayes, then Ségou, Mopti-Sévaré, and Gao;
- The reflex of new inhabitants to automatically request a doorway number for each new building. The city districts now require these numbers to deliver official government documents, and some service providers require the numbers (to open a bank account, for example).

Nevertheless, the period following the addressing operation has been marked by some shortcomings: (a) a fairly ineffective, non-relational database was used to record addresses and was underutilized; (b) Carpol's digital mapping resulted in a black and white Bamako guide map of mediocre quality; (c) coordination between the finance departments and the EDM utility concessionaire was initially well supported with communication and training efforts, but those efforts practically ceased in the years following completion of addressing in Bamako. Thus, the project failed to achieve its objective of establishing a codification of activities common to both taxes and addressing at the time that the business tax was simplified; (d) efforts to continue addressing and to keep information up-to-date ceased at the end of the French Cooperation Agency project; new plots were no longer included, and ultimately EDM took over the task of numbering blocks of houses using its own system.

Specific applications

The main feature that was unique to the Malian experience was the development of novel techniques for creating signs, which will be used by the municipality of Nouadhibou (Mauritania). This solution involves stenciling street names using an effective, low-cost, artisanal technique.

Stencils are cut with a cutter using used offset plates. The street name is painted on using a high-quality paint[10] that is weather and UV-ray resistant. The technique's success, implemented by local business initiative groups formed by young, unemployed graduates, was even more remarkable since the solution proved to be quite economical and ideal for municipalities with modest budgets.

Figure 3.3. Bamako: Divided by "addressing zones."
Cities addressed in Mali

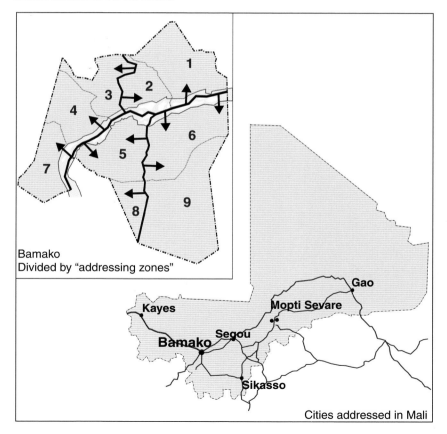

Mauritania

City	Inhab.	Area (ha)	Streets named	Doorways addressed	Total cost	Cost/ doorway
Nouakchott	714,000	7,938		120,000	1,284,700	10.7
Nouadhibou	89,743	838	681	17,140	25,500	1.5
Rosso	73,250	462	426	8,504	14,900	1.8
Atar	23,790	317	276	4,575	9,700	2.1
Boutilmit	16,768	254	264	3,845	4,400	1.1
Tidjikja	9,791	195	165	1,958	5,100	2.6
Aleg	6,598	115	115	1,760	4,400	2.5
Moudjeria	3,400	46		380	2,100	5.5
Tiguent	3,250	52		480	2,600	5.4
Rachid	1,800	14		267	1,300	4.9
Tekane	1,600	25		214	1,100	5.1
Subtotal 1	943,990	10,256	1,927	159,123	1,355,800	8.5
Kaedi	61,974			9,996	37,331	3.7
Kiffa	47,678			7,690	28,720	3.7
Zouerat	44,718			7,213	26,937	3.7
Atar (updated)	23,790			3,837	14,330	3.7
Aleg (updated)	14,809			2,389	8,921	3.7
Selibaby	14,465			2,333	8,713	3.7
Néma	12,001			1,936	7,229	3.7
Ayoun	10,911			1,760	6,572	3.7
Akjoujt	7,648			1,234	4,607	3.7
Subtotal 2	237,994			38,386	143,361	3.7
Total	1,181,984	10,256	1,927	197,511	1,499,160	1.5
Average, excluding Nouakchott						2.8

- *Costs only including cities that implemented an address system as part of PADDEC (Support of the Communal Development Process), PADDEM (Project to Support Deconcentration and Decentralization in Mauritania), or AFD (French Development Agency) projects. The projects receiving IDA (International Development Association) funding (UDP) include 10 regional capitals; they are currently in progress.*
- *Cost per doorway does not include the tax survey.*

Background and objectives

Mauritania has recently undergone a decentralization (laws of 1986 and 1987) mainly intended to "promote the exercise of democracy and local development initiatives by implementing participatory methods that promote sound management of the affairs of populations" (Government Municipal Policy Statement). For about ten years, efforts involving municipalities have mainly consisted of introducing tools and management methods that would help these decentralized bodies operate according to consistent guidelines in a country where the Walis are the predominant group represented in territorial government. Another goal has been the support of capacity building in the municipalities of Nouakchott and Nouadhibou that have each experienced extremely rapid urban growth.

Since 1998, addressing has been an important tool in sound municipal management. With support from the MAE and AFD,[11] and the World Bank, addressing is now being expanded to all 12 regional capitals and even beyond. The broad geographic scope of the operation is mainly due to its tax applications. Addressing is expected to help consolidate procedures for issuing tax notices and collecting taxes handled by municipalities and therefore to help with the organization of decentralized and deconcentrated departments in charge of these tasks. This objective has been the driving force behind making this entire operation more immediately operational. In addition, some local consulting firms have been mobilized to support the municipalities in this task.

Financing and implementation

Financing for street addressing has come from:

- Municipalities themselves: this was the case for the first addressing project in Mauritania. The municipality of Nouadhibou handled the entire project in 1998;[12]
- The MAE, as part of the PADDEC and then the PADDEM (starting in 1999) projects for Nouakchott (pilot project in the municipality of Tevragh Zeina), Aleg, Atar, Rosso, Tidjikja and more recently for several rural municipalities in Tagent. These projects fall under the leadership of the Ministry of the Interior, Post, and Telecommunications (MIPT);
- The AFD, as part of a financing agreement signed in 2001 with the metropolitan government of Nouakchott; the project involves extending addressing to the entire city;

- The World Bank with the Urban Development Project (2002) for the 10 regional capitals that have still not implemented an address system or need additional addressing work or updates. The previous DIU (Urban Infrastructure Decentralization Project) had financed a mission in 1996 to take aerial photographs of Nouakchott and all regional capitals. Those photographs proved invaluable for the addressing project.

The diversity of financing sources makes it difficult to accurately evaluate the cost of the work performed. However, the total amount invested since 1998 in the 17 cities where a street addressing initiative has been implemented or is under way is estimated at US$1.5 million, which is a rate of US$7.6 per doorway addressed. The street addressing effort in Nouakchott accounts for 85% of the total expenditure and 60% of the total target population. This illustrates the significant differences between the methods used for the capital compared with those used in other cities.

These ratios do not take into account costs for ongoing technical assistance from the MAE and AFD. However, these figures attempt to include costs for tax surveys, which were often used instead of addressing surveys in Mauritania. These surveys are the main source of cost overruns generated during these projects. These overruns are even more noteworthy since the visible results of addressing efforts were weak, with few good quality signs found on streets.

With regard to implementation, Mauritania (a) used local consulting firms to handle these operations, (b) automatically included a tax survey component as part of every operation, and, finally, (c) focused its efforts solely at the municipal level, so that the DGI (National Tax Authority) and deconcentrated Public Works departments acted only as observers.

The project in Nouakchott opted to develop two software tools: a GIS to manage addresses and a program to issue tax assessment notices. Up until very recently, the private service provider in charge of providing project support was the sole user of these tools because the metropolitan government's addressing unit was considered unprepared to use them. Changes are currently under way, and the addressing unit, currently part of the Resources Directorate, should become part of the Secretary General as its own directorate, considering the fact that it manages so many functions that ultimately affect all directorates. Information provided by each municipal addressing unit will be used to update the address directory annually after national departments have verified the information. However, splitting the CUN into nine municipalities and splitting taxation between municipal (occupancy tax and municipal tax) and inter-municipal taxes (business tax and land tax on improved property) may ultimately alter this arrangement.

Technical features

- *Division*. In Nouakchott, the divisions correspond to the nine municipalities of the metropolitan government (CUN),
- *Street codification*. The street is identified by a number composed of a composite radical (municipality number and district number) and a sequential number (for example: Street 42.156 is the 156th street in District 2 of Municipality 4). Numbering increases chronologically along two major axes: one north-south axis separates the following municipalities: Teyaret, Ksar, El Mina de dar Naim, Arafat, and Riad. The other east-west axis separates the Tevragh Zeina, Ksar, Toujoumine de Sebkha, and Arafat municipalities.
- *Numbering doorways*. Numbering is metric and alternating (even and odd on opposite sides of the street). However, in small towns, the system simply consists of numbering doorways chronologically without references to streets.
- *Street sign installation*. Initially, military engineers used a stenciling process to install signs in the Tevragh Zeina pilot zone. Signs were installed in a few neighborhoods in 2003. They are bilingual, in French and Arabic.
- *Surveys*. A tax survey was performed when the addressing system was implemented.
- *Directory*. Data are kept on a special software program (Arcom) that can be used to issue local tax assessment notices (CFPB, TH, TC,[13] business tax). The program also tracks collections.
- *Address map*. The map is in a GIS (*Anouana*, which means address in Hassania) but since it has not been printed, it has not been widely distributed.

Results

Thanks to the efforts of the Department of Local Governments (DCL), which oversees the initiatives, to extend addressing to all regional capitals, addressing has quickly become commonplace in municipalities and among people in general. This is even more remarkable since the effort, from the outset, was focused on taxation, which would not necessarily have broad appeal. In Nouakchott, the effort included awareness campaigns carried out particularly within schools.

However, municipal leaders have had difficulty taking over responsibility for the effort and its outcome because of (a) the absence of any department responsible for addressing outside of Nouakchott and Nouadhibou, and (b) the complexity of the tools developed (GIS, tax management software) for the Nouakchott project, which makes them difficult to replicate in other municipalities. These two factors are a direct result of the methods used, and, in particular, they are a result of the fact that private entities handled the entire project.

Consistent methods were not employed when the effort expanded to 17 cities. Each private service provider was free to develop its own techniques. The lack of simple address management software led to a significant gap between the computer technology developed for the project in Nouakchott and the technology used in other cities. In fact, the level of sophistication of the tools developed could make it more difficult to reach sound management objectives established at the outset of the project. Frequent changes in legislation and regulations means that these tools often require complex and costly adjustments.

Finally, the significant increase in tax assessment notices issued, now that the tax base and taxpayers can automatically be identified, have not yet resulted in a comparably significant increase in collections. For example, the land tax on improved property is still only collected at a rate of 15% of notices issued in Nouakchott (Nouakchott in 2003: 80 million UM[14] collected for 609 million UM in tax assessment notices issued). Similarly in Rosso, the country's third largest city, the occupancy tax only brought in 100,000 UM in collections in 2003 out of an estimated 6 million UM in potential collections.

However, the completion of addressing efforts and tax surveys has energized the municipal departments in charge of tax collections, and their commitment is particularly evident in the collection of municipal tax from local merchants.

Finally, addressing in Mauritania still has a low profile. Municipalities have not published maps; the sophisticated mapping tools used have made it difficult to produce simple maps that could have been distributed and posted as useful information in town halls and other government offices. The installation of street signs has been limited.

Specific applications

LOCAL TAXATION. The main objective of addressing has been to gather information about each piece of land and its location. Municipal taxation had been almost nonexistent in terms of actual yield until the introduction of addressing and was considered to be the priority application of addressing, so that each municipality and the CUN could establish equitable taxation. Computerized tax collection is expected to make procedures more secure and reduce the risks of dilution. Thus, specialized software programs were developed to support the project in Nouakchott. They were primarily intended to ensure more efficient collection of taxes and fees and included Anouana software, a plot location tool, and Arcom, a tax assessment notice issuing and collections tracking program. Eventually, the CUN plans to interface both of these software tools.

For the other municipalities, objectives are similar, but they are using different tools. It is unlikely that these cities will use the two software tools developed in Nouakchott (except possibly Nouadhibou). The DCL plans to distribute "local taxation" software that is easier to use and has no mapping link. For the time being, these cities manage their address and tax directories either manually or with a spreadsheet program.

BASIC SERVICES. For the most part, the public services and major private operators who have been asked to use and invited to try the addressing system were very interested (MauriPoste, Mauritel, Mattel, Somelec, Snde, and others). However, they have taken a "wait and see" approach, and some would like to have exclusive rights to the tool.

Figure 3.4. Cities addressed in Mauritania

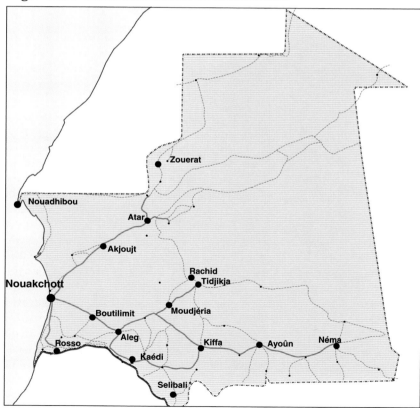

Mozambique

	Maputo	Beira	Nampula	Pemba	Quelimane	Matola
Number of inhabitants 2002	1,300,000	453,000	278,000	80,000	155,000	375,000
Urbanized surface area (ha)	8,300	3,700	2,250	960	1,160	4,600
Number of streets	2,464	970	840	586	573	1,400
Number of intersections	5,900	1,530	1,037	915	777	3,000
Streets named	454	236	62	29	49	303
Number of doorways addressed	90,816	39,253	25,922	13,356	22,599	40,000
Cost: signs & install. (US$)	124,465	135,833	65,112	44,748	44,986	180,000
Total cost (US$)	553,250	-	-	-	-	-
Dates	1995–99	2001–02	2001–02	2001–02	2001–02	2003–05

Background and objectives

The addressing project is part of the Mozambican government's plan to decentralize the administration of its 33 largest cities. Immediately following independence, the heavily centralized government had almost complete authority over the way cities were run. Municipalities were all the more ineffective due to the impact of the civil war, a deteriorating economy, and the fact that large numbers of rural residents had migrated to cities, swelling unplanned urban neighborhoods that lacked adequate facilities.[15] In such a situation where few public resources were available, the Mozambican authorities wanted to create tools, procedures, and references that would help rebuild the capacities of urban institutions in order to better control the development and administration of their cities. Addressing appeared to be the obvious first step in the entire process. Addressing for the city of Maputo was initiated in 1992 but not actually implemented until 1995. The success of this effort led to an expansion of the project to four regional capitals—Beira, Nampula, Pemba, Quelimane—and Matola, the city next to Maputo.

Technical features

- *Division*: In Maputo, the city was divided into five addressing zones and 17 sectors.
- *Street codification*: Streets are identified by a number composed of a radical (zone number) and a sequential number (for example: street 2.156 is the 156th street in zone 2). Numbering runs east to west beginning at the Bay of Maputo and south to north beginning at the Maputo estuary.
- *Numbering doorways*. Numbering is metric and alternating (even and odd on opposite sides of the street).
- *Street sign installation*. Local companies produced and installed the signs.
- *Surveys*. The addressing unit performed surveys.
- *Directory*. The directory was first created in an addressing software developed for Mac; it was later transferred to a new version of the software program (Urbadresse), this time developed for PC.

Technical Features are similar for other cities.

Financing and implementation

The PROL project (Local Government Reform Project), financed by the World Bank, initiated addressing in the Mozambican capital in 1992. The project was actually implemented at the start of 1995 as part of the "Project to support urban institutions and the social development of Maputo neighborhoods," cofinanced by the MAE and the city itself. The implementation, led by a municipal addressing unit, received ongoing technical assistance. Subsequently, a national addressing unit oversaw an expansion of the effort to the cities of Beira, Nampula, Pemba, and Quelimane, using the same methods and procedures. This effort was part of a "municipal development project of provincial capitals." Finally, in 2003, a new effort was launched in Matola under different conditions that included financing from decentralized cooperation of the Department of Seine-St. Denis (France), which occasionally assists an addressing unit.

Results

In 10 years, addressing has affected more than half of Mozambique's urban population, or 2.7 million inhabitants, and about 220,000 buildings have been assigned an address. Nearly 70 municipal employees have been trained in addressing techniques. For the six cities involved in the effort, an address directory, street index, and address maps have all been created, and streets now have street signs.

From an institutional standpoint, the addressing unit of Maputo is now an official part of the city administration, and a national addressing unit was created to coordinate operations throughout the country. The addressing units have established a number of contacts with governmental departments, utility concessionaires, private companies, and NGOs; they have implemented numerous addressing applications. All in all, Mozambique's experience is a model for addressing efforts. This success is due to the significant involvement of the Mozambican authorities, as well as the MAE's sustained support. Various factors should ensure the sustainability of this initiative:

- Mayors have realized how important addressing is for urban management;
- The addressing units know how to use addressing techniques, including the use of automated tools. They now have field technicians that can share their knowledge with other agents;
- The creation of a new statute for addressing units allows them to sell their services to government agencies, utility concessionaires, companies, and individuals, which should cover part of their operating costs.

Specific applications

The previous chapter lists a number of applications that have been implemented: tracking epidemics, developing an economic database (BDE), and facilitating coordination with the postal service (Correios de Moçambique) and concessionary services (Agua de Moçambique). In addition, the addressing unit of Maputo worked with the National Directorate for Construction and Urban Development to organize 2,400 city streets into a hierarchical system, and it collaborated with the Secretariado Técnico de Administraçao Eleitoral to organize the first municipal elections in 1998. Finally, it is important to highlight the institutional benefits gained by incorporating the addressing unit into the capital's municipal administration and creating a national addressing unit.

INCORPORATING THE ADDRESSING UNIT INTO THE MUNICIPAL ADMINISTRATION. The addressing unit of Maputo became the Addressing and Toponymy Directorate (DAT) in 2000. This directorate reports directly to the Mayor's office. That status and the fact that the DAT can sell its products and services have helped to sustain its operations (regular field and map updates) and to develop new initiatives (creating thematic maps upon request of various departments, distributing excerpts of the address directory, etc.). In addition, since the DAT is in charge of toponymy, it prepares lists for street names that will be submitted for approval to the Municipal Assembly.

Finally, the DAT is responsible for issuing residency certificates for any new buildings and any change of use. This document must also be presented with all requests for connections to the water and electricity networks. This tool allows the DAT to remain informed about any changes in buildings and to maintain an updated address directory.

CREATION OF A NATIONAL ADDRESSING UNIT. A national addressing unit was formed in 2000 within the Ministry of State Administration under the National Directorate for Municipal Development. It is responsible for addressing all of the cities in the country and, consequently, for securing the necessary financial backing for the project. Its specific responsibilities include:

- Training of addressing units and other governmental departments on addressing techniques and applications;
- Tracking and monitoring operations in order to ensure that the addressing units are operating smoothly and consistently in their various initiatives;
- Providing support to addressing units: addressing software transfers, product sales, and use of copyrights;
- Handling communications: public relations with cities, utility concessionaires, and companies; administration, in collaboration with the Investment Promotion Centre, of a web site entitled "Street addressing in Mozambique."

Figure 3.5. Mozambique cities involved in addressing initiatives

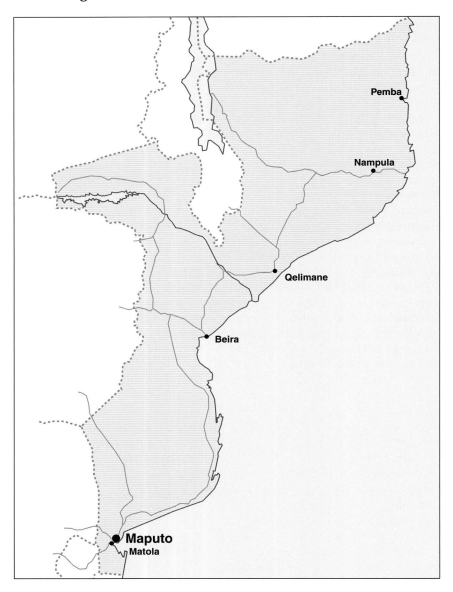

Niger

Number of inhabitants	850,000
Cost of signs	US$190,000
Cost of installation	US$40,000
Total cost of operation	US$405,000
Estimated cost/doorway addressed	US$6.5
Addressing unit established	2002

Background and objectives

Niamey was one of the last remaining capitals in the region without a street addressing system. As this city of 800,000 inhabitants attempted to decentralize, proper street addressing became an urgent need. An addressing component had first been conceived as part of the PRIU (Urban Infrastructure Rehabilitation Project), which financed a feasibility study in 2001. However, time constraints made the project unfeasible. Another donor, the AIMF, already working on other projects in Niger, showed an interest in including addressing in its cooperation with the metropolitan government of Niamey (CUN). The objectives included the creation of an urban data bank, urban management tools, and the improvement of the CUN's resources.

Technical features

- *Division.* The city was divided into 44 neighborhood groups.
- *Street codification.* The street is identified by a two-letter radical (neighborhood code) followed by a number corresponding to the street number. Thus, "Street GM 12" is the 12th street in the "Grand Marché" neighborhood. Streets running parallel to the Niger River have even numbers. Numbering begins either along the banks of the river or at the street coming out from the bridge.
- *Doorway numbering.* Numbering is metric and alternating (even and odd on opposite sides of the street).
- *Street sign installation.* A company selected following an international bidding process produced the signs, and local companies supervised by the addressing unit installed the signs.
- *Number assignment and surveys.* The addressing unit performed both tasks. The survey includes the address, occupant's name, plot use cate-

gory, the cadastral reference, whether or not electricity and water are available, and information on streets.
- *Address directory.* This was created in the Urbadresse address management software program.
- *Implementation.* The metropolitan government's addressing unit implemented the project. It is responsible for maintaining data. An accounting firm periodically audits the addressing unit (solution found to be successful for street addressing in Conakry).

Financing and implementation

In 2001, the PRIU (World Bank) financed a feasibility study for street addressing in Niamey, but there was not enough time to implement the plan. The CUN (which financed the framework for an addressing unit) and the AIMF[16] took over the project and successfully completed the initiative, which is now considered as part of the preparations for the International Francophonie Games (Niamey, 2005). The AFD will help contribute to the effort's continuation and implementation of applications. In addition, in 2003, the MAE launched a street addressing project in Maradi to which a tax application will be added for this city and for the capital.

Results

What is remarkable about this project is the fact that all of the various parts of the project were completed successfully, in a short period of time, under unusual conditions that could be considered "risky." In fact, this effort, which was the country's first such attempt:

- was not part of a project and thus did not have the advantage of that framework (as in Burkina Faso, Guinea, Mauritania, or Mozambique),
- was carried out at the municipal level, where governmental departments had only modest resources,
- didn't have the benefit of ongoing technical assistance, but instead had occasional assistance over several weeks,
- was financed by a donor with no experience in street addressing.

After 15 months, with the various tasks having been carried out concurrently, progress was as follows: surveys and number assignments of doorways are complete for the entire city; the address directory is complete (about 50,000 addresses); signage maps and a list of signs have been sent to the supplier chosen following a bidding process; the 10,000 street signs have been produced and installed; the address map and street index are ready for printing. Such positive results are due to several converging factors: empowerment of a very active steering committee (which quickly made certain decisions following the feasibility study), management outside the administrative rules of the addressing unit budget but rigorous monitoring by a private, local accounting firm, and, above all, the remarkable involvement, within the CUN, of a small and highly motivated local team that was consistently available.

Specific applications

Several important aspects of this operation have made it a success.

INVOLVEMENT OF THE STEERING COMMITTEE, which was composed of representatives from the CUN, the Cadastre, Urban Planning, the PRIU, utility concessionaires, and two neighborhood leaders per municipality. Together, this team managed to combine flexibility and quick response times in meetings and decisionmaking. The general guidelines adopted were submitted for approval to the Municipal Council, but the steering committee, which was easier to mobilize and more involved in the operation itself, actually made the technical decisions.

USE OF A PRIVATE, LOCAL ACCOUNTING FIRM. It is often difficult to begin a street addressing project. The addressing unit does not yet have a place in the municipal government. It is usually necessary to employ short-term contract staff (survey takers, laborers). Teams are on the move in the field on a daily basis. And the numerous needs in terms of small consumables are often hard to predict. In addition, the typically tight deadlines of such a project are not well suited to slow government bureaucracies. Finally, the budget involved is not insignificant and requires expert management.

Niamey's street addressing experience, based on the Conakry model, has been instructive. Using a certified accounting firm to closely track the addressing unit's expenditures has proved valuable. This tool protects resources and enables teams to overcome the difficulties mentioned above. It also protects the addressing unit officer from getting sidetracked, allowing him to focus on technical matters. It helps maintain a certain work pace by paying contract personnel weekly and by quickly paying transportation and consumables expenses. Finally, it protects the addressing unit from having to deal with a variety of requests that are often difficult to avoid.

PARTICIPATION OF UTILITY CONCESSIONAIRES AND OTHER DEPARTMENTS. From the outset of the project, the steering committee coordinated several departments to implement the street addressing operation. The committee managed to maintain the initial momentum, which sometimes tends to fade as the project wears on. Thus, the project's various participants signed memoranda of understanding to facilitate information sharing. Also, the search for a common denominator among directories of various departments and addressing showed cadastral references to be the best way to ensure maximum reconciliation among the various directories.

EXEMPLARY COMMUNICATION. With the help of a Nigerian TV crew, the addressing unit produced a public awareness video about street addressing. A group of actors created an entertaining presentation of a family from Niamey wondering about all the talk they are hearing about the new street addressing project. A neighborhood meeting is held to answer questions. The entire sketch is lively and presents all the relevant information in five minutes. The video is available in both French and the local language. Since few teams, aside from those in Guinea and Mozambique, took such measures to produce this type of information, it is worth noting the effort here.

IN CONCLUSION, FUTURE PROSPECTS. The addressing unit staff have been asked to provide technical assistance for Maradi's future street addressing project. The project's success has encouraged other donors to strengthen the unit's capacities and to support the implementation of addressing for various applications like street system management, inventory of the metropolitan government's public assets, and creation of an urban information system that specifically uses the data gathered.

Figure 3.6. Niamey: Divided into "districts"

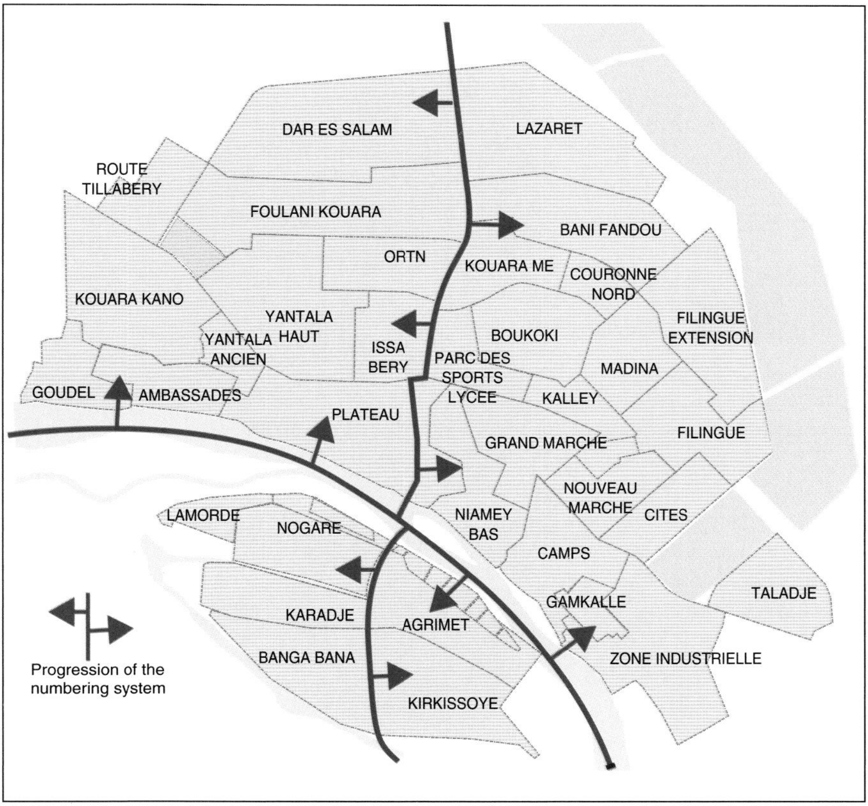

Senegal

		(US$ millions)	PIP* Addressing $	Population
1	Dakar	15.0	623,630	940,046
2	Pikine	7.3	283,108	790,481
3	Guediawaye	4.5	150,586	474,811
4	Kaolack	4.2	92,864	251,143
5	Thies	4.1	117,409	282,675
6	Rufisque	2.8	110,052	170,386
7	Ziguinchor	2.2	86,415	225,916
8	Diourbel	2.1	56,725	116,187
9	St. Louis	2.1	37,631	157,819
10	Louga	1.6	36,240	89,788
11	Tambacounda	0.9		72,167
Subtotal		46.9		3,571,419
All municipalities		81.4		4,704,566
Investments portion		65.1		
Studies & MOD**		8.6		
Assistance portion		7.7		
Financing				
IDA		70.4		
AFD		9.5		
Government		1.6		

* Priority Investments Program
** Delegated Contract Manager

Background and objectives

In Senegal, the first street addressing project after independence dates
back to 1993, but addressing was not implemented in any significant way
until 1998 with the Urban Development and Decentralization Program
(PAC). Street addressing is only one part of this large program and
initially affects only the country's 11 largest cities, while PAC affects 67
urban municipalities, for a total of US$81.4 million. Municipalities
determine PAC investments based on "urban, organizational, and
financial audits," which list needs and municipal resources for meeting
those needs. Following a participatory process involving community
members and various stakeholders, the municipalities agree to the terms
of a "municipal contract" signed with the central government to carry out

three priority programs for investment, maintenance, and institutional strengthening.

The street addressing component falls under this institutional strengthening program. The project had a dual objective: (a) to address the main cities in the country, and ultimately facilitate local tax collection; and (b) to test, in two other cities, an interface of tax rolls and the address directory to identify the potential taxpayers having thus far escaped tax payment ("addressing and tax registers" in Thiès and Kaolack—see chapter 2).

Technical features

- *Division.* Cities are divided into neighborhoods generally defined by government decree.
- *Street codification.* The street identification is composed of a two-letter radical (neighborhood code) followed by a number corresponding to the street number. Thus "Street ES.12" is the 12th street in the "Escale" neighborhood. Numbering runs chronologically along two axes determined by the city's configuration. For example, in Ziguinchor, numbering begins at the river for north-south running streets. And for east-west running streets, numbering begins on opposite sides of the street that starts at the bridge.
- *Doorway numbering.* Numbering is metric and alternating (even and odd on opposite sides of the street).
- Street sign installation. A single company selected following an international bidding process produced the signs, and local companies, supervised by the ADM (Municipal Development Agency) and local addressing units, installed the signs.
- *Number assignment and surveys.* Local addressing units performed these tasks.
- *Address directory.* Data were originally on a spreadsheet before being transferred to the Urbadresse addressing software.

Financing and implementation

Addressing in Senegal received the following financing:

- In 1993, the "Support Project for Decentralization and Urban Development in Senegal" (PADDUS), with the help of the French Cooperation Agency, financed a street addressing training program and pilot addressing effort in M'Bour. The Department of Local Governments and the Department of Urbanism and Architecture completed this project together.

- The World Bank with AFD provided most of the financial backing for the PAC (1998–2004). The Municipal Development Agency leads the project and specifically oversees the street addressing component implemented by local addressing units.

Results

Street addressing initiatives were carried out in 11 cities simultaneously, and the implementation had to overcome three major hurdles:

- The number and size of cities targeted in the street addressing initiatives;
- Although PAC and ADM were responsible for carrying out the project, their general timetable did not dictate when the project would start. Rather, the project's timing was dictated by the mayor's office, which was authorized to sign and execute the municipal contract;
- The PAC's timeframe (five years).

Given these constraints, the fifteen cities initially eligible for addressing carried out the project in various ways. Eight performed all addressing tasks (Thiès, Louga, Diourbel, Kaolack, Ziguinchor, St-Louis, Guediawaye, and Tambacounda); three accomplished only partial street addressing, with the remainder of the project to be finalized as part of the new PAC project (Dakar, Rufisque, and Pikine); and four did not meet deadlines (M'Bour, Richard-Toll, Kolda, and M'Backé). The entire program includes mapping, street sign installation, surveys and number assignment of doorways, and the creation of an address directory. The partial program is limited to the first two tasks.

Table 3.4. Street addressing materials per city

		Street signs	Doorway signs	Posts
1	Dakar	21,747		3,470
2	Pikine	10,387		877
3	Guediawaye	5,573	403	346
4	Kaolack	2,133	5,936	112
5	Thies	2,749	8,282	69
6	Rufisque	2,082		93
7	Ziguinchor	1,432	6,009	215
8	Diourbel	1,849	2,150	64
9	St. Louis	1,303	145	106
10	Louga	934	1,957	25
11	Tambacounda	743	136	213

Specific applications

Aside from the "tax register" mentioned previously, the most notable aspect of the street addressing project in Senegal concerns its implementation. The ADM (under close supervision of the World Bank and with the periodic assistance of an international consultant) had to closely coordinate all street addressing activities so that they would be consistent with the other efforts being undertaken at the municipal level. The organization of the project maps out as follows:

- The ADM's Technical Department and its BDU (urban data bank) unit handled general project oversight. The department determines procedures to be followed, handles training of the municipal addressing units involved, initiates the process of drawing up address maps, prepares and launches the overall request for bids for the supply of signage materials, and, finally, supervises the actual work of street addressing in municipalities.
- Each municipality creates a Local Addressing Unit (CLA) to track operations with support from the ADM.

Except for the sign installation phase, addressing of the first cities in the project (Thiès, Louga, Diourbel, Kaolack, and Ziguinchor) was essentially carried out in-house. The ADM's active participation in assisting the CLAs made it possible for municipalities to iron out all the initial problems. The other cities hired consultants to perform two categories of work: (a) to establish codification, prepare address and signage maps, and create an inventory for signs to send to the manufacturer; (b) to support the CLA in performing surveys and number assignments and create the address directory. In all cases, the installation of street signs was contracted out.

To track activities, the ADM created a detailed and weighted list of the various tasks and established a calculation table showing the progress of the work in each city for the entire project (annex 4).

Table 3.5. Implementation of the project by city

	Thiès	Louga	Diourbel	Kao-lack	Ziguin-chor	Dakar	Ru-fisque	Pikine	Tamba-counda	St. Louis	Guédia-waye
Project launched	A	A	A	A	A	A	A	A	A	A	A
Addressing unit created	A	A	A	A	A	A	A	A	C	C	C
Codification	A	A	A	A	A	C	C	C	A/C	A/C	A/C
Pilot operation	A	A	A	A	A	C	C	C	C	C	C
Provisional base map of city	A	A	A	A	A	C	C	C	C	C	C
Surveys: streets, doorways	A	A	A	A	A	x	x	x	C	C	C
Stenciling doorway numbers	A	A	A	A	A	x	x	x	C	C	C
Directory on spreadsheet	A	A	A	A	A	A	x	x	C	C	C
Base map w/key city features	A	A	A	A	A	A	C	A	C	C	C
Signage map	A	A	A	A	A	C	C	C	A	A	A
RFB for sign suppliers	A	A	A	A	A	A	A	A	A	A	A
Receipt of signs at A	A	A	A	A	A	A	A	A	A	A	A
RFB for sign installation	A	A	A	A	A	A	A	A	A	A	A
Sign installation	E	E	E	E	E	E	E	E	E	E	E
Printing map & index	E	E	E	E	E	E	E	E	E	E	E
Directory on software	x	x	x	x	x	x	x	x	x	x	x
Number of zones to address ->	21	14	14	16	12	48	3	16	8	13	12

A: ADM; C: Consultant; E: Company; x: deferred until next PAC; RFB: Request for bids.

Table 3.6. Division and weighting of tasks

Step	No.	Weight	Tasks	City A	City B	City C	City D
A	1	1%	Project launch				
	2	2%	Awareness, codification				
	3	1%	Addressing unit identification				
	4	1%	Proposals, project-related decrees				
B	5	4%	Provisional base map of city				
	6	1%	Documents for project				
	7	2%	Pilot operation				
	8	10%	Surveys: streets, doorways				
	9	10%	Stenciling doorway numbers				
C	10	2%	Base map w/key city features				
	11	2%	Signage map				
	12	2%	Directories on spreadsheet				
	13	1%	Street index				
	14	1%	Acceptance of work				
	15	3%	RFB for sign supply				
D	16	4%	Order from supplier				
	17	3%	Acceptance by ADM				
	18	5%	Delivery of signs to municipalities				
	19	2%	RFB sign installation				
E	20	27%	Sign installation				
	21	1%	Acceptance of work or certificate of completion				
F	22	5%	Automated map finalized				
	23	2%	Index & map printed				
	24	8%	Directory on addressing software				
		100%					

Figure 3.7. Cities addressed in Senegal

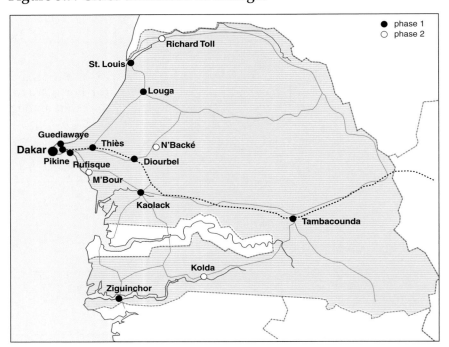

Other projects: Benin, Rwanda, Djibouti, Togo, and Côte d'Ivoire

Urban land register in Benin

Benin acquired an Urban Land Register (RFU), a sort of simplified cadastre, that the FAC began financing in the 1990s for Porto Novo, Cotonou, and Parakou. Creation of the RFU was a partnership among various players: local administration, Central Tax and State Land Department, and Serhau, a service provider. The register is aimed at creating local tax bases through surveys of land, buildings, and their owners or occupants. It was only created for the "formalized" portion of the urban fabric of main cities. A detailed survey has helped to create a database; thus, each plot has six files associated with it (plot, owner/taxpayer, building, housing unit/taxpayer, business establishment, owner/taxpayer). However, since tax departments are not kept informed about changes in ownership (specifically, sales agreements), they have found it difficult to maintain and update information.

The RFU has a dual addressing system: a geocodified address (neighborhood/zone, block of houses and plots) and a postal address (streets and plot entrances). The map known as the address map was created in order to physically locate plots, but there is no plan to actually install street signs or doorway numbers citywide.

Rwanda: addressing and urban land register

The project in Rwanda, which began in the early 1990s, is the result of the combination of a French Cooperation Agency project and a limited World Bank project to build up urban institutions. Rwanda's addressing project attempted to combine the RFU project and other addressing efforts by creating an Urban Land Use Registry (RIOFU). It had three objectives: (a) to determine the property tax for local municipalities; (b) to issue land affidavits; (c) to create maps to be used for urban planning and development.

Table 3.7. RFU costs in US$

	Investment	Cost/capita	Cost/ha	Cost/plot
Cotonou	1,050,000	1.9	150	15
Porto-Novo	560,000	2.9	132	14
Parakou	168,000	1.8	42	11

The urban district of Kigali, the capital, and the city of Butare were equipped with such registers in 1992–1993. The register in Kigali covered an area of 2,300 ha, and the register in Butare covered 500 ha. Plans were to extend the operation to other cities, but dramatic events in 1994 nearly wiped out such efforts. However, the new PIGU program financed by the World Bank (2005) calls for a resumption of the initiative and a street addressing pilot operation in the informal settlements of Kigali. A GIS is also being prepared for the capital city.

Djibouti: addressing in Balbala incomplete

The "historic districts" or *magala* in Djibouti (population of 450,000 in 2002) developed near the port and the European district. Numbered 1–7 bis, the districts were established in an organized fashion and were assigned addresses before independence, despite the impermanence of many of their buildings. In 1983, the city expanded considerably to the Balbala basalt site when that area was no longer cut off from the city's historic district. This occurred when the city developed the Wadi Ambouli crossing and removed the barbed wire fence that had blocked that entrance in the city. The Balbala site gradually became part of the city, and many projects were undertaken to provide the area with facilities.

In 1997, the MAE financed a street addressing study for this new neighborhood (2,000 ha) following the significant infrastructure efforts (*grande trame*) that helped provide services to the most underserved neighborhoods in the metropolitan area. But the addressing project stalled there, obviously waiting for a more opportune moment.

Togo: Street addressing and residence tax

In 1996, the Urban Development Project financed by the World Bank implemented an addressing system and residence tax concurrently. This residence tax, payable by anyone with their main residence in Togo, is based on the type of housing and its water, electric, and telephone facilities.

"This program to help local municipalities build financial resources included a vast city street addressing and taxpayer identification program. Thus, from a level of less than 300 taxpayers previously subject to a property-based taxation system (property tax and tax on household waste removal), street addressing has made it possible to identify over 80,000 potential taxpayers for the residence tax. This reform is expected to help local municipalities improve their financial resources, to provide services, and to make the needed urban investments to improve the living environment of residents."[17]

An addressing unit that was part of the town hall's administration piloted the first project in Lomé. In particular, the project focused on a simple street identification system based on districts: "District Adobou Komé—Street 6" for example. The address map of Lomé was later incorporated into a GIS. In 2001, the Urban Integration and Local Cooperation Project financed by the MAE extended the addressing unit's work.

Addressing in Côte d'Ivoire

Côte d'Ivoire undertook its first street addressing projects in Abidjan using its own resources, and in San Pedro with financing from the European Union (Coastal Towns Development Project). The project was split into three steps: (a) numbering streets and sign installation; (b) numbering buildings, (c) distributing a public guide map, producing an awareness campaign, and training the teams involved.

The first step was carried out in both cities. Thus, the 10 Abidjan municipalities were divided into 55 street address zones defined by natural boundaries and each containing several neighborhoods. A letter was assigned to each zone, with streets running east-west, parallel to the ocean, being assigned even numbers and perpendicular streets being assigned odd numbers. Thus, boulevard Latrille in the municipality of Cocody becomes "Bd A5 Latrille." Streets in the seven municipalities have signs. The addressing unit created as part of the BNETD (National Office for Technical Studies for Development) eventually plans to equip a total of 6,000 streets and 12,820 intersections and dead-end streets with about 25,000 signs and 13,000 signposts.

The buildings have not yet been numbered, but plans are for the numbering to be metric and alternating. A street database has been created, and address maps exist in computerized format but have not yet been printed in large quantities.

In the neighborhoods where addressing already existed such as Zone 4, Plateau, Vieux Cocody, and Treichville, the old names were kept, but all of the streets have been numbered.

Finally, to make it easier for people to find their way around using the new address system, plans are to post neighborhood maps in bus shelters, at the entrances and exits of neighborhoods, and in public places. As for future plans to name streets, the municipal councils will oversee the gradual implementation of that project.

Figure 3.8. San Pedro: Divided into "addressing zones"

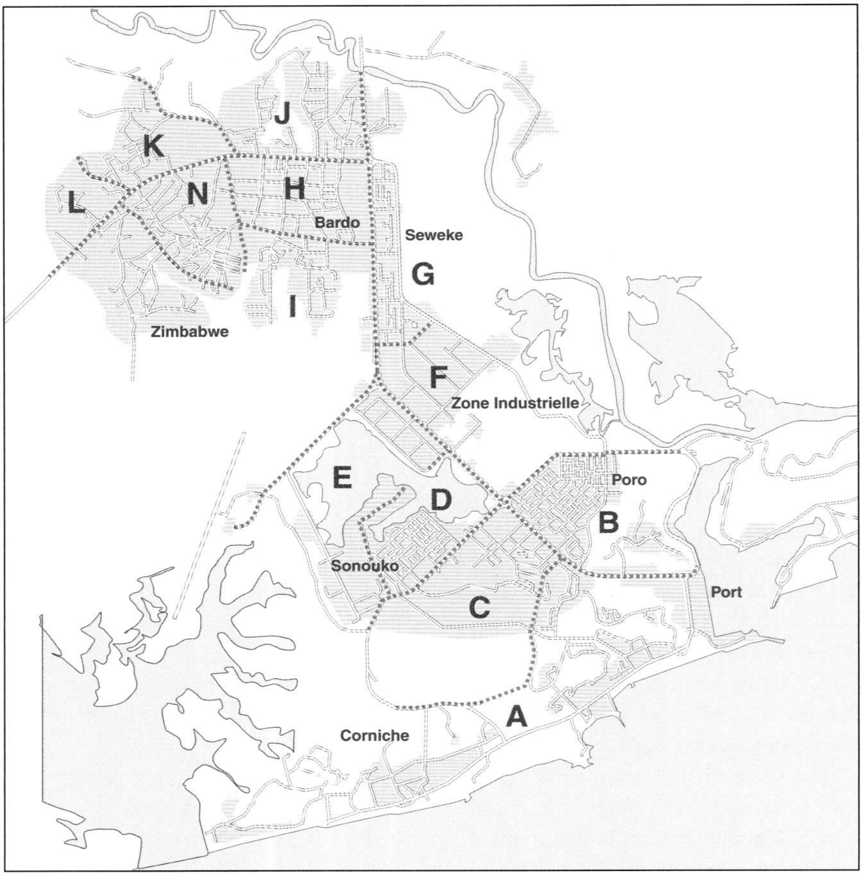

Notes

1. Maputo (population 1,300,000), Conakry, Douala, Bamako, Lomé, Niamey, Yaoundé, Nouakchott, N'djaména (population 600,000), Ouagadougou, Beira, Matola, Bobo-Dioulasso, Nampula, Thiès, Kaolack, Ziguinchor, Quelimane, Diourbel, Louga, Pemba (population 80,000). The numbers represent population figures for the year when addressing began in each city.

2. In most cities, authorities were reluctant to address so-called irregular or squatter settlements.

3. The lowest cost is in Nouadhibou (US$0.25), and the highest is in Nouakchott (US$10.7).

4. One country used its own funds to finance these activities (Côte d'Ivoire), but as of 2004 the effort remains limited in scope.

5. The same applications were developed in Yaoundé and Douala.

6. This application was previously mentioned in Chapter 2 in the section entitled "Support for municipal services."

7. Fonds d'Aide et de Coopération (Aid and Cooperation Fund) (France).

8. This project is designed to increase resources for district management and maintenance of city services, particularly roads. Addressing in Bamako constitutes a major component of the project.

9. Committee created in 1999 as a public corporation.

10. Acrylic and vinyl copolymer base.

11. French Development Agency.

12. The first project was carried out in Nouadhibou, based on the Bamako model, using only municipal financing (US$22,000), which equals US$0.25 per doorway addressed, far below later costs for similar projects in Nouakchott.

13. CFPB: land tax on improved property, TH: occupancy tax, TC: municipal tax.

14. UM: oughiya, Mauritanian currency.

15. In Maputo, annual population growth reached 8%.

16. International Association of Francophone Mayors.

17. Badabon, C. 2001. *La lutte contre la pauvreté urbaine au Togo (Fight against Urban Poverty in Togo)*.

4
Street Addressing Manual

Basic assumptions

This chapter presents a set of activities that delineate the practical aspects of implementing a street addressing program. The manual is based on three assumptions:

1. *Designating street names at the outset (i.e., giving names to streets that are nameless) is nearly impossible.* Street naming is usually the prerogative of municipal authorities, and the process is slow, involving a choice of names of individuals, heroic or historical figures, artists or benefactors, and often lengthy negotiations that are best faced rather than avoided. Usually, the most important streets are given the most prestigious names, creating a hierarchy of streets to match that of the names themselves, an especially delicate task when the names of politicians are used. As the case of Cameroon demonstrates, official decrees for street naming do not always produce results (annex 3). The recommended solution is to adopt a number identification system initially, which does not involve choices based on emotion and allows streets to be identified immediately. This system, which has been adopted notably in the United States, is well adapted to cities with a "checkerboard" or grid layout where streets follow one another sequentially (street 1, street 2, street 3, etc.), but it is unsuitable when the street layout is irregular. In this case, streets in the same district may be designated by an identifying element: a local place-name, the name of the district, or a sequential letter or number. This is considered a temporary solution, until the streets are gradually named, which is often more meaningful for residents. However, it is clear that a street that has already been numbered is subsequently easier to name because it has already been identified, located, and defined by its origin and end point.

2. *Street addressing programs are a municipal undertaking.* Some programs have been implemented as part of projects begun under ministerial supervision before subsequently coming under the control of local governments. But this approach should be considered an exception to the rule: implementing a street addressing program is an opportunity to mobilize the community, specifically through the creation of a street addressing unit, which should gradually evolve into an urban data bank unit, an urban observatory or the city's urban planning unit.

3. *An address is defined by its relation to a street rather than to a block of houses.* The principle involved is to make the address visible in the public space, that is, from the street: this comes down to identifying streets (street signs) and buildings on them (numbers on the building façade). Other systems give priority to identifying the block (private space) on a map, with no special attention given to a particular location. Several cadas-

tral maps work this way, with no street names or numbers, but their users are surveyors and other professionals in the field, who are used to reading maps with an ease that surpasses the abilities of the average citizen.

Presentation of the manual

The manual is organized into 13 illustrated activities that break down the different phases of a street addressing program.

- *Overview of the process*
  Activity 1: Designing the street addressing program
  Activity 2: Conducting a feasibility study
- *Responses to questions asked during the feasibility study*
  Activity 3: Setting up the street addressing unit
  Activity 4: Estimating costs and time frames
  Activity 5: Defining the scope of the program
  Activity 6: Choosing a codification system
- *Street addressing key tasks:*
  Activity 7: Mapping
  Activity 8: Surveying and numbering doorways
  Activity 9: Recording addresses
  Activity 10: Installing street signs
  Activity 11: Producing the address map and street index
  Activity 12: Conducting a media campaign
  Activity 13: Maintaining and adapting the system

Activity 1. Designing the street addressing program

The program has three phases: preparation, implementation, and maintenance. The progression of each phase is described briefly below and illustrated by figures 4.1 and 4.2 (planning and sequencing of tasks). During these phases, the following tasks are undertaken: codification, surveying and number assignment to doorways, mapping, installation of street signs, setting up an address directory, and media campaigns.

Preparation phase

OBJECTIVE AND TASKS. This phase should help to define approaches to implementing the street addressing program and setting up the unit charged with coordination, known as the "street addressing unit." Tasks during this phase will focus on:

- conducting a feasibility study to determine the codification system (cf. glossary) for identifying streets and numbering doorways as well as approaches to implementing the program,
- setting up the street addressing unit responsible for coordinating implementation.

EXPECTED RESULTS. Municipal authorities will approve the feasibility study's recommendations and render the street addressing unit operational.

ACTORS. The municipality, consultant, street addressing unit.

DURATION AND COST. This phase lasts about 21 weeks, 12 of which are used for the feasibility study. Costs incurred will cover the feasibility study (two person-months) and hiring of three people to head the unit, in addition to operating and materials acquisition expenses.

SCHEDULING. The preparation phase will be executed in two stages: feasibility study and setting up the street addressing unit (the following numbers refer to sequences in figures 4.1 and 4.2).

- Stage One: (1) select a consultant to run the feasibility study; (2) conduct the study, (3) have municipal authorities approve recommendations.
- Stage Two: (4) set up the unit, (5) collect initial documents (base maps), (6) conduct the first media campaign, (7) train street addressing unit agents in implementing and monitoring the street addressing program (the consultant who prepares the feasibility study may also provide this training).

Implementation phase

OBJECTIVE AND TASKS. This is the phase in which the program becomes fully operational by definition. Tasks will essentially focus on:

- preparing the address map and the street index (mapping),
- positioning street signs at the main intersections (installation of signage),
- numbering of doorways, according to the codification system adopted and the survey associated with it,
- setting up an address directory,
- conducting a media campaign for the street addressing program.

EXPECTED RESULTS. Results will hinge on undertaking the tasks above and producing the following documents: address map, street index, address directory, media campaign components, signage map, list of street signs.

ACTORS. The municipality, street addressing unit, trainer, survey takers and laborers, media campaign specialist, street sign manufacturer and installer, printer.

DURATION AND COST. The duration of this phase will depend on the size of the city: the estimate is 12 to 18 months. Costs incurred will cover street addressing unit operations (including compensation for survey takers and short-term hires), supply of street signs and materials needed for numbering doorways, and media campaign expenses.

SCHEDULING. Mapping, survey preparation, numbering of doorways, and launching of a request for bids for producing street signs may be undertaken almost simultaneously.

- *Mapping*. Based on initial preparations during the feasibility study and information gathered during the preparation phase, the street addressing unit creates a base map (8), which depicts the streets and toponymy of the districts. The unit then creates an inventory of streets and intersections, which is essential for verifying the layout of the base map (9). The process of codifying streets then begins with indicating their identifiers on the map, their endpoints, and the type of subdivision adopted by the street addressing program. The map and the street index are then finalized before printing (11). After the request for bids is issued (12) and the printer is chosen (13), the printing process begins.
- *Doorway numbering and surveys*. Questionnaires and survey materials are prepared (15) at the beginning of the implementation phase, as soon as the base map is ready. Survey takers must then be recruited and trained

Figure 4.1. Flowchart for tasks

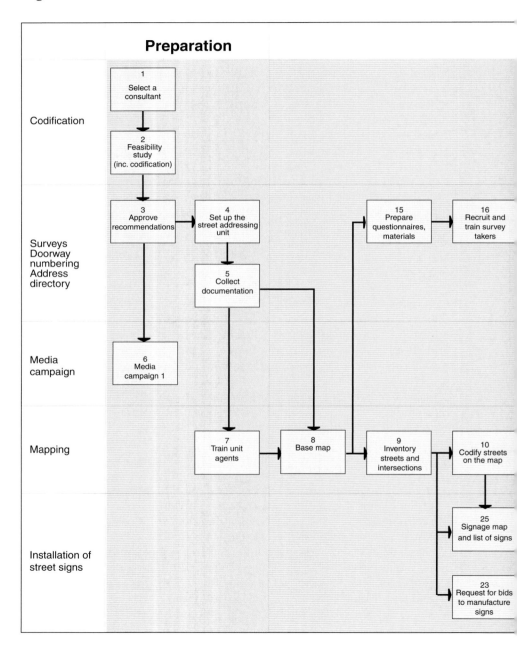

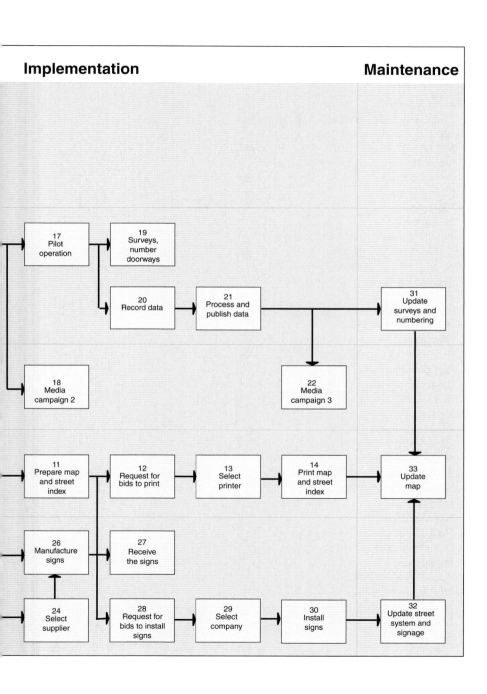

Implementation   **Maintenance**

17 Pilot operation	**19** Surveys, number doorways
	20 Record data → **21** Process and publish data → **31** Update surveys and numbering
18 Media campaign 2	**22** Media campaign 3
11 Prepare map and street index → **12** Request for bids to print → **13** Select printer → **14** Print map and street index → **33** Update map	
26 Manufacture signs → **27** Receive the signs	
24 Select supplier → **28** Request for bids to install signs → **29** Select company → **30** Install signs → **32** Update street system and signage	

Figure 4.2. Planning of tasks

	weeks		
FEASIBILITY STUDY	**12**		
1. Select a consultant	2		
2. Feasibility study (including codification)		8	
3. Approve recommendations	2		
STREET ADDRESSING UNIT	**9**		
4. Set up the street addressing unit	4		
5. Collect documentation	3		
6. Train unit agents	2		
MAPPING	**46**		
8. Base map		3	
9. Inventory streets and intersections		4	
10. Codify streets on the map		5	
11. Prepare map and street index		3	
12. Request for bids to print map and index		8	
13. Select printer		2	
14. Print map and street index		4	
SURVEYS AND NUMBERING	**39**		
15. Prepare questionnaires and materials		6	
16. Recruit and train survey takers		4	
17. Pilot operation		1	
19. Surveys, number doorways	25		
ADDRESS DIRECTORY	**33**		
20. Record data		28	
21. Process and publish data		5	
INSTALL STREET SIGNS	**39**		
23. Request for bids to manufacture signs		8	
24. Select supplier		2	
25. Signage map and list of signs		5	
26. Manufacture signs		15	
27. Receive the signs		2	
28. Request for bids to install signs		6	
29. Select company to install signs		2	
30. Install signs		6	
MEDIA CAMPAIGN	**48**		
6. Media campaign 1		1	
18. Media campaign 2		1	
22. Media campaign 3		2	
MAINTENANCE	**14**		
31. Update surveys and numbering		12	
32. Update street system and signage		6	
33. Update map		6	

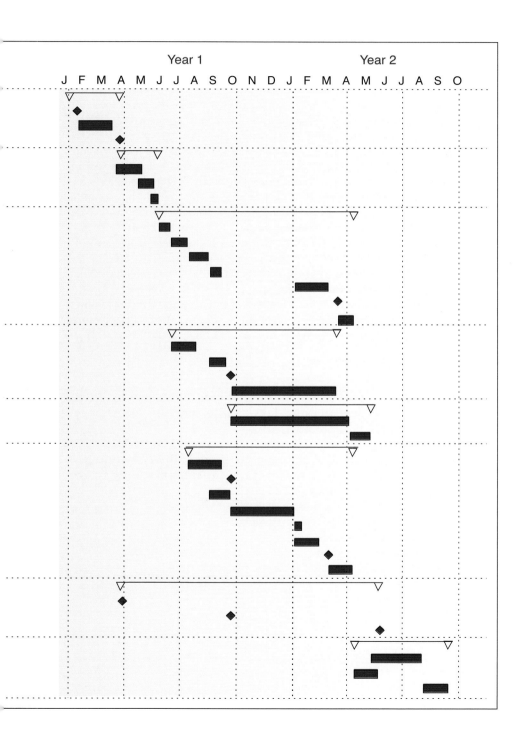

(16), and then a pilot operation is launched (17), which leads to a second media campaign (18). The longest phase of the operation then begins (19): numbering doorways and conducting surveys of building occupants.

- *Address directory.* Data are entered daily (20) as surveys are completed. When the program has been completed, all of the data are processed and distributed to the administrative bodies and departments involved (21).
- *Installation of street signs.* This is a lengthy step because it includes the manufacture and installation of the street signs. First, a request for bids for manufacturing the signs is issued (23) at the outset of the implementation phase and after an inventory of streets and intersections has been conducted, but an exact list of streets does not need to be available in order to issue the request for bids. However, the list and signage map (25) should be ready upon selection of the supplier (24) so that production can get under way (26). Once the signs have been produced and before they are delivered (27), a request for bids is issued for placing the signs (28), which will begin after the company has been selected (29).
- *Media campaign.* Awareness raising campaigns will target the population on at least three occasions: at the end of the preparation phase when the street addressing unit has been set up (6), during the pilot operation (17), and when the map and street index have been distributed (22).

Maintenance phase

OBJECTIVE AND TASKS. This phase usually requires fewer resources than those needed for implementation. Tasks will essentially focus on the following issues:

- Updating and completing the numbering process: doorway numbers have disappeared, new doorways have been created, and addresses need to be assigned to new districts (31);
- Updating and distributing the address directory;

Table 4.1. Street addressing tasks by phase

Task	Preparation	Implementation	Maintenance
Codification	x		
Mapping	x	x	x
Numbering of doorways—surveys		x	x
Installation of street signs		x	x
Address directory		x	x
Media campaign	x	x	x

- Updating and completing street sign installation: street signs have disappeared or have been damaged, new streets must be given signs (32);
- Updating the address map (33).

EXPECTED RESULTS. Results will consist of updated versions of existing documents and possibly the extension of street addressing programs to neighborhoods that do not yet have addresses. Once the main street addressing needs have been met, the street addressing unit should expand its role, using the knowledge gained from the street addressing program, and broaden its mandate to become a documentation center, for example, or urban database.

ACTORS. Municipality, street addressing unit.

DURATION AND COST. Maintenance should be conducted annually. Costs incurred will cover the operations of the street addressing unit and possible supply of new street signs and materials for numbering doorways.

Activity 2. Conducting a feasibility study

The local conditions and financial resources available are unique to each city; the design and implementation of a street addressing program must take this specificity into account. Different approaches to numbering, sign installation, and mapping are possible. Before undertaking a street addressing program, municipal authorities must have data available for decisionmaking: a feasibility study helps to determine the conditions under which the program is feasible.

The feasibility study should offer more than general guidelines; it must offer specific and practical recommendations that make implementation of the program possible once municipal authorities have approved the study's conclusions. These recommendations should focus on the following points:

- Codifying streets and doorways;
- Scope of the program;
- Practical methods for mapping, numbering, surveying, sign installation, and creating an address directory;
- Organizing and staging the program;
- Cost, financing, deadlines.

Preferably, a consultant who specializes in street addressing should conduct the feasibility study. The study can be implemented in about five weeks, since this street addressing manual can answer questions that arise during the process.

Terms of reference for the feasibility study

Background
In the last two decades, the municipality of Doloba (population of 350,000) has grown rapidly (7% per year). Outside of the inner city neighborhoods, streets are nameless and building doorways have no numbers. The lack of an address system creates many obstacles to the delivery of public services related to health care, law enforcement, and municipal technical services. Residents do the best they can to overcome these difficulties using the name of the neighborhood or local placename as landmarks, but the situation has become so serious that the municipality has decided to launch a street addressing program. These terms of reference are designed to be used for a feasibility study that describes the precise conditions under which this program should be carried out.

Objective

Based on the results of the study, municipal authorities should be able to make clear decisions. A schedule for approval of the recommendations formulated will be prepared for use upon completion of the study. After the recommendations are approved, the program may be implemented as soon as possible.

Tasks to be implemented

The program has three phases: preparation, implementation, and maintenance. The feasibility study and the creation of a street addressing unit responsible for coordinating the program are part of the preparation phase.

Tasks to be implemented focus on the following issues: (a) codification of streets and doorways; (b) scope of the program; (c) practical methods for mapping, numbering, surveys, sign installation, and creating an address directory; (d) organization and staging of the program; (e) cost and financing.

CODIFICATION

- *Codification of streets.* Most streets are nameless. Experience shows that it is almost impossible to assign names quickly and systematically because the naming process requires lengthy negotiations between the municipality and residents. The solution is to adopt a street numbering system that will gradually assign names in a subsequent phase. Given that streets are not laid out regularly, as in a grid fashion, for example, numbers cannot be assigned to streets in a sequential manner, that is, with street 42 following street 41. To facilitate street identification, a prefix or suffix is usually added to the street number to refer to the municipality, district, or neighborhood. For example, if the reference is a district, the 42nd street of the 3rd district will be identified as street 3.42; if the reference is sector C, the 42nd street would be identified as street C.42.

  The consultant will study the main options for identifying streets and pinpoint their advantages and disadvantages before he/she formulates his/her recommendations. Toward this end, he/she will provide a map of the city at a 1:10,000 scale, indicating the proposed subdivision that will serve as a reference for the street (municipality, district, neighborhood, local placename, address zone).
- *Numbering of doorways.* The consultant will study the main options (sequential, decametric, metric numbering), their advantages and disadvantages, and recommend a solution for numbering doorways.

  For neighborhoods where doorways are already numbered, the consultant will make other recommendations.

SCOPE OF THE PROGRAM

Priority neighborhoods. Many neighborhoods need addresses, and some may receive higher priority than others. Some neighborhoods on the outksirts of the city are still under construction, and it may be appropriate to delay implementation of a street addressing program in these areas. The consultant will propose a list of priority neighborhoods and substantiate his/her recommendations.

Street addressing coverage. Street addressing programs assign a number to buildings (houses, places of business, facilities). Addressing may be extended to urban fixtures such as public standpipes, fire hydrants, or waste transfer points. The consultant will indicate if he/she plans to include such fixtures in the first street addressing program or if he/she plans to postpone their inclusion to a subsequent program.

Location of pilot operation. The consultant will indicate on the map an area consisting of several streets where the pilot operation may be conducted. He/she will briefly specify the reasons for his/her choice.

PRACTICAL CONSIDERATIONS

- *Mapping.* The consultant will prepare a map of the city at a 1:10,000 scale (if possible, in electronic format, which will include the following information):
  - streets and squares that already have names,
  - administrative boundaries (municipalities, districts),
  - proposed boundaries for street codification,
  - priority zones and zones to be targeted in a subsequent phase,
  - geographical direction in which numbering will proceed,
  - toponymy of important neighborhoods and local placenames,
  - identification (numbering) of streets with end points indicated in addition to direction of numbering on doorways for two city neighborhoods.
- *Numbering of doorways.* The consultant will prepare:
  - a survey form to be filled out upon number assignment,
  - a draft of the standard informational memo to be sent to residents,
  - a model for inscribing and finalizing doorway numbers.
- *Address directory.* The consultant will prepare a draft survey form and will describe how the data should be handled, the purposes for which it will be used on a regular basis and transmitted to the administrative bodies concerned.
- *Sign installation.* The consultant will provide the following information:
  - estimate of the number of existing intersections in the areas where street addressing is needed,
  - estimate of the number of signs to be posted,

- street sign proposal: size, wording, material, type of mounting, naming of suppliers,
- proposal for manufacture and installation.

ORGANIZING THE STREET ADDRESSING UNIT AND STAGING THE PROGRAM

- *Supervisory Committee*. The municipality has created a Supervisory Committee for the street addressing program, to which the consultant will submit the results of the study. The Committee includes representatives of the municipal council and decentralized departments of the Ministries of the Interior and Urban Affairs. It will meet periodically with the street addressing unit during the implementation phase to review progress on the program. The consultant will propose a schedule of meetings for the Supervisory Committee during implementation of the program. He/she may suggest additional meetings, for example, with neighborhood leaders.
- *Street addressing unit*. The unit will be responsible for coordinating activities. For this purpose, it will recruit survey takers and hire short-term workers to assist with the program. It will be responsible specifically for mapping, numbering of doorways, the survey database, and placement of signs. The unit will have three full-time employees.

  The consultant will identify and propose candidates who may assist the unit, whether or not they are drawn from municipal departments. He/she will make recommendations on:
- unit operations,
- implementation planning,
- the frequency of meetings with the Supervisory Committee.

  The consultant will draw up a brief set of procedures specifically describing:
- the relationship between the Supervisory Committee and the street addressing unit during the implementation phase,
- the unit's prerogatives and the role of different actors participating in the program.

COST AND FUNDING

The consultant will assess projected costs of the program for the preparation (setting up the street addressing unit), implementation and one-year maintenance phases, breaking out investment and operating expenses.

The street addressing unit will enjoy some financial autonomy, in particular during the implementation phase (during which short-term workers should be paid in timely fashion and minor expenses covered). The consultant will make recommendations on cost control measures.

When projected costs are reviewed, the consultant will break out, as needed, the various sources of projected funding for the program.

DURATION. DOCUMENTS TO BE SUBMITTED
The study will take five weeks. At the end of the third week, the consultant will submit an interim report in triplicate to the Supervisory Committee in which a detailed cost estimate will be provided. The Supervisory Committee will have eight days to respond to the report. The consultant will have one week to prepare his/her final report, of which he/she will submit five identical copies. Time allowance is five person-weeks.

DOCUMENTS TO BE PROVIDED BY THE MUNICIPALITY
The municipality will assist the consultant with contacting its own departments, neighborhood leaders, and heads of other administrative bodies that have data needed for the study. It will provide the consultant with documents in its possession that may be needed for the study (specifically, plans and maps of the city).

VALIDATION OF RESULTS
When the interim report is submitted, the consultant will provide his/her results to the Supervisory Committee. To facilitate decisionmaking, the consultant will use the schedule for approval below to summarize the issues covered.

Schedule for approval
The schedule summarizes recommendations made by the consultant to the Supervisory Committee. Each of the 23 points is submitted for approval. The list below presents, in italics, sample responses or refers the reader to tables or figures.

- Codification
  1. What does the street addressing program propose for the street codification system and for approaches to subdividing the city?
     Subdividing the city: • into neighborhoods, • into groups of neighborhoods,• into districts, • into address zones, • other.
     Codification of streets: • numbering system using a figure or letter: street 3.12, street C.12, • numbering system with initials of the neighborhood: street Med.12 or street 12.MED (in the "Medina" neighborhood).
  2. Which numbering system is to be applied to doorways?
     Numbering is • sequential, • metric, • decametric.
  3. In which direction will the numbering proceed?
     Determine two perpendicular axes in the city center (major street, river) from which the numbering will begin: • For streets running north to south, numbering will begin at the axis, and for streets running east to west, it will begin at . . . .

4. What will happen to the existing numbered doorways in some neighborhoods?
   The existing numbering system is • maintained and will be changed at a later date, • is changed, but the old numbers may be retained in the interim.

- Scope of the program
  5. Which are the priority zones, and where can street addressing be postponed?
     • Formal districts will be targeted as a priority (list). • Historic informal districts will be targeted under the same conditions as formal districts. • Only existing major streets (list) in the historic informal districts will be targeted. • New informal districts will be targeted at a later date (list). • Reasons for this proposal are as follows . . .)
  6. Where will addresses be assigned: only to buildings or to urban fixtures as well?
     The program will focus on • only buildings, • on buildings and urban fixtures.
  7. Where will the pilot operation take place?
     The pilot operation will take place in the . . . . neighborhood. The five streets chosen are: . . . .

- Practical considerations
  8. What will the street addressing map look like?
     The proposed map at a scale of 1:10,000 is attached.
  9. What is the estimated number of doorways to which a number will be assigned?
     The estimated number of doorways per neighborhood is as follows (see table).
  10. How will the doorways be numbered?
      The numbering will be done by stenciling with paint on the wall • on a white rectangle, • in a circle, • on wooden signs nailed over the doorway, etc.
  11. Who will do the numbering and conduct the survey?
      This will be done by • the street addressing unit, with the assistance of survey takers and laborers that the unit has recruited and trained; or . . . .
  12. What kind of data will be collected by the survey?
      The data to be collected are provided in the following table (to be prepared): e.g.: complete address, type of use (housing, place of business, municipal facility, urban fixtures), type of building (single- or multi-unit), access to utilities (water, electricity, telephone), width and length of street system— condition of streets and facilities.
  13. What are the expected results?
      Better information on • the tax base, • municipal infrastructure and facilities.
  14. What is the estimated number of street signs to be installed (sign density)?

The number of signs per neighborhood is provided in the following table. It has been calculated on the following basis: four signs per intersection in the city center (list of neighborhoods), two signs at all intersections in the following neighborhoods, two signs for every other intersection in the following neighborhoods, etc.

15. What type of street sign has been proposed?

The proposed street sign has the following characteristics: material, size, color, mounting.

16. How will the sign manufacturer be selected?

After an • international, • national request for bids has been issued.

17. Who will be responsible for installing the signs? How will the selection be made?

The signs will be placed by • a company selected after a local request for bids is issued, • technical departments of the municipality.

• Organization and staging

18. Who will manage the pilot operation? What are his or her main responsibilities?

A coordinator will manage the street addressing unit, • he/she will be the main liaison with the Supervisory Committee, • he/she will report to the Director of Technical Departments, who will also be a liaison to the Supervisory Committee.

19. How will the municipality and street addressing unit interface?

The following schedule lists the various meetings and field visits (table).

20. How many full-time and short-term workers will the street addressing unit have?

The unit will have . . . . full-time employees, including the coordinator and . . . . short-term teams mobilized to conduct surveys and number the doorways.

21. What is the time frame for implementation and the main stages planned?

The projected schedule is as follows . . . .

• Cost and financing

22. What are the projected costs?

Costs of implementation are broken down in the attached table: ....

23. What are the different sources of projected funding?

• Municipality : . . . .% ; Project in support of local governments: ... % ; utility concessionaires : . . . .% ; Sponsors : . . . .%

Figure 4.3. Addresses assigned to urban fixtures

Activity 3. Setting up the street addressing unit

This section focuses on the second stage of preparation for the program: setting up the street addressing unit.

Responsibilities

This stage involves two areas of responsibility: decisionmaking and implementation.

DECISIONMAKING. Municipal authorities are responsible for decision-making. They are the main contract managers, and in this role undertake and finance the program (sometimes with donor support); they make critical decisions identified during the feasibility study related to the budget, codification, scope of the program, media campaigns, selection of suppliers, and other matters. Owing to the broad impact of a street addressing program, other administrative entities and key utility concessionaires (water, electricity) should also be involved. Setting up a Supervisory Committee is usually a good approach to broadening participation.

IMPLEMENTATION. Various approaches may be workable here, but the idea of setting up an implementation structure as a municipal service is not usually the most appropriate solution for a variety of reasons:

- Municipalities do not usually provide for this type of position, and creating it sometimes leads to considerable delays that interfere with the launching of the program.
- Technical departments, where this position might be created, are often very busy with day-to-day affairs and are unaccustomed to handling multiple activities (such as mapping, surveys, setting up a database).
- Finally, the implementation phase clearly differs from the maintenance phase: it is shorter (lasts about one year) and calls for a greater number of more diversified activities and narrowly focused, more specialized skills.

For these reasons in part, experts who are not associated with the municipality have assisted in the implementation phase of several street addressing programs, before these are taken over during the maintenance phase by one of the municipal departments already in existence or created for this purpose.

In other words, although this implementation structure known as the street addressing unit is placed under municipal authority, its role may

Table 4.2. Distribution and phasing of tasks

Task	Phase	Responsible
• Train full-time staff	Preparation	Consultant
• Procure supplies needed for the program to succeed	Preparation Implementation	Coordinator
• Organize and supervise public awareness raising campaign	Implementation	Coordinator
• Prepare codification and mapping	Preparation Implementation	Chief Cart.
• Prepare consultations with actors (supplier, sign installation company, others,	Implementation	Coordinator
• Recruit short-term workers needed for implementation	Preparation	Coordinator
• Train short-term workers	Preparation	Chief Cart. Directory Mgr.
• Supervise street sign installation	Implementation	Chief Cart.
• Supervise surveys and doorway numbering	Implementation	Chief Cart.
• Ensure creation of the computerized address directory	Implementation	Directory Mgr.
• Report to the Supervisory Committee on progress of the program	Preparation Implementation Maintenance	Coordinator

evolve from that of service provider during implementation to a permanent department during the maintenance phase. The unit may eventually serve as a sort of municipal documentation center responsible primarily for collecting information related to planning and development.

Tasks of the street addressing unit

The unit intervenes in accordance with decisions made upon completion of the feasibility study and recorded in its procedures. Its main tasks during the implementation phase are as follows:

TASKS DURING PREPARATION

- *Setting up the unit:* Preparing the location, setting up office and computer equipment.
- *Collection of documentation.* The focus here is on maps, city plans, and expansions under way, and aerial photographs. The purpose of this collection is to create a base map with an outline of streets and major facilities. The map is at a 1:10,000 scale and should serve as the basis for a street inventory (activity 7).
- *Training of unit agents.* This is for core unit members (see below).

Composition of the street addressing unit

The unit comprises a set of full-time core members and teams that are deployed on a short-term basis. The unit is managed by a coordinator.

Full-time core members are involved during the preparation phase, when the feasibility study is completed and during the implementation and maintenance phases. They include as a minimum: (a) the coordinator, who is responsible for moving the work forward and ensuring that the unit is operating properly, (b) someone in charge of mapping and placement of street signs, and (c) someone in charge of taking surveys and creating the address directory.

Short-term teams are involved in the implementation phase during survey taking and doorway numbering. To minimize supervision problems, it is usually advisable to form no more than four or five teams. Each team comprises (a) a team leader, (b) a field surveyor, (c) one or two survey takers, and (d) two to four painters and laborers.

This is one example of team composition. The qualifications and number of full-time team members may also vary depending on the scale of the program.

- Preparation: the unit consists only of full-time core members.
- Implementation: the unit may have more than 30 people (three full-time members and four teams of six to eight people).
- Maintenance: staff may be reduced to the full-time team or even limited to one person; under these circumstances, the program is not expected to be extended nor is the unit's role expected to evolve beyond its initial mandate.

COORDINATOR. As the main liaison with the Supervisory Committee, the coordinator plays an important role in organizing and managing the program. He has the following duties:

- Prepare decisions of the Supervisory Committee and associated meetings,
- Provide a progress report on task implementation and obstacles encountered,
- Prepare the media campaign, submit decisionmaking guidelines,
- Prepare request for bid files and organize bid opening and sorting produres,
- Supervise training of unit agents,
- Organize team interventions in the field,
- Oversee the work of actors,
- Prepare payment arrangements for agents,
- Oversee project execution.

Required skills and profile. Professional with a degree in management, the coordinator will have the following qualifications: management experience, team leadership skills, mapping capabilities, computer knowledge commensurate with the job. Topographers (or surveyors), engineers, and architects would be the best suited for the preparation and implementation phases.

CHIEF CARTOGRAPHER. Assists the coordinator and is in charge of mapping and installing street signs. He is responsible for:

- Gathering mapping documentation to create the base map;
- Street by street, checking that the base map conforms to the reality on the ground, making any corrections necessary;
- At each intersection, identifying existing street signs and future sign placement;
- Based on these observations, drawing up a list of existing street signs and those to be ordered, preparing the signage map and the street index;
- Taking delivery of orders (signs and posts);
- Supervising installation of street signs;
- Reporting to the coordinator.

Required skills and profile. Experience in mapping and computers (design software), project oversight, solid knowledge of the city. Map-makers, surveyors, and topographers would be the best suited for this position.

SURVEY AND DATABASE MANAGER. The coordinator's other assistant. He is responsible for:

- Preparing the surveys,
- Assisting the coordinator in the organization of surveying and numbering teams,
- Data input,
- Ensuring that data are processed and disseminated according to the coordinator's instructions,
- Ensuring that surveying and numbering teams are trained,
- Reporting to the coordinator.

Required skills and profile. Experience in preparing, monitoring, and use of surveys, solid computer knowledge (databases), good organizational skills. A computer scientist or sociologist would be the best suited for this position.

SHORT-TERM TEAM

Team leader. Responsible for:
- Managing the surveying and numbering teams in the field,
- Preparing materials needed for numbering doorways,
- Establishing and maintaining contact with residents during the survey,
- Providing a daily progress update to the survey manager and delivering completed survey forms to him.

Required skills and profile. Team management, good interpersonal and organizational skills, ability to read maps and charts. Topographers and project leaders are well suited for this position.

Survey taker (one or two per team). Responsible for:
- Completing survey questionnaires provided to residents,
- Providing reports to the team leader.

Required skills and profile. Team management, good interpersonal and organizational skills, ability to read maps.

Field Surveyor. Responsible for:
- Regardless of the numbering system adopted, providing the painter with number to be placed on the building;

- Regardless of the system adopted, indicating on the map as the program progresses the first and last number of each street segment (this information will be transmitted to the chief cartographer);
- Providing reports to the team leader.

Required skills and profile. Degree recipient, map reading ability.

Painters and laborers. Responsible for inscribing with chalk and then painting the doorway numbers according to the field surveyor's instructions. They must be literate.

TRAINING
Once the feasibility study has been completed, the full-time core members will be trained in street addressing techniques before the implementation phase begins. The consultant who prepared the feasibility study may also provide this training. Additional computer training in using software for the design and creation of the address directory is sometimes necessary.

Short-term teams receive training at the beginning of the implementation phase. Training focused on survey techniques, distance measure-

Figure 4.4. Organizational chart for the street addressing unit

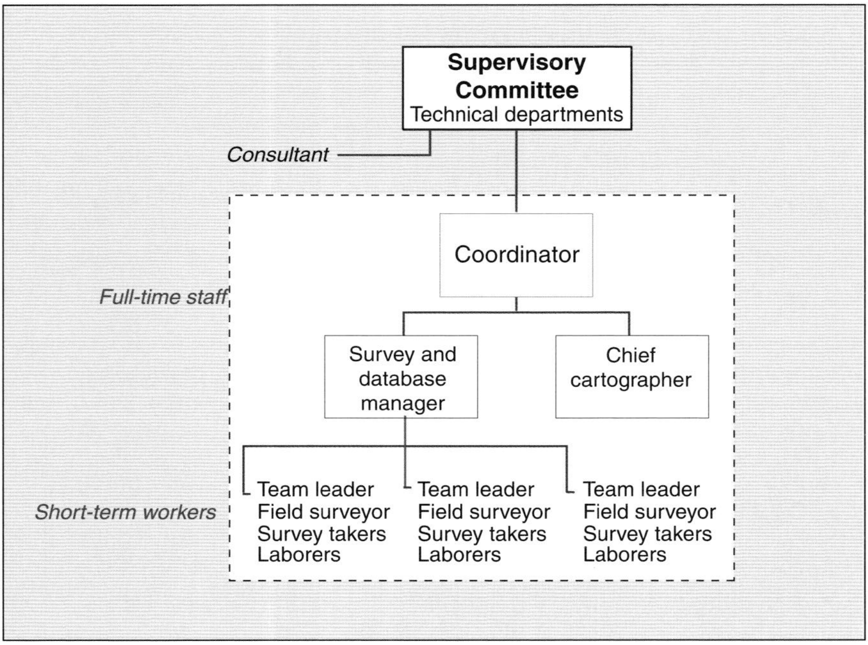

ment, doorway numbering, map reading, and organizing of data collected daily. It is completed on the ground during the pilot operation.

Unit operations

Experience shows that to create the best possible conditions for implementing a street addressing program, the unit needs some autonomy at the outset. One key issue, for example, is payment of the short-term team, which should be done weekly in the interest of efficiency; this task raises the question of oversight, among other issues. Street addressing programs have worked best when administrative procedures are kept to a minimum and outside service providers are involved and responsible for managing the budget under a contract with municipal authorities.

Arranging offices and equipment for the unit

The unit must have its own offices and technical and computer equipment (suggested list provided; see table 4.3).

OFFICES. During the preparation and maintenance phases, the office has a small staff and requires little office space. The requirements change during the implementation phase, when a meeting room is absolutely essential for training, preparations, progress reports on daily activities, display of completed maps and those still in progress.

Figure 4.5. Street addressing unit during implementation

Table 4.3. Computer equipment for the unit

Type of equipment	No.	Allocation
Computer	2	Mapping and address directory
21" screen	2	Mapping and address directory
Computer (desktop or laptop)	1	Coordinator
Black and white laser printer	1	Addressing unit
Color printer	1	Mapping
Plotter (format A1 or A0)	1	Mapping
CD-ROM recorder	1	Addressing unit
DC-AC inverter	3	Addressing unit
Scanner	1	Addressing unit
Memory module	4	Mapping
Type of software	No.	Allocation
Word processing, spreadsheet, presentation	3	Coordinator, mapping, address directory
Design (like Illustrator)	1	Mapping
Design (like AutoCAD) or GIS	1	Mapping
Photo processing	1	Mapping
Addressing, database	1	Address directory

Figure 4.6. Street addressing materials

EQUIPMENT

Transportation: a vehicle such as a pickup truck to transport staff and equipment for survey taking, doorway numbering, and installation of street signs. If a pickup is not available, motorbikes and carts may be used.

Furniture for the office and meeting room (including something to store maps and plans).

Media campaign: overhead projector, video projector.

Addressing (by team): an odometer, one or two sets of stencils, paint brushes, paint rollers, consumables.

Activity 4. Estimating costs and time frames for an addressing program

Objective and expected results

The objective is to estimate the cost of a street addressing program and to design an intervention program in which costs stay within the projected budget.

Implementation

The consultant makes a first estimate of the costs during the feasibility study, and the results are compared to the projected budget for the program before being presented to the Supervisory Committee. A framework for calculation (tables 4.4 and 4.5) makes it possible to vary the different parameters until costs are brought into line with the budget. The framework details staff, operating and equipment costs for the unit, materials supply and installation costs, costs associated with the media campaign, and printing of the address map and index.

Before any simulation is run, a preliminary inventory and mapping exercise will determine the scope of the program: number of streets, number of intersections (anchored or not by buildings), number of streets that already have addresses, kilometers of streets to be assigned an address (to estimate the number of doorways to be numbered).

Task 1. Prepare the database

The framework is set up using a table containing basic data (table 4.4), which differentiates street addressing data (lines 1 to 18) from cost data (lines 19 to 35). A footnote provides further detail on each item. Since calculations are made automatically, the boxed cells need only be completed in table 4.4 to obtain the results in table 4.5. The calculations take into account the different assumptions formulated based on the population to determine the number of teams, the duration of the program, and the standard costs for the media campaign and printing (table 4.6). This calculation framework provides an initial cost estimate, relates the estimate to the available budget, and thereby determines the program's level of service.

Table 4.7 shows that the cost of the program ranges from US$109,000 for a city of 50,000 inhabitants to US$519,000 for a city of 500,000 inhabitants. The larger the city, the lower the cost per inhabitant: US$1.76 for a city of 50,000 inhabitants and US$0.90 for a city of 500,000 (this ratio does not take into account the cost of equipment for the unit, which is considered part of the initial investment).

Table 4.4. Basic cost calculation data

1	Inhabitants	200,000		17	% of intersections with posts	10%
2	Inhabitants/hshld.	6.8				
3	% of neighborhoods without addresses	10%		18	Signposts (no.)	270
				19	Consultant (hrs./mo.)	$4,000
4	Surveys to be conducted (no.)	26,471			*Addressing unit*	
				20	Coordinator (hrs./mo.)	$600
5	Surface area in ha to receive an address	3,000		21	Chief cartographers (hrs./mo.)	$450
6	Survey/team/ hour (no.)	10		22	Survey mgr. (hrs./mo.)	$450
				23	Support staff (hrs./mo.)	$150
7	Survey/team/ month (no.)	2,000			*Short-term*	
8	Team/month needed (no.)	13 Team/mo.		24	Team leader (hrs./mo.)	$350
				25	Field surveyor (hrs./mo.)	$300
9	Teams (no.)	3		26	Survey taker (hrs./mo.)	$250
10	Duration of surveys	4.4 mo.		27	Unskill. painter (hrs./mo.)	$100
11	Duration of program	16 mo.		28	Cost of street sign	$15
12	Intersections for zones receiving add. (no.)	2,700		29	Cost of doorway sign	$4
				30	Cost of street signposts	$25
13	Signs per intersection (no.)	2		31	Cost of street sign installation	$6
14	% intersections with signs	80%		32	Cost of doorway sign installation	$3
15	Street signs (no.)	4,320		33	Cost of signpost install.	$15
16	Doorway signs (no.)	200		34	Media campaign (%)	3%
				35	Printing	$12,000

1 & 2	Population and inhabitants per household (using available data).
3	Percentage of population in districts subsequently receiving addresses (to be determined).
4	Number of surveys = number of doorways (automatic calculation based on '1, 2, 3').
5	Surface area of districts to receive an address (automatic calculation based on '1,3' and densities of table 4.5).
6	No. of surveys conducted by team and by hour (to be determined).
7	No. of surveys conducted by team and by month (automatic calculation based on '6' at a rate of 8 hours per day and 25 days per month).
8	No. of team-months needed (automatic calculation).
9	No. of teams (automatic calculation based on '4' and '7').
10	Duration of survey (automatic calculation based on '8' and '9').
11	Duration of program (automatic calculation using table 4.5).
12	No. of intersections to be equipped (automatic calculation based on '5' and assuming 0.9 intersections/hectare).
13	No. of signs per intersection (to be determined).
14	Percentage of intersections that would actually be equipped (to be determined).
15	No. of street signs (automatic calculation based on '12, 13, 14').
16	No. of doorway signs (to be determined; the doorway numbers are usually painted as a cost-saving measure, but a few signs may be provided for public buildings that will serve as a prototype).
17	Percentage of intersections with signposts (to be determined after a quick survey; if an intersection has no façade where street signs can be installed, they should be installed on a signpost; this would only be in exceptional cases owing to cost constraints).
18	No. of signposts (automatic calculation based on '12' and '17').
19–27	Monthly remuneration of staff on the addressing unit or temporarily employed during the surveys (to be determined based on information to be gathered).
28–33	Cost of supplying and installing street and doorway signs (to be determined based on information to be gathered).
34	Media campaign (automatic calculation based on hypotheses in table 4.5).
35	Printing (automatic calculation based on hypotheses in table 4.5).

Table 4.5. Calculating cost of street addressing (example)

	$/month	No.	Team No.	Months	$	%
Summary					222,537	
1. Staff expenses					**54,268**	24%
Consultant	4,000	1		2.5	10,000	
Addressing unit						
Coordinator	600	1		16.0	9,600	
Chief cartographer	450	1		16.0	7,200	
Survey and database manager	450	1		16.0	7,200	
Support staff	150	1		16.0	2,400	
Short-term hires						
Team leader	350	1	3	4.4	4,632	
Field surveyor	300	1	3	4.4	3,971	
Survey taker	250	2	3	4.4	6,618	
Unskilled painter	100	2	3	4.4	2,647	
2. Unit operating expenses					**24,221**	11%
Rent, water, electricity, telephone	700			16.0	11,200	
Consumables	300			16.0	4,800	
Vehicle maintenance/fuel	500			16.0	8,000	
Consumables for surveys, numbering	50			4.4	221	
3. Unit equipment					**33,000**	15%
Computers		3			9,000	
Printers		2			1,000	
Plotter		1			3,000	
Engraver, DC-AC inverter, scanner		1			3,000	
Software kits		1			4,000	
Photocopier		1			3,000	
Vehicle		1			10,000	
4. Supply and installation of addressing materials	Unit Cost ($)	Quantity			**92,221**	41%
Supply of street signs	15	4,320			64,800	
Supply of doorway signs	4	200			800	
Supply of signposts for street signs	25	270			6,750	
Installation of street signs	6	4,320			16, 848	
Installation of doorway signs	3	200			390	
Installation of posts for street signs	15	270			2,633	
5. Media campaign	4%				**6,352**	3%
6. Printing of address maps and index					**12,000**	5%

Table 4.6. Cost calculation assumptions

No. of surveys	No. of teams	No. of months	Density (inhab/ha)
Less than 10,000 inhabitants	1	12	150
from 10 to 25,000 inhabitants	2	16	120
from 25 to 50,000 inhabitants	3	16	120
from 75 to100,000 inhabitants	4	18	80
from 100 to 150,000 inhabitants	5	24	80
from 150 to 200,000 inhabitants	5	24	80
from 200 to 300,000 inhabitants	6	24	60
more than 300,000 inhabitants	6	24	40

Population	Media campaign	Printing
Less than 100,000 inhabitants	5%	$ 8,000
from 100 to 500,000 inhabitants	4%	$ 12,000
more than 500,000 inhabitants	3%	$ 18,000

Figure 4.7. Training of a street addressing unit

Table 4.7. Summary of costs according to the city's population

Inhabitants	No. of surveys	No. of teams	Survey duration (week)	Staff	Unit operation	Unit equipment	Supplies	Media and printing	Total	US$ per HH
							Cost in US$1000			
50,000	6,618	1	3	34	18	33	13	11	**109**	1.76
				31%	17%	30%	12%	10%	100%	
100,000	13,235	2	3	41	24	33	35	21	**154**	1.21
				26%	16%	21%	23%	14%	100%	
200,000	26,471	3	4	42	24	33	92	18	**210**	0.89
				20%	12%	16%	44%	9%	100%	
300,000	39,706	3	7	63	24	33	206	24	**350**	1.06
				18%	7%	9%	59%	7%	100%	
400,000	52,941	4	7	75	27	33	274	27	**437**	1.01
				17%	6%	8%	63%	6%	100%	
500,000	66,176	4	8	84	27	33	343	32	**519**	0.97
				16%	5%	6%	66%	6%	100%	
700,000	92,647	4	12	102	28	33	479	36	**678**	0.92
				15%	4%	5%	71%	5%	100%	
1,000,000	132,353	5	13	139	37	33	684	44	**936**	0.90
				15%	4%	4%	73%	5%	100%	
1,500,000	198,529	6	17	184	37	33	1,025	55	**1,334**	0.87
				14%	3%	2%	77%	4%	100%	

Task 2. Run necessary simulations

Several simulations are usually needed to reconcile estimated costs with the projected budget for the program: for example, Table 4.8 shows that the amount of materials varies (according to hypotheses A, B, C) with the percentage of the population that has not received an address, intersections with signs, and intersections with posts. Simulations show a gap of 40% in cost between scenarios A and C.

Other factors may lead to variations in the total cost: staff and equipment used, quality of materials, scope of the media campaign, or distribution of documents printed.

Task 3. Estimate time frames

To estimate the overall time frame, a distinction must be drawn between the preparation and implementation phases. The preparation phase lasts about three months, from recruiting the consultant responsible for the feasibility study to setting up the street addressing unit. The time frame for this phase cannot easily be condensed. Conversely, time needed for the implementation phase depends on the size of the city, the number of short-term teams mobilized, and the time needed to analyze the data, for mapping, production, etc. (full-time unit staff).

The previous framework shown in table 4.5 gives a quick estimate of time needed for the implementation phase, which breaks out the coordinator's intervention time (full-time team) and time needed from team leaders (short-term team). Time involved depends on the size of the city (table 4.9) and the amount of materials needed for implementation.

Table 4.8. Variation in cost according to materials used

City of 100,000 inhabitants	A (adequate)	B (moderate)	C (low)
% of population w/o address	10%	20%	40%
% of intersections with signs	100%	80%	50%
% of intersections with posts	40%	20%	10%
Cost	$173,000	$153,000	$123,000

Table 4.9. Implementation time frame according to the size of the city

City population	Time required for surveys (months)	Total time involved (months)
50,000	3.3	12.0
100,000	3.3	16.0
200,000	4.4	16.0
300,000	6.6	16.0
400,000	6.6	18.0
500,000	8.3	18.0
700,000	11.6	18.0
1,000,000	13.2	24.0
1,500,000	16.5	24.0

Activity 5. Defining the scope of the program

Objective and expected results

The objective is to define the scope of the street addressing program by comparing the resources available with coverage of planned activities. Three issues must be resolved:

- *Priority neighborhoods to receive addresses.* How can these priorities be set?
- *Coverage of the street addressing program.* The program assigns a number to the doorways of buildings (homes, places of business, facilities). Should it be extended to other significant urban fixtures: public standpipes, fire hydrants, waste transfer points, etc.?
- *Definition and location of pilot operation.* What does the pilot operation entail? Where will it be implemented?

Implementation

The scope of the program is evaluated and approved by the Supervisory Committee during the feasibility study (preparation phase) and then applied and shaped during the implementation phase. Tasks include determining: (a) zones to receive an address; (b) coverage of the addressing program; (c) the broad outlines of the pilot operation. *Selection criteria* help to further refine the tasks. They include:

- *Available resources*: will they be sufficient to cover all neighborhoods?
- *Time frames*: is the time frame for implementation of the program compatible with the municipality's agenda?
- *Technical choices*: the idea of street addressing in so-called irregular neighborhoods or developing neighborhoods often provokes widely differing responses from government officials:
  - they are motivated to implement an addressing program in the neighborhood during upgrading projects;
  - they are motivated to implement an addressing program to strengthen land tenure for the population;
  - they are hesitant to implement an addressing program owing to the complex urban fabric;
  - they refuse to implement an addressing program because they do not want to legalize an irregular settlement.

Task 1. Define the zones to be addressed

ESTABLISH A NEIGHBORHOOD TYPOLOGY. The typology will define homogeneous zones or neighborhoods (type of housing, population density, street layout) based on which the street addressing program will go forward or be postponed:

- Densely populated formal neighborhoods (old and new): these are often located in the city center and are very busy and well served; initiating street addressing in these neighborhoods has a significant impact on the population.
- Formal neighborhoods that are becoming more densely populated: if the neighborhood is reasonably formal, street addressing can be quickly initiated; if not, it is usually preferable to wait until the neighborhood has been occupied and the urban development process has run its course or is stabilizing.
- Squatter settlements and/or irregular neighborhoods: the government's attitude on this will provide the basic approach. Technical obstacles usually arise because there is no network of streets, and the solution is to identify the main routes and assign addresses to them.
- Specific zones (industrial, military).

LIST THE NEIGHBORHOODS TO BE INCLUDED IN THE PROGRAM. The typology of the neighborhoods will determine which of them should receive priority in the program and which should be assigned addresses at a later time. This list, which must be approved by the municipality, is tested on the basis of the three previously mentioned criteria: cost, time frames, and technical choices (activity 4: cost assessment).

Task 2. Determine the coverage of the program

Various technical departments would like to assign addresses to urban fixtures that are the municipality's responsibility, to facilitate maintenance: public standpipes, fire hydrants, and waste transfer points, for example. The issue is whether fixtures should be addressed at the same time as buildings or if this task should be carried out separately. Once again, cost considerations, time frames, and technical choices will determine this decision.

There is a certain efficiency to assigning addresses to buildings and urban fixtures at the same time, but this may also increase costs and delay completion. It is necessary to train a team especially for this task since survey taking and managing the whole operation become more complicated.

It is often preferable to assign addresses to buildings first and deal with urban fixtures subsequently or during the maintenance phase, when the operation can be conducted with a smaller staff. During the maintenance phase, a GIS may also be put in place to monitor the maintenance of urban fixtures.

Task 3. Define and determine the setting for the pilot operation

The pilot operation is an important stage in the implementation phase; it takes place between the training of short-term teams for the street addressing unit and conducting surveys in the field. The goals of the pilot operation are (a) to test the results of training and (b) to conduct a media campaign that reaches local authorities and the general public. These objectives are equally important, so it would be unwise to emphasize the former over the latter.

It is important to define the parameters of the operation during the feasibility study:

- Determine the budget for the pilot operation;
- Set the time frame (one or two days, for example);
- Specify the streets involved (three or four, for example);
- List actions to be undertaken for the addressing operation (organizing teams, surveys, numbering of doorways, and so on) and for the media campaign (radio, television).

Activity 6. Choosing a codification system

Objective and expected results

The objective is to adopt a codification system for identifying streets and numbering doorways. The expected result is improved navigation around the city through the aid of easily visible signage that identifies streets and building entrances.

Assigning names as street identifiers can be a lengthy and sensitive process, and the preferable solution initially is to use a numbering system that will enable people to find familiar places or subdivisions. Such an undertaking is seldom easy, however, since streets do not usually follow a regular pattern. It is a much simpler task to number buildings, inasmuch as the available choices are limited to three alternatives (see task 4, below).

Implementation

During the course of the feasibility study, the consultant chooses a codification system, which is then subject to approval by the Supervisory Committee. The system is put into practice during the implementation phase while the address map is in preparation. The creation of a codification system involves the following tasks: (a) divide the city into address zones, (b) decide on a system for identifying streets, (c) decide on a system for numbering streets, (d) decide on a system for numbering buildings, and (e) make adjustments for special cases. At the end of this section, we will present five examples of codification systems used in cities that have a regular street layout.

Task 1. Divide the city into address zones

The objective of this task is to link a numbering system to familiar places such as neighborhoods, districts, and local placenames. The city can be divided into groups of streets in the same zone, which are then given a shared identifier in the form of a prefix or suffix for easy location. A variety of natural or administrative subdivisions—such as municipalities, city districts, sectors, neighborhoods, or local placenames—can delineate boundaries.

MUNICIPALITIES OR CITY DISTRICTS. This type of subdivision is suitable for large metropolitan areas. Under this system, a street is identified according to the number or initials of the municipality or city district (municipalities in Conakry, city districts in N'djamena, or sectors in Ouagadougou).

Figure 4.8. Defining phases of a street addressing project

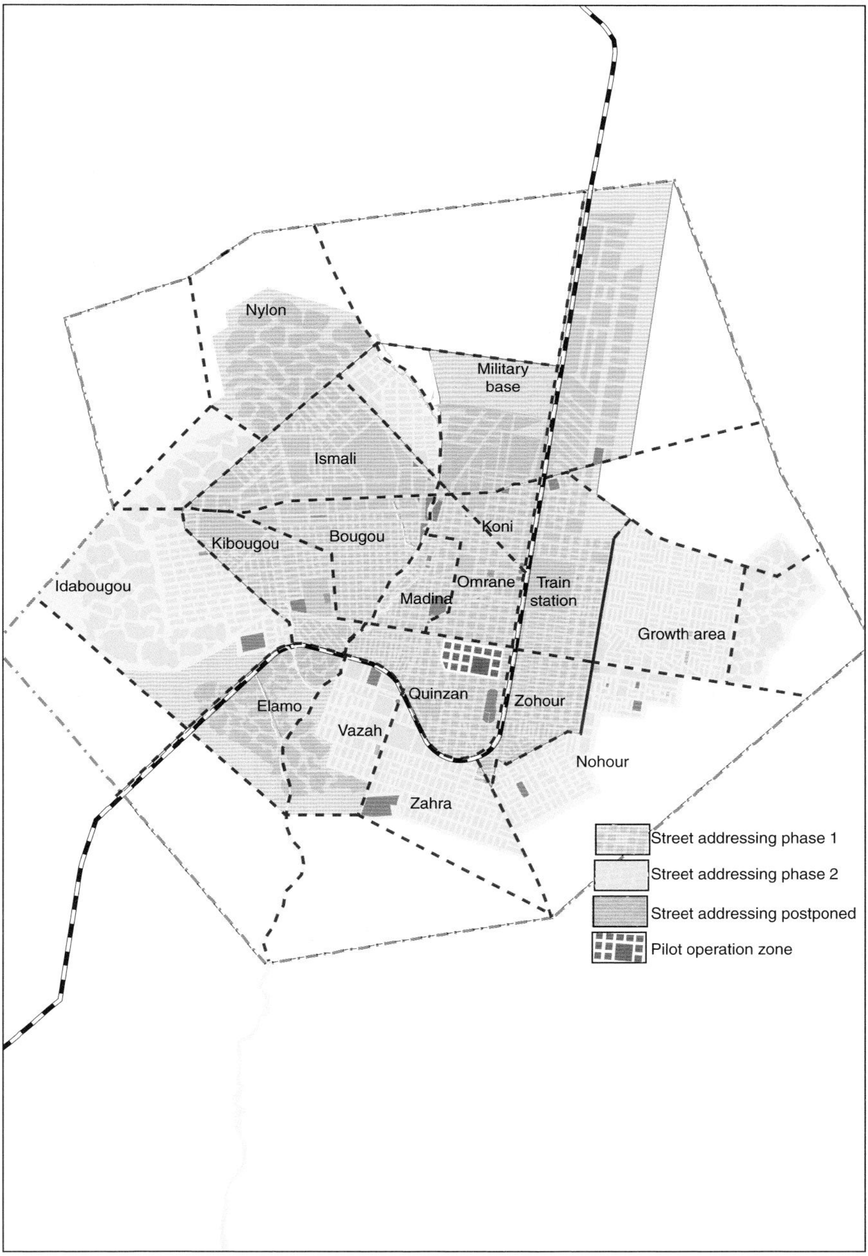

Nylon

Military base

Ismali

Koni

Kibougou   Bougou

Idabougou

Omrane   Train station

Madina

Growth area

Elamo   Quinzan   Zohour

Vazah

Nohour

Zahra

Street addressing phase 1

Street addressing phase 2

Street addressing postponed

Pilot operation zone

Advantages. (a) The system uses an administrative subdivision generally familiar to most residents; and (b) the use of this type of subdivision makes it easier for these entities to reconcile their own statistical data with the addressing information.

Disadvantages. (a) Municipalities or city districts are sometimes too spread out for easy location of street coordinates; and (b) these entities sometimes have more than 1,000 streets, making the identifier long and difficult to read, for example, Street 6.1567.

NEIGHBORHOODS. This system identifies streets according to their surrounding neighborhood (as in Lomé, Niamey, and cities in Senegal).

Advantages. (a) Residents can usually identify and find neighborhoods easily because they are a familiar reference point; and (b) since neighborhoods often comprise fewer than 100 streets, they are easy to identify and locate.

Disadvantages. (a) Neighborhood boundaries are sometimes ill-defined or poorly understood, and the mapping process requires consultation with local representatives who may not easily reach a consensus; and (b) neighborhoods may simply be local placenames encompassing a handful of streets that would need regrouping, again necessitating consultation and agreement between local representatives.

AD HOC ADDRESS ZONES. If the aforementioned systems will not suffice, a breakdown into ad hoc address zones may be the appropriate solution (as in Yaoundé and Maputo, for example).

Advantages. (a) A variety of characteristics can be combined, such as homogeneous residential areas, administrative boundaries, and natural dividing points; and (b) if administrative boundaries change, the numbering system is not subject to challenge.

Disadvantages. (a) The breakdown occurs along unfamiliar boundaries; and b) as a result, residents are less likely to comprehend the street identification system.

GRID SYSTEM. Under this system, the city is divided into uniform sections in a grid pattern, and each numbered section becomes part of the street identifier.[1] Thus, the streets in section 125 would be numbered 125.1, 125.2, 125.3, and so on.

Advantages. (a) The sectioning process is not hindered by geographic features or administrative subdivisions; (b) sections can be georeferenced easily; and (c) the street numbering system is appropriately simple when there are few streets involved (e.g., fewer than 10).

Disadvantages. (a) The grid pattern does not usually follow the general layout of city streets, and the same street may span several sections, thus complicating the numbering system; and (b) a grid system is a much less meaningful locator than a neighborhood reference.

WHICH SYSTEM IS BEST? These subdivisions, though important, are nothing more than a tool for identifying streets that will ultimately be assigned names. The best type of subdivision is often the one that will be the most meaningful to residents, and therefore a grid system is not strongly recommended. The choice of subdivision should yield a simple, easily readable numbering system. One way to ensure that this condition is being met is to create zones comprising fewer than 900 streets. In zones of that size, the sequential numbers will have a maximum of three digits, and there will be a comfortable margin for the inclusion of any new streets within the zone (figure 4.9).

Task 2. Decide on a system for identifying streets

Once the city has been divided into municipalities, city districts, sectors, neighborhoods, or other type of address zone, they can be referenced in the street identifier, as prefixed or suffixed numbers or letters.

- The choice of a street identification system should be guided by several *principles*. The system should:
  - Be simple and easily understandable;
  - Allow for rapid codification of all streets, including those in slum neighborhoods, pending a name assignment;
  - Take into account the city's features and the ways in which its residents customarily establish points of reference (existing subdivisions, local placenames, and so on);
  - Be amenable to gradual implementation as financial and human resources become available.
- Several street identification options are available, as in the following *examples:*
  - Municipalities identified by number. In municipality 3, the streets would be numbered 3.1 to 3.999, for example, Street 3.21.
  - City districts identified by letter. In district C, streets would be numbered C.1 to C.999, for example, Street C.21. Or alternatively, a suffix can be used, as in Street 21.C.
  - Neighborhoods identified by their initials. In the Medina neighborhood, the streets are numbered ME.1 to ME.999, for example, Street ME.21or Street 21 ME.
- *How to ensure maximum readability?*
  - Choose Street 3 rather than Street 003 to avoid similarity to a computer-generated number.

Figure 4.9. Addressing subdivision by address zones and by neighborhoods

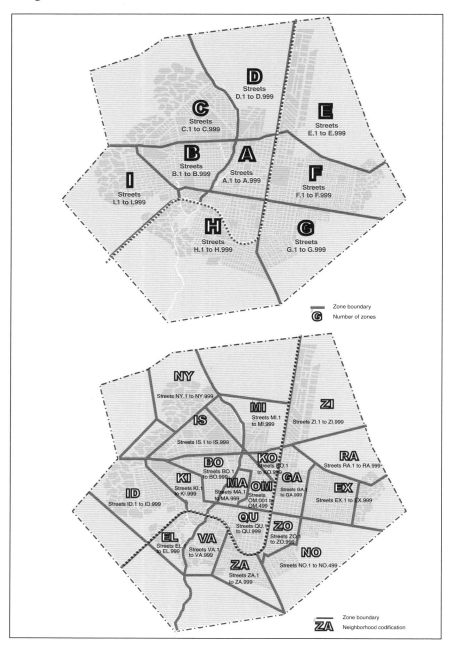

- Limit the number of signs: sequential numbers should not exceed three digits.
- Avoid compound prefixes, such as Street 42037 where 4 refers to the municipality, 2 to the district, and 037 to the sequential street number. Such an identification system may be intellectually satisfying, but less easily readable.
- Test the proposed identification system on model street signs (activity 10). This precaution is essential if the signs are to be bilingual (Maghreb, for example).
- *How to identify streets along address zone perimeters?* A street that divides sectors C and E certainly cannot be assigned prefix C for the right side and prefix E for the left. Arbitrary choices of this kind can be governed by alphabetical or numerical order, so that the street dividing sectors C and E will be assigned prefix C (hence, Street C.120); and, similarly, the street dividing zones 3 and 5 will carry the prefix 3 (Street 3.98).
- *How to treat named streets?* Named streets will retain their name, but the addressing unit assigns them a number as well to facilitate indexing.

FROM NUMBERS TO NAMES

- *Which streets should receive naming priority?*
  - Streets that border an address zone, beginning with those that carry the heaviest traffic,
  - Streets regarded as major in terms of right-of-way or traffic flow, such as "backbone" streets that span several sectors or neighborhoods,
  - Public squares and main intersections.
- *How to begin the naming process?* The city of Ouagadougou provides a notable example, in which city officials created a Toponymy Commission that gathered a list of names documented and classified into categories such as famous figures, historical references, or geographic features (annex 2). The recommended method consists of the following steps: (a) identify those streets to receive naming priority; (b) choose a list of names; (c) when applicable, present the list to residents of the affected streets for their consideration; and (d) obtain approval from the municipal authorities.

Task 3. Decide on a system for numbering streets

The following steps will facilitate implementation of the street numbering system and make it easier for people to understand the underlying logic: (a) determine the geographical direction in which numbering will proceed; and (b) differentiate even/uneven numbering according to the orientation of the street.

Two perpendicular axes must first be defined to set the point from which numbering will begin. The method of definition will vary depending on a city's particular configuration. Examples include:

- City traversed by a river (such as Bamako or Niamey): in each address zone, numbers start from the banks of the river and from each side of the main avenue through the city center that runs perpendicular to the river (such as a bridge over the Niger River).
- City on the seacoast (Dakar and Conakry, for example): in each address zone, the numbers increase in conventional fashion from south to north and from west to east.
- City growing outward in all directions from the center (as in Ouagadougou and Yaoundé): the axes are defined on the basis of characteristic features such as principal arterial streets in the city center, a railway, a thalweg, or other marker. The axes should be consistent with the subdivision boundaries and should not cross address zones. In each such zone, the numbers increase perpendicularly to the axes.

Based on the defined axes, a decision is then made concerning which streets will carry even numbers (north-south streets, for example) and which will receive uneven numbers (east-west) (figure 4.10). For very large sectors, the numbering system is best applied in successive blocks.

Task 4. Decide on a system for numbering buildings

The first step in this task is to define the streets on the address map in terms of their beginning and end, and then determine the geographical direction in which numbering will proceed, in accordance with the chosen street numbering system.

The numbering progression starts from the designated point zero of each street. By convention, buildings on the left side of the street are assigned uneven numbers, and those to the right receive even numbers, all of which increase in the direction of progression. Any of several numbering system options may be considered, including sequential, decametric, and metric systems.

SEQUENTIAL OR "CLASSIC" NUMBERING. The existing doorways are numbered sequentially, alternating between uneven numbers on the left side of the street (1, 3, 5, 7, and so on) and even numbers on the right side (2, 4, 6, 8, and so forth) (figure 4.11).

Figure 4.10. Progression of the numbering system

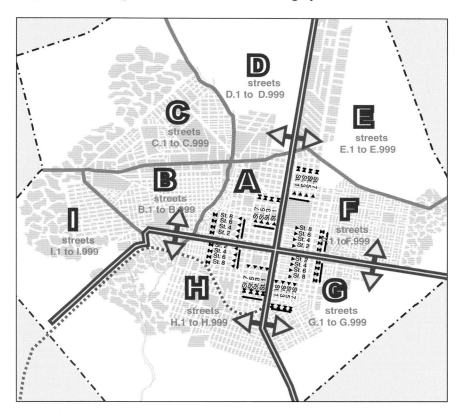

Advantages. The system is (a) simple, well-known, and widely used; and (b) suitable if the numbering system goes into effect after all buildings have been completed and/or when all plans for future building have been set.

Disadvantages. (a) New structures built between existing numbered buildings must be assigned numbers with "bis," "ter," and the like; (b) when several plots are merged, the numbers of the first and last plot in the series are usually retained; (c) since building frontage usually varies in length, successive even and uneven numbers are not necessarily directly across the street; and (d) in developing neighborhoods without a master plan, it is nearly impossible to use sequential numbering because buildings spring up in no particular order, sometimes dozens of meters apart over periods of months or years.

Box 4.1. Historical curiosities

Should the numbering scheme begin with "1" for each street? Or would it be preferable to adopt continuous numbering within each neighborhood? The latter solution was used in Paris during the Revolution and exists today in certain neighborhoods in Japan. The houses are numbered by block rather than by street, creating a system especially perplexing to passersby and tourists.

Numbering generally begins from a point as close as possible to the city center in order to follow the street as it extends outward to the periphery, though this is not always the case. In Venice, for example, the first number is assigned to a landmark building in each neighborhood; hence, the Doges' Palace in the San Marco neighborhood bears the number "1." Such peculiarities are not to be recommended.

METRIC NUMBERING. Under this system, conceived in 1800 by Leblond, inventor of the meter, address numbers signify the distance in meters between the street's "point zero" and the building entrance (figure 4.12).

Advantages. (a) This numbering system is especially suited to areas of rapid urbanization and allows for numbering isolated buildings; (b) successive even and uneven numbers follow a logical progression, making it easy to find addresses; (c) construction of a new building does not require the use of "bis" or "ter" with the address; and (d) the inherent recognition of distances simplifies the provision of municipal services, particularly for utility network installation and maintenance.

Disadvantages. (a) Numbers containing three or four digits (in reference to distance in meters) are harder to remember than two-digit numbers; and (b) numbers are not sequential, which sometimes confuses those unfamiliar with the numbering system.

DECAMETRIC NUMBERING. During the reign of Napoleon, the architect Huvé proposed this system, which calls for "placing numbers at equal distances, for example every ten meters, thereby signaling the length of the street." Streets are divided into 10-meter segments, which are numbered successively 1, 3, 5, 7, etc., to the left and 2, 4, 6, 8, etc., to the right. Distance markers are placed every 100 meters to facilitate numbering (figure 4.13).

Advantages. (a) This simple system combines the ease of reading sequential numbers and the possibility of measuring distances through metric numbering; (b) in developing neighborhoods, it facilitates reference to the decametric system in order to assign addresses to isolated buildings; for example, a building located in the 10th segment from the beginning of the street will be assigned number 19 or 20, depending on its position on the left or right side of the street; (c) successive even and uneven numbers will be more or less directly across the street; and (d) the inherent recognition of distances simplifies the provision of municipal services, particularly for utility network installation and maintenance.

Disadvantages. (a) Since the system is seldom used, there is little practical know-how on which to draw; (b) two buildings located in the same segment will require letters to differentiate the addresses, for example, 12A, 12B; (c) in developing neighborhoods, a master plan will not be needed, but as a minimum the system will require segmentation of streets and installation of distance markers to facilitate the numbering of future buildings.

Task 5: Make adjustments for special cases

WHAT TO DO WITH THE OLD IDENTIFICATION SYSTEM? If the street addressing program has adopted a metric or decametric numbering system, what should be done in a city center that already has named streets and a sequential numbering system?

Figure 4.11. Sequential alternating numbering systems

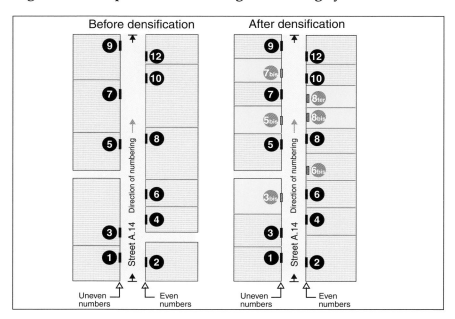

Figure 4.12. Metric alternating numbering system

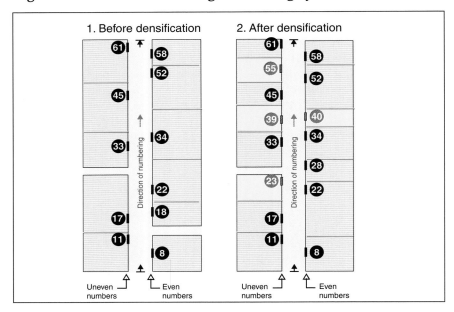

Table 4.10. Decametric numbering system

Segment	Distance (m)	No. left side	No. right side
1	0–10	1	2
2	10–20	3	4
3	20–30	5	6
4	30–40	7	8
5	40–50	9	10
6	50–60	11	12
7	60–70	13	14
8	70–80	15	16
9	80–90	17	18
10	90–100	19	20
11	100–110	21	22

Streets. All streets in the city center should be numbered according to the system being implemented citywide, but street signs need not be changed. Street numbers will be included in the street directory, and any replacement signs will include the number inscribed unobtrusively beneath the street name.

Figure 4.13. Decametric alternating numbering system

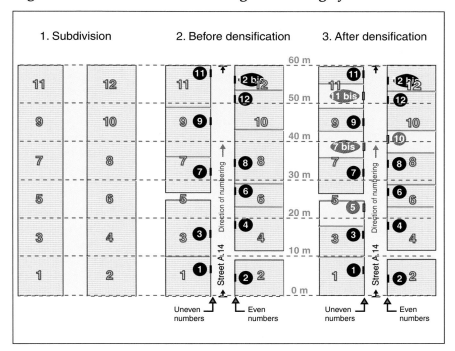

Doorways
- If the majority of buildings in the city center are numbered sequentially, avoid drastic changes and allow the city center to retain its current numbering system;
- If only a few doorways in the city center are numbered sequentially, retain the existing number—at least initially—and place the new number next to it so as to prevent confusion among citizens attached to their old number.

HOW TO CODIFY CUL-DE-SACS? The simplest solution is to identify cul-de-sacs as such and assign numbers as for regular streets. As an example, Cul-de-sac 3.12 would be located between Street 3.11 and Street 3.13 (figure 4.14).

Using a more complex solution, a cul-de-sac can be linked to the street onto which it opens. For example, Street 3.12 would lead to Cul-de-sacs 3.12(1) and 3.12(3) or Cul-de-sacs 12(2) and 12(4), depending on their location on the even- or uneven-numbered side of the street.

City officials may wish to specify the location more precisely. For instance, a cul-de-sac located 325 meters from the beginning of Street 4.61 would be given the number 4.61.325. Owing to the complexity of this system, however, it is often rejected in favor of a simpler solution.

HOW TO CODIFY PUBLIC SQUARES? Squares are codified in the same manner as streets. To avoid confusion, and in keeping with the cul-de-sac example, different numbers are assigned to squares and streets, hence, Street C.26, Square C.28, Street C.30 (figure 4.14) .

The doorways on a public square are numbered according to the following procedure: (a) specify a point zero at the place where a principal street converges with the square; and (b) assign numbers starting from point zero and moving clockwise around the square.

HOW TO CODIFY INTERSECTIONS? A city's technical departments may need to identify intersections, particularly during the course of street system studies that differentiate street segments. The solution is to codify the intersection in reference to one of its component streets; for example, the intersections on Street 3.10 would be coded Intersection 3.10 A, Intersection 3.10 B, and so forth.

Since an intersection involves two or more streets, it will be coded more than once, but only the code of the more important street will be retained. For example, at the intersection of Streets 3.10 and 3.15, the intersection will be coded Intersection 3.10 C if Street 3.10 is more prominent (figure 4.15).

HOW TO CODIFY INFORMAL SETTLEMENTS? These areas, also called squatter settlements or slums, tend to have streets unsuited to motor vehicles and are often regarded as illegal. City authorities may be hesitant to introduce a street addressing system in such areas for fear of lending legitimacy to informal occupancy.

In an effort to improve the living conditions of slum residents, however, cities sometimes perform emergency work, most notably to improve access conducive to the introduction of water lines, street lighting, and other utilities. A street addressing program should support, or even precede, this type of work to help identify and assign addresses along the major routes in the area. The numbering scheme need not be as rigorously applied as in the aforementioned solutions, but building numbers can reference the closest route.

One possible method of codifying informal settlements uses the following steps: (a) specify or confirm the principal routes through the area; (b) assign street numbers as indicated above, for example, Street 4.12 in reference to District 4 or Street ZA12 in the Zahra neighborhood; (c) at

Figure 4.14. Codification of cul-de-sacs and intersections

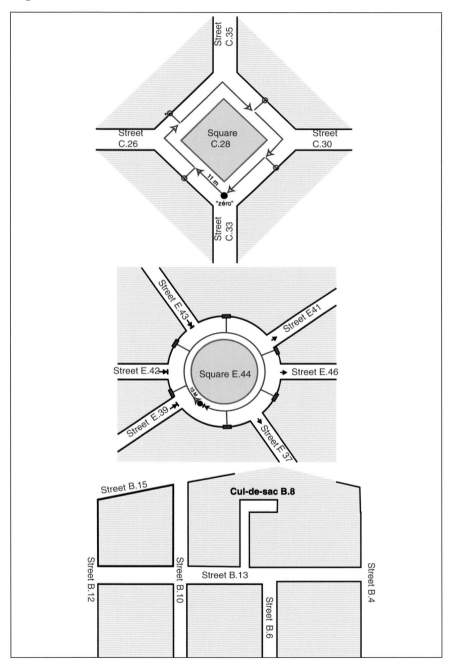

Figure 4.15. Codification of intersections

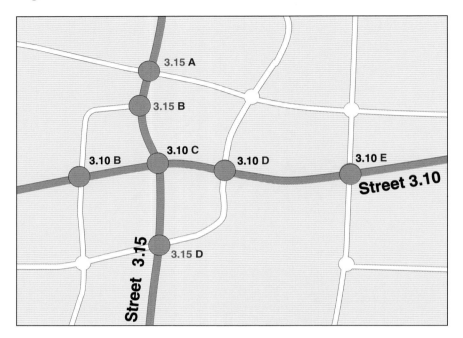

intersections, establish appropriate division of space for the bisecting routes; and (d) assign a number that links each dwelling to the street.

As an example, along Street 4.43, dwellings would be numbered 43/1, 43/3 or 43/2, 43/4 depending on their location on the even- or uneven-numbered side, as previously determined (figure 4.16).

A COMBINED SYSTEM. For documentation purposes, we will briefly discuss another codification system used in the suburbs of U.S. cities, where the street layout is often "landscaped" rather than systematized as in a city center. Streets have names, but the house numbers often include a radical that refers to a neighborhood-type subdivision. Using 7809 Moorland Street as an example, 78 is the radical and 09 is the sequential number that designates the fifth building from point zero on the right-hand side of the street. (figure 4.17)

Examples of cities with a regular street layout

If streets follow a regular "checkerboard" pattern with systematically arranged blocks of buildings, the street numbering process is simple. A

Figure 4.16. Addressing in informal settlements

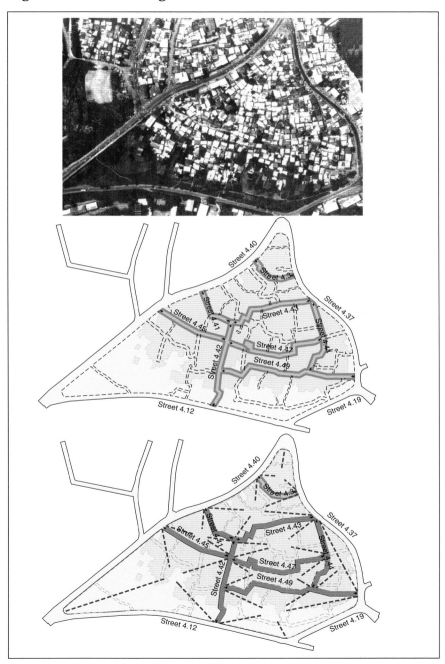

Figure 4.17. Combined addressing system

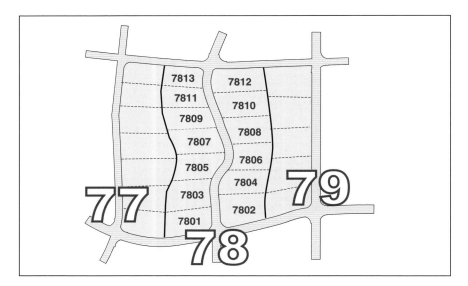

variety of solutions are available, however, as illustrated by the examples of Puebla de los Angeles, Mexico; Mannheim, Germany; Paris, France; Washington, D.C., USA; and Chandigarh, India.

PUEBLA DE LOS ANGELES

With a present-day population of three million, this UNESCO-designated World Heritage City and capital of the Mexican state of Puebla was founded in 1531 by the Franciscans, who dreamed of building a city that would serve as a model of harmony among all peoples and races and as an example for other cities in New Spain. The city is patterned in straight lines and divided into quadrants along two axes that change names at the central square, the Zocalo. Legend has it that angels drew the cross where the two axes meet. The east-west axis is formed by Avenida Camacho to the east of the Zocalo and Avenida Reforma to the west. The north-south axis is composed of Avenida 5 de Mayo on the north side of the Zocalo and Avenida 16 de Septiembre on the south side. The other east-west arteries are *avenidas* (avenues) and north-south arteries are *calles* (streets) (figure 4.18).

- In the northwest quadrant, the streets parallel to Reforma are even-numbered and designated "west," and streets parallel to 5 de Mayo have uneven numbers and a "north" designation.

- In the northeast quadrant, the streets parallel to Camacho are even-numbered and designated "east," while streets parallel to 5 de Mayo are even and "north."
- In the southwest quadrant, the streets parallel to Reforma are uneven and "west," and those parallel to 16 de Septiembre are uneven and "south."
- In the southeast quadrant, the streets parallel to Camacho are uneven and "east," while those parallel to 16 de Septiembre are even and "south."

The streets parallel to the north-south axis are numbered evenly to the east of the axis and unevenly on the west side. Street numbers increase on each side of the axis. The second street is called 2 North or 2 South depending on its position relative to the east-west axis. The same logic prevails for the east-west streets, that is, even numbers are designated "north" and uneven numbers "south." Thus, the second street is called 2 East on the east side and 2 West on the west.

Figure 4.18. Puebla Los Angeles in 1531

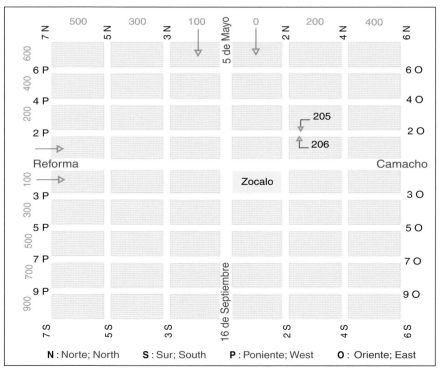

N : Norte; North   S : Sur; South   P : Poniente; West   O : Oriente; East

Buildings are numbered according to the following system:

- To the west of 5 de Mayo–16 de Septiembre: between the axis and Street 3, numbers begin with 100 (even and uneven numbers on opposite sides of the street); between Streets 3 and 5, numbers begin with 300; between Streets 5 and 7, numbers begin with 500, and so on.
- To the east of 5 de Mayo–16 de Septiembre, the same idea applies: between Streets 2 and 4, numbers begin with 200, between Streets 4 and 6, numbers begin with 400, between Streets 6 and 8, numbers begin with 600, and so forth.
- To the north and south of Reforma–Camacho, the same logic applies.

MANNHEIM
The checkerboard plan of this citadel city, founded in 1606 by Frederick IV and reconstructed by Vauban in 1689, is generally regarded as the prototype for 19th-century cities in the United States and Europe. It was the only city in which streets were identified by letters and numbers. The blocks have retained their original numbering system, hence the block bounded by Streets F and 2 is called F2 (figure 4.19).

PARIS
Paris has been the focus of several street addressing projects since the eve of the Revolution, which bears witness to a prevailing desire "that a judicious, steady, and rational process will truly facilitate relations among citizens." One of the most curious such plans for this irregularly patterned city was proposed in 1787 by Choderlos de Laclos, who envisioned a system "whose apparent logic is a poor disguise for its extreme complexity".[2] His system divides the city on each side of the Seine into twenty sections or neighborhoods (400 x 1000 *toises*,[3] assigns them a letter and then numbers the streets by assigning "uneven numbers to streets running more or less parallel to the river and even numbers to streets that are substantially perpendicular." Houses are then numbered "following the flow of the river for streets parallel to it" and starting from the river on perpendicular streets. Addresses are given as a combination of numbers and letters, for example, District D, Street 8, house 25 (figure 4.20).

WASHINGTON, D.C.
Washington has three street series (figure 4.21):

- North-south streets are numbered 1, 2, 3. For example, 16th Street is located on the White House axis.
- East-west streets are designated alphabetically[4] as A, B, C, and so on. Progressing beyond the letters, the streets have two-syllable names

Figure 4.19. Mannheim

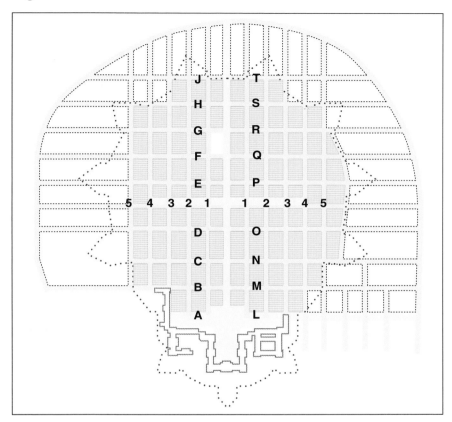

(Adams, Belmont, Chapin), then three syllables (Allison, Buchanan, Crittenden), and finally names of trees and flowers (Butternut, Cedar, Dahlia). Residents sometimes refer to the four alphabets of this system.
- Diagonal streets have names of states: Connecticut, Pennsylvania, Massachusetts, Wisconsin.

The progression moves outward on each side of the Capitol, which is intersected by North Capitol Street, East Capitol Street, South Capitol Street, and the Mall. Two streets having the same identification are differentiated by points of the compass, for example, C Street NW, C Street NE, C Street SW, C Street SE.

Each street segment is numbered in increments of 100 starting from the Capitol, hence 100 between A and B Streets, 200 between B and C, 700 between G and H. The same logic applies for the perpendicular streets:

Figure 4.20. Paris: Choderlos de Laclos' proposal

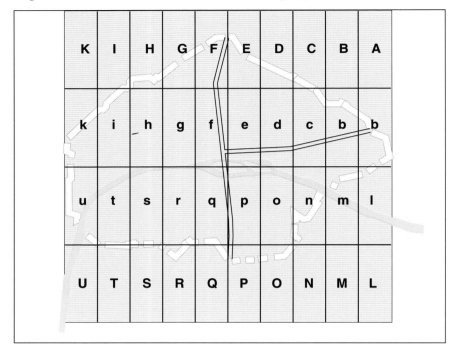

100 between 1st and 2nd Streets, 200 between 2nd and 3rd Streets; 1800 between 18th and 19th Streets. Doorway numbering follows the same logic; hence, the first digits refer to the segment number, and the remaining digits designate the sequential number, with uneven numbers on the right side and even numbers on the left in increasing progression. Thus, 1818 H Street is located on the 18th block from the Capitol on H Street. The building entrance is theoretically the 9th doorway from 18th Street on the even side.

CHANDIGARH
The foregoing examples apply only to the centers of the respective cities. The street extensions do not follow the checkerboard pattern, and the rigid numbering systems have broken down. Chandigarh offers an example of a different arrangement. Built by Le Corbusier, the city developed in a systematized manner and today occupies four times the surface area planned at the time of its creation in 1950. The 25 original 800x1200-meter sectors have increased to 100, but the plan has retained its

Figure 4.21. Street addressing system in Washington, D.C.

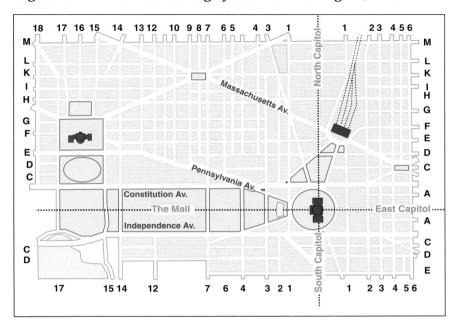

initial precision, making it possible to locate each sector instantly through the numbering system at the core of the city's address system. The principal arterial streets that form the grid system have names such as Himalaya Marg, Jan Marg, and Udyog Path. Within each sector the numbering system is less predictable, using blocks and doorways as references (figure 4.22).

Figure 4.22. Sectors in Chandigarh

Activity 7. Mapping

Objective and expected results

The objective is to create an address map with a scale along the lines of 1:10,000 that shows streets and neighborhoods, their toponymy, administrative boundaries, and principal buildings. The addition to this document of street sign information will result in the signage map.

Implementation

The street addressing unit's chief cartographer will manage this activity, which consists of the following tasks:

- *Preparation phase*: (a) gather the documentation; and (b) confirm the level of staff expertise in cartography;
- *Implementation phase*: (c) make the base map; (d) inventory all streets; (e) prepare the address map; and (f) prepare the signage map (see activity 10).

Task 1. Gather the documentation

The first task consists of gathering the existing cartographic documents from sources including the city's technical departments, the mapping and cadastral units, the minister of urban development, and the water and electricity concessionaires. The documents may differ considerably in scale, format, support media, creation dates, and topographic references. They are classified by order of importance, with priority given to those that are the most topographically accurate and thus able to provide a basis for the base map. The documentation is supplemented, if possible, by fairly recent aerial photographs of the city or a high-resolution satellite image[5] (annex 6, aerial photography).

The following information should be gathered during the same period: (a) list and boundaries of neighborhoods, city districts, and municipalities; (b) list of local placenames, (c) list of streets currently and previously named; (d) location of principal paved streets; (e) location of streets on which buildings are already numbered; (f) location of notable buildings, such as a ministry, city hall, prefecture, university, market, hospital, major place of worship, train station, airport, or the like.

Task 2. Confirm the level of staff expertise in cartography

The maps are best prepared on an electronic medium, in which case the chief cartographer should confirm the level of staff expertise when applicable. The choice of software will depend on two factors: (a) ease of use so that the chief cartographer can delegate certain tasks; and (b) compatibility with production using a four-color printing process in view of the broad dissemination of the address map. The training is estimated at one week.

Task 3. Prepare the base map

The base map will provide the basis for the address and signage maps. The selected cartographic documents are converted to the same scale through photocopying, or by electronic means after scanning. The base map is prepared on carbon paper or electronic medium, assisted if applicable by a surveyor, a cartographer, and an architect. The base map includes:

- Street layout,
- Boundaries of municipalities, neighborhoods, city districts,
- Indication of notable buildings,
- Toponymy of neighborhoods and local placenames,
- Toponymy of previously named streets.

Task 4. Draw up the street inventory

It is essential to verify the contents of the base map and conduct a systematic on-site inventory of streets and intersections. This painstaking task can be carried out using a vehicle, preferably with the participation of the coordinator and the chief cartographer and survey manager to increase their familiarity with the city. The information to be gathered is reported on a printout of the base map, which includes:

- The exact street layout,
- Verification of previously named streets,
- The location of existing street signs,
- The location of streets with previously numbered buildings,
- Identification of street condition (paved or unpaved),
- Verification of the toponymy (neighborhoods, streets, local placenames) and boundaries of municipalities, neighborhoods, and city districts.

Task 5. Prepare the address map

The base map is revised according to the gathered information. A printed map is submitted to the Supervisory Committee and/or neighborhood representatives for validation of any unclear boundaries of municipalities, city districts, and neighborhoods.

The base map is then ready to become the address map, which will include:

- The boundaries and toponymy of the subdivisions (municipality, sector, city district, neighborhood, and the like);
- The name or number of each street;
- Arrows indicating the beginning and end of each street;
- Doorway numbers at the end of each block (if applicable);
- Major facilities (such as a ministry, city hall, school, hospital, market, stadium, train station, railroad, or airport), places of note, and applicable toponymy;
- Main waterways and green spaces;
- An alphanumeric grid (1 km x 1 km, for example) to make it easier to locate points of reference;
- Map legend, north indicator, and graphic scale.

The next phase involves preparation of the signage map and publication of the address map.

Figure 4.23. Stages of implementation for a street address map

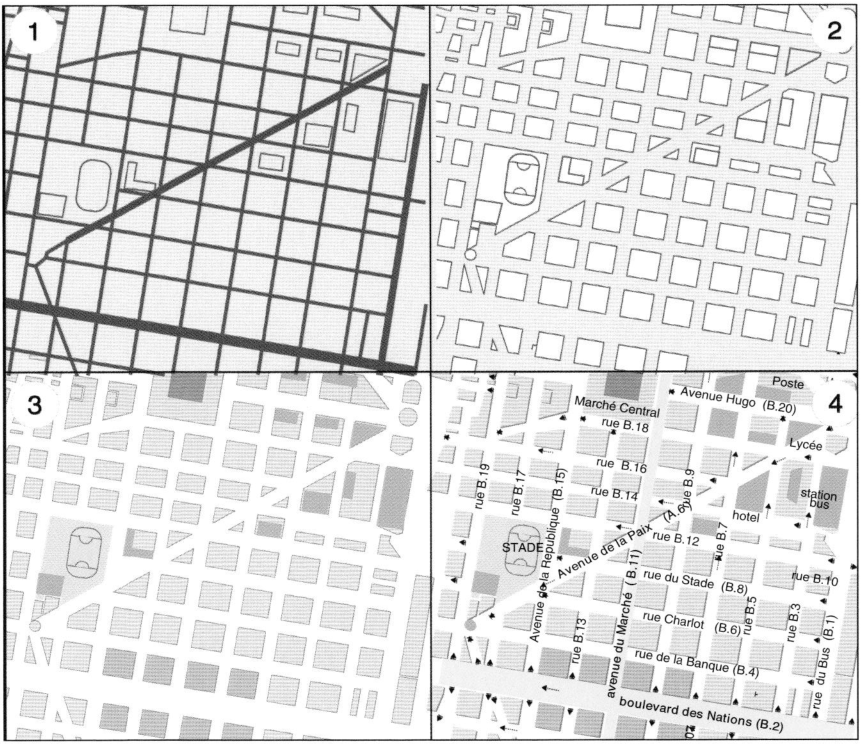

Figure 4.24. Example of an address map (Conakry)

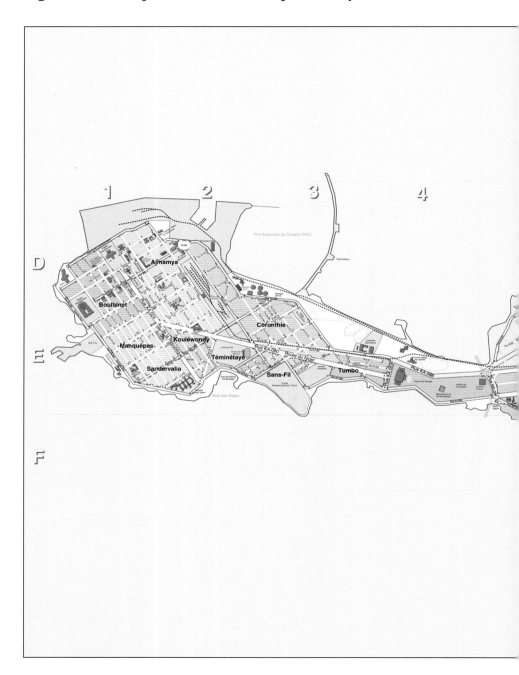

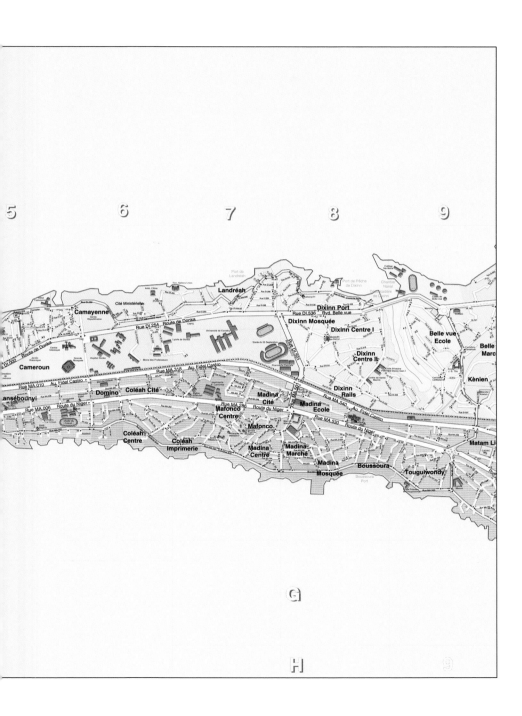

Activity 8. Surveying and numbering doorways

Objective and expected results

The objective is to number the doorways of buildings and, in the process, conduct a survey whose results will be recorded in the address directory. This is undoubtedly the most time-consuming and meticulous part of the street addressing program.

Implementation

A number of tasks must be carried out prior to the surveys and doorway numbering: (a) approval of the codification system by the Supervisory Committee upon completion of the feasibility study; (b) definition and production of the base map; (c) preparation of questionnaires and of surveying and numbering materials; (d) recruitment and training of surveying and numbering teams; and (e) a pilot operation. Tasks (b) to (d) are performed at the start of the implementation phase.

Task 1. Codification

This task consists of establishing a street identification system and assigning numbers to doorways. See activity 6 for further discussion.

Task 2. Mapping

This task comprises the preparation of a base map, which will enable teams to find physical coordinates on the ground as they conduct surveys and install street signs. See activity 7 for further discussion.

Task 3. Preparation of questionnaires and other materials

PREPARATION OF QUESTIONNAIRES. Once the general framework for the survey is established during the feasibility study, the questionnaire can be finalized. At this stage it may seem desirable to conduct a comprehensive survey, but such an approach would involve considerable time expenditure. Since the surveys and doorway numbering are to be conducted concurrently, the recommended approach is to conduct a quick, cursory survey, for subsequent completion during the maintenance phase.

In view of these circumstances, the questionnaire should be short, with wording tailored to the working method employed in the survey. For example, the presence of a water company representative during the survey will make it easier to find out the meter number. The following essential data should be obtained during this initial survey (figure 4.25):

- Address. Name of district, number assigned to each doorway, old number if applicable, street number, street name if applicable.
- Land use category. For example: residential, institutional facility, business (specify).
- Type of building. Examples include: single-story, multi-story, detached house; multi-unit; permanent or temporary structure.

Other information may be added:

- Water and electricity meter numbers. Meters may not be accessible without a utility company representative present.
- Cadastral references. Generally added to the questionnaire after the survey.
- Name of occupant. This information is sometimes difficult to determine for a number of reasons (e.g., refusal to respond; or no point of contact, or several).
- Environment. Examples include: paved road, sidewalk, drainage canal, street lighting. For this type of information, however, it seems more appropriate to organize a specific survey that would inventory and assign addresses to urban fixtures such as public standpipes and fire hydrants, waste transfer points, bus shelters, and the like, preferably during the maintenance phase.

Once the forms have been prepared, the information can be codified for easier computerized data entry. Forms pertaining to economic activity and type of occupancy are prepared in collaboration with the tax department, if possible. The survey form has space reserved for codification, but the survey taker will make handwritten entries for the type of activity.

PREPARATION OF MATERIALS. Each team should have the following materials:

- Survey forms, locator maps;
- Informational memos signed by the mayor, for distribution during the survey process;
- Odometer (when a metric or decametric numbering system is used) for measuring distances to determine doorway numbers;
- Chalk, paint, paintbrushes, and stencils for numbering.

Figure 4.25. Example of survey form

Neighborhood **Madina**		Length of street		**450** m.		
Street number **B.88**		Width of right-of-way		**7m**		
Street name		Type of street		**cobblestone**		

No.	Doorway no.	Type of occupancy	Code	Water	Electr.	Other
1	4	Detached house	H1	A4045	565CC	
2	15	Telephone booth	E2			F
3	18	Vehicle rental agency	P5	A4867	876DD	
4	37	General commercial	C1	G504	45EDD	
5	38	Apartment building	H2	B404	34KL	
6	44	Detached house	H1	A9904	876CC	
7	49	General commercial	C1	A476	78EDD	
8	68	Medical office	L2	A8901	A404	
9	99	General commercial	C1	G404	56EDD	
10	135	Temporary structure	H4			P61
11	148	Detached house	H1	A5679	987CC	

Date ....
Name

Task 4. Recruitment and training of teams

Each team may consist of up to eight persons, including a team leader, field surveyor, survey takers, painters, and laborers. The tasks, though easy to perform, are quite varied, hence the diverse profiles of the team members required. During the recruitment process, special attention should be focused on the potential cohesiveness of the team, whose members will be required to work together throughout the operation. The participation of agents from the utility concessionaires or the tax department during the survey process usually expedites data-gathering and enables agents to quickly complete their own directories with new address entries. A written agreement may be used to govern the participation of the utility concessionaires (box 4.2).

The training focuses on the team members' mastery of the tasks involved, as well as the organization of the team during and after the survey periods: (a) coordination of progress in the field; and (b) organization of collected data at the end of each session and review of materials for the next day's session.

**Box 4.2. Memorandum of agreement between
the municipality and the utility concessionaire**

By agreement between the City of . . . . , as the first party, represented by
. . . . , and the Water Company, as the second party, hereinafter referred
to as the "concessionaire" and represented by . . . . , the parties have
agreed as follows:

Article 1 – The City has begun a street addressing program in which the
concessionaire has decided to take part by committing three of its agents to
participate in field surveys, in collaboration with the street addressing unit.

Article 2 – Agents of the concessionaire shall help match each
subscriber's address information—gathered during the street addressing
program—to the water meter number. The street addressing unit shall
record the gathered data in an address directory and send the data to the
concessionaire along with the address map. The unit shall also provide the
concessionaire with interim reports of survey results.

Article 3 – The participation of the concessionaire's agents will have a
bearing on the duration of the street addressing survey, which is estimated
to last three months. The coordinator of the street addressing unit shall
notify the concessionaire at least three weeks prior to the start of the field
survey and shall provide periodic progress updates.

Article 4 – This agreement shall expire on *(date)*, the anticipated completion date of the street addressing program. The agreement may be
amended subject to mutual consent of the parties.

Article 5 – This agreement shall be announced and distributed as
needed.

Done at . . . . on . . . .
For the City,   For the concessionaire,

Task 5. Pilot operation

The pilot operation has two objectives: to test team training and to
promote the operation through the media, although the second objective
should not eclipse the importance of the first.

- The operation is conducted in a busy, fairly structured neighborhood marked
  by permanent buildings and a well-established street system. The locus of
  the operation is generally the city center, although streets whose lively activity might interfere with the surveying and numbering tasks should be
  avoided. The initial strategy is to fine-tune the training approach while gradually preparing the team before it is required to tackle problem cases.

- There is no need to choose an extensive area. The pilot area generally encompasses only a few (i.e., four to five) streets, which should be sufficient for testing all of the teams.

TESTING. The testing concentrates on: (a) the team's performance under realistic circumstances; (b) giving survey respondents the mayor's memo with a specific explanation of their new address; (c) conducting the survey; and (d) placing the number on the building.

MEDIA CAMPAIGN. The pilot operation provides an additional opportunity to make the authorities and the general population aware of the address system. The campaign should emphasize the doorway numbering and sign installation operations. During this period, model street signs can also be designed and possibly installed. In many cases, the signs are made by local craftsmen for temporary use prior to full-scale production. The objective at this stage is to have a prototype of the permanent signs (dimensions, color, type of inscription).

Task 6. Assign numbers to buildings

This task is performed concurrently with the survey but will be discussed here for ease of presentation. The numbering operation occurs in two phases:

- The municipality is responsible for the initial numbering phase of a street addressing program. The number is painted, using a stencil if possible, on the wall or door of the building. The occupant is obliged to keep the number visible; if this is not provided by law, a municipal regulation may so stipulate.
- The occupant subsequently obtains and affixes a more permanent doorway sign.

The acquisition and mounting of doorway signs should not be included in the street addressing budget, in view of the cost and operational constraints. The procurement of doorway signs involves administrative complications, especially if a metric numbering system is used (since the numbers are nonconsecutive), and affixing them often leads to a series of occupant-generated delays.

A few exceptions might be made in the case of public buildings, which the street addressing team could outfit with doorway signs. These could serve as examples to encourage other residents to replace their painted number with such a doorway sign.

PRACTICAL PROCEDURES. The numbers are usually affixed in two steps during a street addressing operation:

- The writing is first done in chalk by the marker, using the number indicated by the field surveyor, which corresponds to the distance to the doorway from point zero in the case of a metric numbering system.
- The painter, proceeding more slowly, then stencils the number; in some cases, a rectangle is painted as a background for the number, preferably on the wall of the building.

Where should the number be placed? A certain degree of homogeneity is desirable for the stenciled numbers: position, height, uniform background color, size of the numbers. As an example, the number might be positioned above and in line with the entrance, or 1.8 meters above the ground and 20 cm to the right of the entrance, in a place that will not be obscured by an open door or shutter.

Standardization offers the advantage of readability. For this reason, address numbers on Parisian buildings are white on a blue background—

Figure 4.26. Field surveyor and survey taker

Figure 4.27. Team progress chart

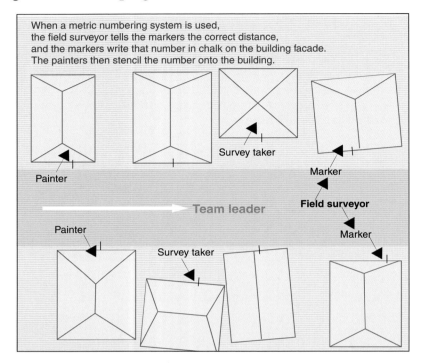

a color combination that is particularly easy to see, even at night under dim lighting conditions. A municipal regulation dated September 27, 1982, requires that doorway signs placed over or near the door frame be rectangular in shape and have a standard height of 17 cm, their width varying depending on the number of digits in the address. All numbers are white on an unframed blue background.

Task 7. Conduct the survey

The survey has several goals:

- To present the occupant with his new address and provide a brief explanation of the newly adopted numbering system;
- To write the number on the wall of the building after discussion with the occupant;

Figure 4.28. Model memo to be presented during the survey

CITY OF DOLOBA
REPUBLIC OF CAMATO

STREET ADDRESSING PROJECT

The municipality has decided to begin a modernization project in order to provide easier access to municipal services. As part of this effort, we will be implementing a street addressing project.

What is street addressing?

Street addressing involves assigning a number to each street in the city, until a future time when street names will be assigned. The number will be displayed at the street corner, mounted either on a panel on the wall of a building, or on a signpost. Each house will also be assigned a number.

What is the purpose of street addressing?

Street addressing will make it easier for you to find your way around the city. It will also make it easier for the city to provide services such as ambulances, fire trucks, and taxis. Mail, messengers and emergency assistance will be able to reach you faster and more directly.

From now on, you will have an address similar to the example below:

M. Sory Diallo
15, rue B.25
Doloba
Camato

- To present a personalized memo containing the address—and if possible the name—of the occupant (see model; figure 4.28); the head of the household need not be present for the survey, as the memo should provide all necessary information about the survey;
- To gather the essential data described above under task 3, including address, type of occupancy, type of building, and other information.

PROGRESS CHECK. The tasks of numbering, surveying, and affixing of doorway signs are sometimes spaced out over long time intervals, therefore necessitating a monthly progress check for each task. A chart such as the model shown in figure 4.29 should be used.

Figure 4.29. Progress chart for street addressing tasks

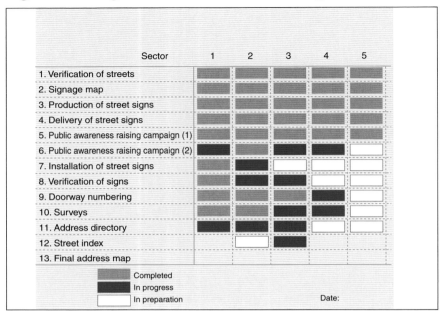

Activity 9. Recording addresses

Objectives and expected results

This activity has two objectives: (a) to set up an address directory based on the survey findings, and (b) to make it available—using procedures to be determined—to government agencies and utility concessionaires, who will add supplementary information according to their own needs.

The expected results are:

- a computer printout, generally in spreadsheet form, intended to facilitate the dissemination of information;
- a data analysis document that provides information such as number of named or numbered streets, number of doorways per neighborhood, list of business activities by neighborhood, and the like.

Implementation

The implementation phase begins with the preparation of a data analysis code for the survey (activity 8) and the development or procurement of system software. The data are recorded during the survey process. This phase consists of four tasks: survey organization and checking; coding; data entry; and analysis and follow-up.

Task 1. Organization and checking

Each day, the documents are organized by the survey staff according to street and neighborhood, checked by the team leader, and filled in or annotated the same day or the next so that the information is not forgotten. The survey manager oversees this task.

Task 2. Coding

Some questionnaire responses that are written out during the survey process—for example, type of business activity or use category—must then be coded.

Task 3. Data entry

USE OF SPECIAL SOFTWARE. A software program specially designed for address directories is recommended for two reasons:

- *Size of the address directory.* The number of lines in the address directory will ultimately equal the number of households. Hence, for a city with a population of one million, the address directory will comprise 100,000 to 400,000 lines. For each line (one line per doorway assigned an address), there will be 10–20 items of data, such as address, use category, type of building, meter number, and so on. Consequently, the database can quickly exceed a million data items. Under these circumstances, traditional spreadsheets are greatly outmoded in their data handling capacity.
- *Use.* The address directory will be used by professionals at many levels: technical experts, tax department personnel, data entry staff, and others. The situation calls for a specific application that provides fast, easy access for data search and retrieval. To meet these needs, an existing application may be adapted or a new one created (though the possibility of software bugs would have to be taken into account under the latter scenario).

FUNCTIONS. The street addressing software will need to include functions that enable the following operations:

- *Data entry:* check for consistency of data entry and for keyboarding errors, change an address, keep a history file (old names);
- *Tailoring the parameters:* make modifications, particularly for occupancy codes and street or sector names;
- *Search:* search for any address according to any data item linked to it (such as name, street number, address, use category, and so on);
- *Statistics:* retrieve data and statistics using multiple criteria;
- *Geographic or "territorial" subdivision:* be able to process data for a specific geographic area to serve the needs of technical or tax departments or utility concessionaires; a "territory" is user-defined and may be stored in memory; it may include one or more neighborhoods, one or more streets or sections of street, or even- or uneven-numbered sides of the street;
- *Data export:* export data in standard formats (such as txt, xls, dbf);
- *Protection:* limit access to some or all data through password protection.

DEFINITIONS

- *Address.* Each address corresponds to a unique code that makes it possible to locate a single element of the city on a particular street.
- *Type of occupancy.* An address may refer to a dwelling, a business establishment (company, shop, service facility, for example), an institutional facility (such as a school, hospital, or government agency), or an urban fixture. Data entry is identical for all types of address.

- *Multiple address.* A single building may have space devoted to several different use categories.
- *Neighborhoods and streets.* Names of address zones are entered prior to addresses, so as to build into the database the codes that will enable the software to function, i.e., the neighborhood code and the street code.

Task 4. Analysis and follow-up

Various types of requests are made for data analysis, such as:

- List of streets by neighborhood (named or numbered streets),
- List of streets by neighborhood according to feature (right-of-way, type, paved),
- List of addresses by neighborhood according to occupancy type (residence, business, facility, urban fixture),
- List of addresses by neighborhood and by street,
- List of businesses by neighborhood and by street.

Similar lists are provided by "territory," if applicable.

Back-up. The address directory is backed up daily during the data entry phase.

Follow-up. The survey progress is tracked each day by marking on an address map those streets that have been "processed."

Training. The staff responsible for keying-in and updating the address directory is familiarized with street addressing techniques and is given the appropriate software training.

Box 4.3. Urbadresse

The Urbadresse software program was developed in the course of several street addressing programs[6] (free of charge). It enables fast, reliable entry and updating of addresses and generates statistical data. It can process 150,000 addresses and about 5,000 streets in less than 10 seconds for the most complex data requests. The level of access can be differentiated according to user, from the database manager to the data entry worker.
   Data entry focuses on the following elements:

- *Sectors, zones, or neighborhoods* corresponding to the type of subdivision used for street numbering. *"Territories"* may also be user-defined, for example, a neighborhood or group of neighborhoods to which streets may be added.
- *Streets:* Neighborhood or zone number; street number; street name (if any); type of roadway (avenue, boulevard, street, lane, cul-de-sac, for example); category (primary, secondary, tertiary, and so forth); beginning with street no. . . . / ending with . . . ; length of street; first and last doorway no.; right-of-way and width of roadway; coordinates on the map grid.
- *Doorways:* Number of doorway; old number (if any); street number and name (if any), occupancy type and code (dwelling, facility, business, urban fixture, other); occupancy group (for example, business activity: agriculture, industry, commercial); occupancy subgroup (such as commercial wholesale, commercial retail, and so on).
- *Optional parameters:* For example, meter numbers, cadastral references, or other information.

The software program can generate statistics for all or part of the city, or for address zones, neighborhoods, or specific territories. For example, it can process requests such as:

- Based on type of occupancy, select dwellings or types of dwellings, businesses or types of businesses, facilities, or urban fixtures, for example. Selection can be by street, group of streets, neighborhood, "territory," or the entire city.
- Based on address, select the data associated with an address, or with a street or group of streets, by neighborhood or "territory"; thus, for any given street, it is possible to determine the number of occupied units, business activities, or facilities, for example.
- Store in memory all changes of occupancy in order to establish history files, thereby making it possible to observe population dynamics.
- Easily input or modify a new address at any time.
- Add free parameters (data associated with an address) at any time and in unlimited number.

Box 4.3. Urbadresse (continued)

- Print excerpts and/or all data.
- Distinguish between even and uneven doorway numbers for opposite sides of the street.
- Import or export data in standard format.

Figure 4.30. Recording data

Activity 10. Installing street signs

Objective and expected results

The objective is to install signage on street corners to designate each street by name and/or number. The expected result is either the installation of street signs on building façades or posts or the use of more rudimentary solutions. This decision is generally budget-driven.

Implementation

Owing to the diversity of tasks included under this activity, they should each be undertaken in expedited fashion without necessarily waiting until the surveys have been completed. The following tasks are to be performed: define the signage system, prepare the maps and list of street signs, procure the sign materials, and install the signs.

Task 1. Define the signage system

Work on this task begins during the feasibility study, in the form of cost estimates and budget preparation—decisions that will undoubtedly influence the choice of signage. The task extends into the street inventory process at the beginning of the implementation phase. At this stage, the team identifies corners where the building façades do not allow for wall-mounted signs and will therefore necessitate the installation of signposts. And finally, the team estimates the specific needs to be met during the operation: (a) number of sign plates; (b) number of stenciled signs; and (c) number of signposts. The type of signage to be used will be determined by weighing cost against durability.

COMPARISON OF SOLUTIONS

1. *Wall-stenciled signs*. This is the cheapest but least permanent solution, in which street names and numbers are stenciled onto the façades or enclosures of buildings at street corners. The factors of note in this regard are the making of the stencil and the choice of paint.
   - *Stencil*. The experience of craftsmen has convincingly shown that precise crafting of the stencils is a decisive factor in their successful implementation. When economy is chosen over quality, the inscription quickly fades or fails otherwise. A first stencil is used for roller-painting the sign's background color. The repetitive nature of this operation calls for a solid frame that can be manipulated with corner irons and handles (see figure 4.31).

Figure 4.31. Stenciling materials

Other stencils are used to repeat the word "street" or the district name. Used aluminum offset plates[7] work well for cutting out letters with a cutter; a wood frame reinforces the stencil, making it possible to achieve high-quality lettering. Experience indicates a production cost of approximately US$10 per stencil.

- *Coating.* If the wall surface is unsatisfactory, a smooth coating a few centimeters thick can be applied. This extra thickness creates a raised design and reduces the likelihood that it will be painted over during a building renovation, for instance after a change of ownership.
- *Paint.* Paint is weather-sensitive and may fade after a number of years. It is therefore advisable not to try to economize on this item by excessively diluting mixtures or using lower-quality paint. Acrylic and vinyl copolymer-based paints generally hold up well against solar and ultraviolet radiation.

2. *Panels or plates.* This solution is costlier but more permanent than stenciled signs. The inscriptions are written on a panel or plate, which is subsequently mounted on a building façade or a post. A panel is distinguished from a plate by its bent or turned-down edges, which make it sturdier but increase the cost.
   - *The material* may be wood, plastic, aluminum or other metal; more durable materials are usually more costly. Sign installations on plywood, painted metal, or certain types of plastic are often less expensive, but they offer little resistance to rain, sun, and other bad weather conditions. A reflective film coating over a metal base seems attractive, but this solution is often expensive and at times unreliable. Various manufacturers suggest using aluminum with baked-on lacquer, but enameled metal is a durable and widely used solution.
   - *The shape, surface, color, and style* of the lettering also affect the cost.
   - *The dimensions* may vary, as no international or even national standards exist. A 25 x 40 or 30 x 50 cm format is fairly common, though smaller dimensions may suffice if a numbering system is used.

3. *Post-mounted signs.* This solution—required occasionally when signs cannot be placed on a wall—is more expensive to implement. The cost includes not only the plates, but also the mounting hardware and the post, and post mounting is also more expensive than a wall installation. The post dimensions must meet safety standards, with a height of at least 2.7 meters to allow for safe clearance beneath the signs. The concrete pedestal must be outfitted with a device to prevent the post from swiveling, and the post must be at least 60 mm in diameter to discourage theft and vandalism. In some cases, cement has been poured into the tube to prevent sawing or theft.

A variety of approaches can be used to help reduce costs, such as varying the sign density, gradual implementation, and sponsoring.

Table 4.11. Unit cost of materials, not including installation (in US$)

| | Plate | | Panel | |
	On wall	On post	On wall	On post
Lacquered aluminum	23	54	31	62
Metal and enamel	29	60	33	64
Alu + reflective film	51	82	70	91

VARYING SIGN DENSITY. Maximum sign density provides for a street sign on the even- and uneven-numbered sides at each street corner. Under this scenario, a two-street intersection would have eight signs—a costly solution that can be modified for each neighborhood. Such a solution may be suitable in the town center, but the sign density could be reduced in less-frequented neighborhoods—for example, two signs per intersection. To achieve further cost savings, street signs could be installed at every other intersection. Such a solution would not make it too difficult to find street coordinates if streets are numbered consecutively.

GRADUAL IMPLEMENTATION. As an initial approach, street signs could be erected on major streets only, with a simpler solution such as stenciled signs used on secondary roads. These latter would be outfitted later, starting with named streets.

A SPONSORING SYSTEM. Sign installation may be sponsored, with the sponsor's name or logo printed unobtrusively in a small font (0.5 cm) on the plate so as not to interfere with the main wording. This system can be used to place high-quality signs in historic districts[8] or to encourage more sponsors after an initial group of neighborhoods has received sponsorship.

Task 2. Prepare the map and list of street signs

The signage map is generally prepared on a 1:5,000 enlargement of the address map. It contains the same information, as well as: (a) the position,

Table 4.12. Comparison of sign densities by cost

Signage solution	Intersections with signs	No. of plates or panels per intersection	Signposts
Maximum	All	8	As needed
Intermediate	All	2	In moderation
Economical	1 out of 2	2	Strict minimum
Minimum	As many as possible	Stenciling on walls	None

Figure 4.32. Sponsored street signs

name, type (plate, stencil), and mounting type (i.e., wall- or post-mounted); and (b) doorway numbers at the end of each block (figure 4.33).

This map is especially useful for determining the number of signs to be installed for each neighborhood and street. It can also be used for:

- drawing up the list of street signs for procuring plates, panels, posts, and stencils;
- a reference document for the company that installs the panels, plates, and posts.

The list of street signs catalogues all signs to be made for installation on walls and posts.

Task 3. Procuring sign materials

This task involves procuring the street addressing materials, usually by way of requests for bids. This process should be started without delay, in view of the time required for bidding, manufacture, and delivery of the materials. The bidding process can proceed without the list of street signs, subject to the following conditions: (a) the feasibility study has established the type of signage and estimated the number of plates and

Table 4.13. Sample list of street signs

Commune no.	Group of districts	Name of district	Type of street	Title of street (name or number)	No. of street (if named)	# on post	# on wall
4	Talladjé (TJ)	Talladjé	Boulevard	du 15 Avril	TJ.2	2	7
4	Talladjé (TJ)	Talladjé	Rue	TJ4		1	2
4	Talladjé (TJ)	Talladjé	Rue	TJ.10		2	2
4	Zone Industrielle (ZI)	Zone Industrielle	Avenue	de l'Afrique	ZI. 2	2	2
4	Zone Industrielle (ZI)	Zone Industrielle	Avenue	des Offices	ZI. 4	2	7
4	Zone Industrielle (ZI)	Zone Industrielle	Rue	ZI6			2
3	Poudrière (PO)	Kalley Est	Rue	PO.4			3
3	Poudrière (PO)	Poudrière	Avenue	du Damagaram	PO 6		4
3	Poudrière (PO)	Sabon Gari	Avenue	du Damagaram	PO 6		3
1	Plateau (PL)	Plateau	Corniche	Corniche Yantala	PL 2	1	2
1	Plateau (PL)	Plateau	Avenue	des Ministères	PL 6	2	
1	Plateau (PL)	Plateau	Avenue	du Général de Gaulle	PL 30	4	10
3	Nouveau Marché (NM)	Baie d'Along	Boulevard	de l'Indépendance	NM 42	1	3
3	Nouveau Marché (NM)	Cimetière musulman	Boulevard	de l'Indépendance	NM 42	2	1
3	Nouveau Marché (NM)	Sabon Gari	Rue	NM 44			2
2	Liberté (LI)	Koiratégui 1	Rue	de Kabekoira	LI 2	3	4

Figure 4.33. Signage map

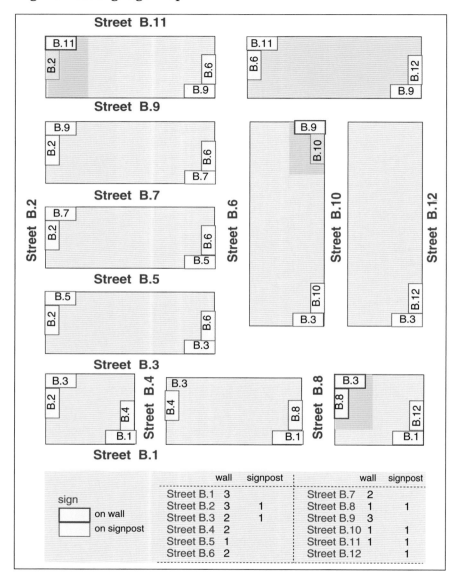

	wall	signpost		wall	signpost
Street B.1	3		Street B.7	2	
Street B.2	3	1	Street B.8	1	1
Street B.3	2	1	Street B.9	3	
Street B.4	2		Street B.10	1	1
Street B.5	1		Street B.11	1	1
Street B.6	2		Street B.12		1

panels needed, and (b) at the time of the contract award, the list of street signs must be ready, at least for a partial order if the supplier agrees to a staggered delivery schedule.

Stencils. It is appropriate to consult local craftsmen about making the stencils. Bidders will be required to submit a prototype during the selection process, however, to ensure that the materials meet the users' expectations.

Signs. If durability of materials is essential and the order will be sizeable, it is generally advisable to arrange an international request for bids, which would open the way to dealing with specialized companies that can often work more reliably at lower cost.

Each bidder will be required to include with the bid a prototype for signs and posts, which will be used as a reference for judging the quality of the materials. The materials delivered must be of at least the same quality as that of the prototypes. The request for bids may suggest that different options be presented for the quantities to be supplied, contingent upon a more definitive indication of the quantity on which bids will be judged (annex 4).

Task 4. Install the signs

RECEIVE, STORE AND DELIVER THE MATERIALS. A specific site is to be provided for receiving, storing, and delivering the sign materials. Upon delivery from the supplier, a certificate of completion must be signed by the street addressing unit and the supplier.

If possible, this site should be located near the areas where street addresses are being assigned. There should be sufficient space for systematic storage of the materials (arranged by street) so as to facilitate subsequent installation work. Security services should be provided to prevent theft.

Certificates of completion will be issued for daily deliveries of materials to the installation teams. The materials will be inventoried at least once per week. The street addressing unit will have the responsibility for each of these tasks.

ORGANIZE SIGN INSTALLATION. The sign installation work includes mounting of signs and posts and stenciling of inscriptions on buildings. Contracts are generally awarded to local companies through a bidding process. If possible, requests for bids are issued separately for supplying the materials and for the installation work. The street addressing unit will supervise the work, which will be performed according to an installation schedule drawn up with the contractor before the work begins. To that effect, a map excerpt will be prepared and given to each team on a daily basis, along with a list of work to be performed and materials to be obtained from the storage facility.

INSTALL THE SIGNS. The street signs are placed on walls or enclosures at a height of three meters and a distance of 20 cm from the building corner, though these measurements should be regarded as indicative rather than limitative. The installation of signposts should conform to the country's usual signposting practices and must not disrupt traffic.

On a daily basis, the street addressing unit assesses the work completed and charts the progress on a map, and each week it conducts a field inspection. The sign installation is deemed to be completed upon acceptance of the work. The street addressing unit will verify that the work has been performed in accordance with the signage map and inventory sheets.

Figure 4.34. Street signs and signposts

Activity 11. Producing the address map and street index

Objective and expected results

The objective is to print and disseminate the address map and its index of streets to government offices and beyond to the general public. This activity dovetails with the media campaign to promote the street addressing program.

Implementation

At the beginning of the implementation phase, the street addressing unit prepared or arranged for the preparation of the address map that was to be used for the surveys and sign installation. The remaining tasks are: (a) check and complete the map; (b) prepare the street index; (c) begin printing; and (d) disseminate and, if possible, sell the documents.

Broad dissemination involves using printing processes unlike those generally used by government printing offices. Consequently, it is advisable to begin the map production process while keeping in mind the printing requirements, which calls for judicious selection of map design software.

Task 1. Check and complete the address map

The address map is supplemented and revised several times during the course of the surveys and sign installation. A number of final adjustments will therefore be needed before the document is sent to the printer.

PLAN AHEAD FOR THE PRINTING PROCESS BEFORE PRODUCING THE MAP

- If the map is designed on paper, it will be useful to transfer it onto a computer using editing software;[9]
- If the map is already computerized, there is no certainty that the printer will be able to use it easily. A map designed on editing software can usually be edited in color with little difficulty. Otherwise, the data will need to be transferable to an editing program. It is advisable to settle these issues prior to beginning work on map production.
- If the map is designed on GIS software, the graphics will need to be easily exportable to an editing program. Although it is often tempting to use GIS software for street addressing because it combines data processing and map production, this type of software is quite complex; it would not be advisable to begin map production with an inexperienced staff. The wise solution is to begin the initial street addressing operation

with simple, inexpensive tools (editing software, for instance), and then plan to graduate to a more sophisticated computerized system after the street addressing unit staff has been trained.

PREPARE THE DOCUMENT FOR PRINTING. It is customary procedure to convert the computer document into films that will be used for four-color printing. The chief cartographer will need to find out the constraints of this process at the beginning of the implementation phase in order to gauge its effects on the map preparation, and particularly on the organization of the different layers comprising the address map (activity 7).

Task 2. Prepare the street index

The index can be used to locate streets on the map according to an alphanumeric grid. It is presented in the form of a list printed either on the front or on the reverse side of the address map, or in a booklet containing the list of streets and map excerpts. The booklet is usually produced in a small format that can be easily slipped into a handbag or an automobile glove compartment.

Task 3. Print the map and index

The job of printing the map and index is contracted out through a bidding process. The production of the films from the electronic document calls for pre-press production techniques that may be beyond the expertise of some printers. All bidders will therefore be required to include with their bid a negative made from a map excerpt so that a qualified printer can be chosen (annex 8).

In order to obtain competitive rates, the map should be approximately 70 x 100 cm, a format widely used in the printing industry. At least 2,000 copies should be printed. In addition to specifications for the map and index, the request for bids can include the provision of about 15 large-format copies printed on high-quality paper using a plotter, for distribution to the municipality and government departments.

Task 4. Disseminate the documents

The map and index should be widely disseminated, preferably through sale. Advertising space can be sold to keep costs down and facilitate updates. It would be desirable, however, to broaden the dissemination by offering (or selling) a computerized version, particularly for government departments and utility concessionaires.

Figure 4.35. Sample map and index

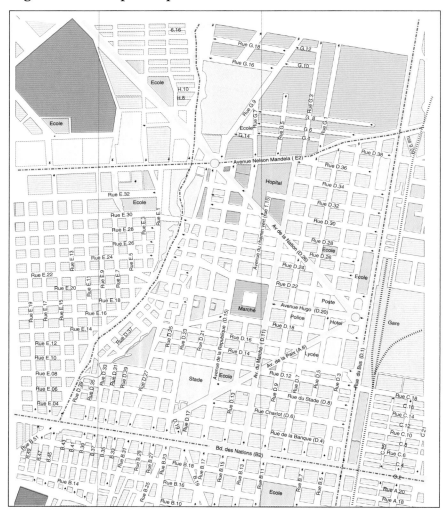

Activity 12. Conducting a media campaign

Objective and expected results

The objective is to keep the public informed of progress and to explain the reason, substance, and schedule of the street addressing program. A media campaign is therefore an essential tool for achieving this objective. The surveys, doorway numbering, and sign installation will have a direct effect on city residents, and these innovations will undoubtedly generate many questions and comments. The absence of relevant information could lead to misunderstanding or unfounded resistance to such a program.

Implementation

RESPONSIBILITY. The municipal authorities will oversee the media campaign. The street addressing unit may assist in this endeavor, but it will not be equipped or trained to assume direct responsibility. A specialized agency, if possible a local firm, should be hired to carry out the campaign.

COST ESTIMATE. The consultant in charge of the feasibility study will submit an initial estimate to the Supervisory Committee, based on a percentage of the operating cost (3–5%).

TARGETS. The media campaign should be targeted to municipal authorities, government departments, economic operators, neighborhood leaders, and civil society.

THE MEDIA. The experience gained during a variety of successful street addressing programs provides some helpful guidelines:
   Meetings, seminars. This type of intervention lies within the means of even the smallest municipality. Arrangements should be made for meetings with:

- the municipality, to provide a forum for decisionmaking and approval of proposals;
- tax departments and utility concessionaires, to identify mutual advantages and to look for ways they can work together;
- the municipality's technical departments or the security, health, or postal departments, usually to explore the practical applications of street addressing;
- neighborhood leaders and the general public, typically of an informational nature; and

- school children or taxi drivers (Mauritania, for example), for educational purposes.

Official "stamp of approval." The launching of the street addressing program, the posting of the first street sign, a visit during the pilot operation, and the dissemination of the address map are examples of opportunities to "put an official stamp" on the program.

News articles. This type of intervention usually poses no problem, but the street addressing unit should often provide assistance so that all technical explanations are accurately stated.

Radio and/or television interviews. These interviews play a key role in any media campaign, and the street addressing unit should be well prepared.

Memo from the mayor. This memo, presented during the survey, explains the occupant's new address, and in particular the meaning of the number painted on the building (activity 8).

Leaflets. The dissemination of printed information about the municipality's address system can be a very effective way to keep costs low.

T-shirts. In several instances, the street addressing units have outfitted their installation teams with "street addressing" t-shirts, which advertise the program and attract and motivate participants.

Maps and index. The dissemination of the address maps and index in both paper and electronic form helps to popularize and sustain the program over time.

Films. Some countries have prepared short television films on street addressing, which can be translated into multiple languages (Guinea, Mozambique, and Niger, for example).

SCHEDULE. The intensity of the media campaign should coincide with the phases of the program: (a) for the preparation phase: startup of the program; (b) for the implementation phase: pilot operation, completion, and evaluation; and (c) for the maintenance phase: expansion of the program into new neighborhoods, or assigning addresses to urban fixtures.

THEMES. The following principal themes should be developed during the media campaign:

- *The benefits of having an address*: provides easier access for health and safety services as well as utility concessionaires. The advantages for the postal service seem obvious, but many countries use a post office box or general delivery system, which is less effective but more economical than door-to-door mail delivery. Postal officials must be involved in any discussion of the merits of street addressing for mail delivery. A similar degree of caution should prevail in regard to taxation, for although an

address system can help improve tax collection, this would probably
not be an attractive advertising slogan.

- *How the system will work.* The codification system will need to be justified and explained. Why number the streets and wait to name them
  later? How does street numbering work? How does building numbering work?
- *Action plan.* The street addressing program will take several months to
  complete, so the municipality would be well advised to present an action
  plan showing the duration of operations, neighborhoods involved, actors,
  costs, and other information. The plan should also provide for longer-
  range goals, such as expansion of the operation to new neighborhoods,
  assignment of addresses to urban fixtures, detailed inventory of municipal assets, and other applications to be managed by the street addressing unit.

Figure 4.36. Conducting a media campaign through film, posters, logos

Activity 13. Maintaining and adapting the system

Objective and expected results

Implementing a street addressing program in a city is necessarily an ongoing operation, especially if the urban area is continually developing. Without maintenance, the system will quickly become obsolete. The objective of this activity is to maintain the system once it has been established. The expected result is the identification of ways in which the street addressing unit in particular can help achieve that objective through its intervention plan after the initial addressing operation.

Implementation

The importance of maintaining the system is generally well understood, but the means of achieving this objective are often left unspecified. The street addressing unit is the entity best suited to assume responsibility for system maintenance, yet its suitability for that endeavor requires some justification since it is not a part of the municipal organizational structure. Therefore, an action plan and budget will need to be prepared and approved by the municipal authorities.

Task 1. Prepare action plans

The maintenance phase begins after the implementation phase, but it may cover a wide range of activities with three possible approaches that may overlap: maintain, extend, or broaden the mandate of the address system.

MAINTAIN THE EXISTING ADDRESS SYSTEM. The action plan focuses on neighborhoods already assigned addresses in order to:

- Repair or replace damaged or vandalized signs and posts;
- Replace street number signs with name signs when the names have been selected by the Toponymy Commission;
- Redo faded doorway numbers, number newly constructed doorways;
- Update the address directory after several changes have occurred, e.g., closure of previously existing doorways or addition of new ones, reassignment of plot or building numbers.

In order to ensure that new addresses or changes of occupant are declared, some countries have instituted an "address certificate," which utility concessionaires require residents to have when making service requests.

EXTEND THE ADDRESS SYSTEM. This approach focuses on completing the work begun:

- *Efforts are focused on neighborhoods already assigned addresses,* but operations are extended to urban fixtures, at least those under municipal authority or relating to neighborhood services, such as public standpipes, fire hydrants, public streetlamps, household waste transfer points, telephone booths or centers, public toilets, and the like.
- *Efforts are focused on neighborhoods not assigned addresses* during the initial operation, either because they had few or no residents, or because they were deemed too difficult to outfit by reason of their informal nature or uncertain legal status. Slum neighborhoods will require special attention. A street address system could help give underserved populations a greater sense of security. There will undoubtedly be a need for innovation using the methods described earlier (chapter 2, section 6).

BROADEN STREET ADDRESSING APPLICATIONS. Once all neighborhoods have been assigned addresses, the action plan focuses on broadening street addressing applications, primarily by expanding data collection to matters other than street addressing. At this point, the addressing unit will need to expand its role and take an adaptive approach. The objective is to gather additional information about the city, which municipal authorities often need for decisionmaking purposes. Many local governments have only sketchy information about the population of certain neighborhoods or the condition of the infrastructure and facilities under their responsibility. Against this backdrop, a number of street addressing units have gradually evolved into documentation centers, urban databases, urban observatories, or urban planning units (Maputo, Yaoundé, Douala). Designations aside, such developments create a tailor-made opportunity for using the knowledge gained during addressing operations to broaden the unit's mandate and answer the need for more information on municipalities.

The action plan could then cover a variety of topics and an inventory of municipal assets can receive priority, particularly as this type of activity is regarded as a continuation of street addressing work.

- *Street inventory:* The data-gathering is done by section and in much more detail than was the case in the street addressing survey, encompassing physical features, road condition, and so forth. This type of research may call for the use of specialized software.[10]
- *Inventory of drainage works:* The drainage canals along roads were identified in the preceding inventory, but sometimes the responsibility for main outflow points falls to the municipality by default, and therefore it is advisable to list them.

- *Inventory of public works associated with household waste management,* such as collection points, pickup routes, placement of trash bins, transfer centers, and landfills.
- *Inventory of neighborhood facilities,* beginning with educational and health facilities (e.g., elementary schools, health posts) whose construction and upkeep fall under the responsibility of the municipality. In these cases, the inventory accounts not only for the physical description but also the operation of the facility, such as the number of students, classrooms, and teachers, and other such information.

Each inventory generates descriptive reports that help officials assess needs and the cost of maintenance, repairs, or public works construction, and the data can be used to guide municipal investment programs. In terms of implementation, a qualitative step is still needed to organize the data into an urban information system.

The addressing unit's action plan may encompass additional efforts, such as assistance to a street toponymy commission in order to gradually replace the existing street numbers, neighborhood population estimates and needs assessment surveys, or a compendium of ongoing studies.

Task 2. Evaluate interventions

A simple list or description of possible action plans is insufficient. The street addressing unit will need to quantify needs in terms of staff, materials, cost, and time before submitting its proposals to the municipal authorities:

- If the existing address system is to be *maintained*, the full-time team that carried out the implementation phase will suffice. Its size could be reduced to one or two persons assigned to the municipality's technical departments, for example;
- If the address system is to be *extended*, the street addressing unit will follow the formula used during the implementation phase to carry out this task, i.e., full-time and short-term teams;
- If the address system is to be *broadened*, the situation will be different, since the nature of the interventions changes radically. This scenario will require a closer analysis to determine the team composition, whether or not it should be assigned to an existing municipal department, and the operating costs.

The foregoing proposals have been implemented to varying degrees in about 50 cities in some 15 countries over the course of the 1990s. Much work remains to be done, however, so that street addressing can make a more substantial contribution toward improving urban management and encouraging a broader recognition of the civic rights of all citizens. These efforts are only a beginning.

Notes

1. The use of this system in Asmara has resulted in limited success, however, because only a few streets in the city center did not have names, and the sections were not systematically numbered.
2. J. Pronteau. Op.cit.
3. A *toise* is an old measurement equaling 6.5 feet or just under 2 meters.
4. J, X and Z are not included; I is spelled "Eye."
5. Images from Spot 5, QuickBird, or Ikonos, for example.
6. Financed by the French Cooperation Agency and developed using Access, this software runs on a standard PC with a 250–500 MHz Pentium II or III processor, and can be installed from a CD-ROM.
7. Mali. Bamako, Kayes, Sikasso—Municipal Support Project (PACUM) and Urban Development and Decentralization Project (PDUD).
8. Historic city center of Puebla, Mexico: VW automobiles.
9. A software program such as Illustrator.
10. Such as Urbavia, Viziroad, or similar programs.

Annexes

Annex 1. Terms of reference for tax registers

1. Background and objectives

Background. (Based on the Senegalese experience)
The need to reform local taxation systems prompted the National Assembly to strongly recommend efforts to eliminate financial burdens and thereby enable local governments to carry out their missions. Various studies identified problems and bottlenecks in the current system and offered recommendations. These studies especially emphasized the need to improve the taxation process, from taxpayer identification to allocation of tax revenues to the appropriate municipal accounts.

The municipal contracts signed with municipalities include support to cities with more than 50,000 inhabitants to improve their issuance of tax notices and their collections for the CFPB (land tax on improved property), TOM (household waste tax), and the business tax. Successful completion of street addressing projects in these cities should make it easier to identify the tax base and improve tax collection without requiring any changes to current legislation or regulations. The first effort to improve direct local tax systems will be carried out in the municipalities of . . . . and . . . . before the effort is expanded to other cities.

The Ministry of Finance and Economy and, particularly, the National Tax Authority participated in discussions about objectives and working methods for this initial project. The National Tax Authority is participating in the initiative through the two regional tax inspectorates. The project will involve the combined efforts of the municipality (financial department and addressing unit), the regional tax inspectorate (regional inspector and controllers assigned to these specific tax areas), the RPM (office of municipal tax revenues), and a consultant.

This document represents the consultant's terms of reference.

Objectives
The objectives are as follows:

(1) Do a valuation of the current status of tax rolls and collections;
(2) Evaluate the resources and procedures currently used by the tax and treasury departments and the municipality for assessment and collection of the CFPB and TOM taxes and the business tax and commercial licenses;
(3) Establish a statistical reconciliation between the number of potential taxpayers identified by addressing efforts and the number of taxpayers on tax rolls or identified by the advance payments list (PPA);
(4) Perform the necessary surveys so that addresses can be included beside taxpayer names on existing tax rolls.

When this activity has been completed, the work will be evaluated and a decision will be made to expand the mission to:

- revise existing property assessments if the valuation conducted during the test phase justifies such action,
- automate the method for assessing these particular taxes.

2. Tasks and phases

The consultant shall provide the following services to meet the aforementioned objectives.

Phase 1: valuation

The consultant will conduct a comprehensive analysis of tax rolls and collections for the CFPB and TOM taxes as well as the business tax and commercial licenses. This analysis will study tax assessments and collections over the past three fiscal years and will include:

(1) A *fully supported statistical analysis* of current tax assessments and collections for each of the taxes and fees concerned. Data will include: number of taxpayers, a breakdown by tax bracket, breakdown by business activity (for the business licenses and fees), volume and number of tax-exempt properties and businesses, with a breakout of both permanent exemptions and temporary tax relief.

   The analysis will also study advance payment lists made during this same period (tax rolls created after annual tax collection campaigns). The statistical analysis will conclude by highlighting the greatest contributors to the city's potential tax revenue. This will include a list of the city's largest taxpayers and business activities. For each of these taxpayers, a table will specify the amount of various direct taxes paid by these taxpayers in order to compare the ratio of local taxation to national taxes.

   The IT Department will provide the consultant with computerized tax rolls to perform this analysis. The consultant will study collections made based on the collections reports provided by the RPM, and will do the same for data regarding advance payments.

(2) An estimate of the *tax burden* represented by these taxes and fees on the main categories of taxpayers. This analysis will involve a sample of about 10 representative taxpayer profiles for the CFPB tax and business licenses and fees. The analysis will include interviews with taxpayers to determine their opinion on the tax burden placed upon them by local taxation in their city.

(3) An evaluation of the *resources and procedures* of local tax and treasury departments for collecting local taxes covered in the study. Such resources

and procedures include number of employees, logistical resources, procedures used (including the local tax circular and evaluation form,
annual census, etc.).

The consultant will review the resources provided by the municipal
authorities and the corresponding budget. He will evaluate how the
validation of tax rolls at the national level affects the timetable for issuing tax assessment notices, handling, and ultimately collecting all the
taxes. The consultant will give his/her opinion on the reliability of the
tax rolls in light of actual collections and taxes considered unrecoverable
by the RPM.

(4) A *summary report on the various elements in the analysis* and recommendations on how to improve the chain of tax collections for the city being
studied.

The analysis is expected to take two months (finalization of the first
two steps of the valuation phase).

Phase 2: Including addresses in tax rolls
The tasks in this phase include:

(1) *Adding addresses to tax rolls for the four taxes and fees concerned*
This task involves placing an address beside the name of each taxpayer
entry on the tax rolls. The addressing unit, the RPM, and the tax department will collaborate on this project. The consultant will be responsible
for project direction and oversight. An address will be entered into the
computerized directory created during the analysis phase. The consultant will provide detailed instructions on how to match addresses to names:
- pre-identification of listed taxpayers by comparing the cadastral map
  and address map: work methods and organization;
- gathering additional data through field surveys;
- sharing of tax rolls among the addressing unit, RPM, and tax department;
- data entry procedure: the address will be entered into the taxpayer
  database provided in Phase 1; the cadastral reference will also be
  entered in order to make it easier to match information in the directories of various departments;
- timetable for covering various zones: the consultant will draw up a
  schedule and scope of work for the project (zones) based on the term
  set for the project.

The consultant will monitor the project weekly and will draft a monthly
activity report that is at least two pages long. All of this work will be
put into a *consolidated, computerized directory* that includes:
- sequential number (DGI) [National Tax Authority];

- sequential number (RPM) ;
- taxpayer identification;
- address of property taxed (city address system); if the taxpayer's address is not the same as the address of the property being taxed (non-occupant owner), both addresses will be listed whenever possible;
- cadastral references of the plot (DGI);
- business activity or sector (business licenses and fees, CFPB and TOM taxes for business premises);
- the amount of each local tax owed by the taxpayer.

(2) *Establishing a statistical comparison between the number of taxpayers on tax rolls or on advance payment lists and the number of addresses contained in the address directory in order to draw conclusions.*

The consultant will use a simple, automated procedure to compare information in the address directory to determine:

- the number of residential occupancy units and the number of taxpayers on the tax rolls for CFPB and TOM taxes,
- the number of business occupancy units and the number of taxpayers on tax rolls for business licenses and fees.

This comparison will take into account any information about the premises contained in the address directory that would enable the consultant to estimate the number of tax-exempt residential properties (rental value less than 1.5 million CFAF, premises less than 10 years old).

3. Implementation, phases, and reports

Implementation

The study's contract manager is ……. The consultant will primarily remain in contact with the IT Department and the addressing unit manager, who will both monitor the project on a regular basis. The contract manager is responsible for maintaining contact with the appropriate departments and for providing access to information. He will provide the consultant with directories obtained from the IT Department as well as a copy of the address directory created under his direction along with the corresponding map.

The addressing unit, RPM, and regional inspectorate in charge of issuing local tax assessment notices shall provide the computer stations needed to perform these services. The municipality has appointed a representative to enter data on the spreadsheet and to perform other data processing tasks outlined in phase 2.

The consultant will present his/her diagnostic report and his/her final report to the municipality, the contract manager, and representatives of the deconcentrated departments involved in the project (taxes and treasury).

Phases
Objectives 3 and 4 will be carried out concurrently over a three-month period following submission of the diagnostic report. For the second task, the consultant will be responsible for monitoring the staff that the municipality, the RPM, and the regional tax department shall assign to this work.

Reports
The consultant shall submit:

- A launch note, one week following receipt of the instructions to the contractor. This note will outline the timetable and expected working methods for performing the services (three copies);
- A diagnostic report, two months following receipt of the instructions to contractor (three copies);
- A monthly activity report throughout the duration of the study (three copies);
- A final report, three months following submission of the diagnostic report; this report will include remarks and comments from the contract manager regarding the diagnostic report as well as comments on activity reports (five copies).

Reports shall be brief, clear, and geared toward quick implementation. They will include all specified annexes.

Consultant profile
The team shall be comprised of:

- a project manager specializing in local finances who has a strong knowledge of the country's local taxation system,
- a socio-economist with a strong background in computers and survey organization. He/she will assist the project manager for the phase 1 analysis work and structuring of the project in phase 2.

Term of services
The project will be carried out over six months, including time for response from the contract manager. The consultant is expected to provide services equivalent to four person-months per city spread out over a five-month period.
Annexes:

- Excerpt of the address directory
- Sample address survey form
- Excerpt of tax rolls.

Annex 2. Toponymy Commission—Burkina Faso

"For human beings living in community, the street is home on a grand scale—not because they find rest there, but because their lives are first and foremost a fabric of communal activities. While it is true that these activities are tempered by rest, the street is still the tie that binds. In Africa, the street is one of the factors that determine who people are and where they live: it runs from home to home. Paths, spaces, and boulevards shape life from afar and leave their mark on movements of thought and activity. As a result, the identity of streets, squares, and monuments defines and reflects the essence of the nation in its sovereignty, its history, and its culture."

— Maître Pacéré Frédéric Titinga
President of the Toponymy Commission
of the City of Ouagadougou (1997).

Outline, criteria, and categories for names

History
(a) Great rulers, tribal leaders, ministers, renowned personalities in Burkinabe tradition and custom; (b) mythical, legendary, and epic figures; (c) men who fought against colonialism; (d) men who fought for independence and the formation of a new nation; (e) men who fought against the slave trade; (f) men who fought against forced labor; (g) men who fought against recruiting soldiers into foreign armies; (h) past military heroes; (i) important dates in history.

Culture, philosophy, and the arts
(a) Famous defenders of traditional values and culture; (b) traditional values and cultural names; (c) great narrators and storytellers; (d) advocates of traditional dwellings, clothing, and cooking; (e) famous writers and media figures; (f) renowned musicians, singers, dancers, artists, painters, and athletes; (g) renowned filmmakers; (h) renowned actors and playwrights; (i) traditional dress; (j) instruments of music, dance, and rhythm, and instruments that preserve tradition; (k) traditional beverages and culinary arts.

Science
(a) Innovators and inventors in various technologies; (b) famous traditional healers, shamans, and medicine men; (c) renowned researchers and inventors and their field of science.

Nation, politics, and government
(a) Great political thinkers; (b) great political leaders; (c) great developers of national buildings; (d) civil servants who died serving the national

cause; (e) historic government buildings; (f) special modern government buildings.

Economics, society, and religion
(a) Well-known religious figures and missionaries; (b) famous union leaders; (c) renowned managers; (d) famous entrepreneurs and economic leaders; (e) defenders of social causes (abandoned children, orphans, people with disabilities, the disenfranchised, the destitute, etc.); (f) organizational, moral, and religious principles and values of traditional and professional institutions; (g) traditional professions and seasonal products; (h) social rites and initiations.

International life
(a) Countries and cities friendly to Burkina Faso; (b) OAU member countries; (c) great African and international organizations; (d) famous foreigners who have influenced world history or Burkinabe history.

Places, traditional sites, environment
(a) Flora and fauna of Burkina Faso; (b) rivers, oxbow lakes, streams, and high hills of Burkina Faso; (c) places, historical and cultural sites in Ouagadougou and Burkina Faso including: administrative districts near Ouagadougou symbolizing resistance to colonialism, traditional ancestral districts, traditional decentralized districts, special traditional districts, locations of the last homes and burial sites of the Mogho-Naba, or rulers, administrative districts symbolizing the protection of distant Ouagadougou and resistance to colonialism, historic districts of Ouagadougou, sacred places and places of traditional rites in Ouagadougou, sacred rivers and water sources in Ouagadougou, local names in Ouagadougou, traditional homes of the Mogho-Naba in Ouagadougou, famous sacred places and sites in Burkina Faso.

Examples of listings in the Commission's compendium
Moro Naba Karfo (1834–1842)
Brother of Naba Sawadogo, son of Naba Roulougou and of Konneyassa. Naba Karfo was a "liberal" ruler. His tomb is in Ouagadougou.

Bibliography: Yamba Tiendrebeogo, "Histoire et coutumes royales des Mossi de Ouagadougou" ["History and royal customs of the Mossi of Ouagadougou"], p. 47-49. 12 Izard. t. 1. P. 172. A a. Dim-Dolobsom, p. 288.

Karamokoba.

Karamoko Sanogo de Lanfiera (the almamy karamokoba). Chief marka de lanfièra, man of letters and great holy man, a national resistance fighter, arrested on November 24, 1896; sentenced to death in a hasty and groundless trial that was the work of the madman Voulet. According to Lieutenant Voulet, he was shot for instigating the Samo revolt.

Bibliography: A. S. Balima: "Légendes et Histoire des peuples du Burkina Faso," ["Legends and History of the People of Burkina Faso,"] 1996, p. 161 181. Me Pacere: Documents et archives sur l'almamy karamokoba [Documents and archives on the almamy karamokoba].

Annex 3. Cameroon: Naming of streets and public squares in cities

The President of the Republic signed the following circular, but no specific actions followed.

(Excerpts from the circular of July 19, 1971)
" . . . the choice of names must comply with two essential criteria:

1. Services rendered
Family and tribal ties or friendships must not form the basis for choosing a name for a street or public square. The name must, as much as possible, reflect the entire municipality's tribute to or honor of a Cameroonian or foreigner who has rendered valuable services, either to the nation as a whole, or to the particular municipality.

The municipality may also choose to honor a global, international, or any other organization of obvious importance either to Cameroon or to the municipality.

I must note that with regard to the use of peoples' names, generally accepted practice gives priority to those who are deceased. The trend of selecting names of living political leaders is not recommended. Nevertheless, given our short national history, services rendered by an individual to a community or to the nation may be recognized during his lifetime. But these are exceptions that must always be fully justified in order to avoid a negative reaction that could call the government's impartiality into question.

2. Historic reminders
It is no less important that the names of streets and public squares in cities remind future generations of certain milestones in our national history. Important historic dates in world history should also be considered appropriate choices.

Procedure
Government representatives of municipal jurisdictions and mayors shall draft proposals for naming public squares and streets in their city, working closely with individuals who are chosen on the basis of their expertise and who may or may not be municipal council members.

The prime ministers of both federal states shall submit proposals for names to be approved by the head of state. The proposals shall include all supporting documentation demonstrating why the name is an appropriate choice. All proposals for names that are approved by the President of the Republic shall be returned to the municipal government representatives and the mayors for adoption by the municipal council . . . . "

—El Hadj A. Ahidjo
President of the Federal Republic (Cameroon)
Yaoundé, July 19, 1971

Annex 4. Tracking and monitoring addressing operations

How can the progress of addressing work be measured, especially when several cities are involved at the same time?

A spreadsheet is a useful measuring tool (see table A.1). The table is gradually completed as follows:

The addressing activities are broken down into six main steps (A through F) that encompass a total of 24 individual tasks. Each task is weighted based on how long it takes to complete that particular task. Thus, the operation launch represents only 1% of the entire operation, while sign installation represents 27%.

Three cities, X, Y, and Z, with populations of 100,000, 200,000, and 300,000, respectively, are represented in the table. The numbers of zones targeted in each city are 8, 12, and 20, respectively. There are two columns, data and results, for each city.

In the data column, the percentage of work completed is entered for tasks 1–7, 13–19, and 22–24. For tasks 8–12 and 20, the number of zones where this work has been completed is indicated. Thus, for city X all of the tasks (1–7, 13–19, and 22–24) were 100% complete. The same is true for the other tasks (8–12 and 20) carried out in the eight zones of the city. On the contrary, in city Z, only the first seven tasks were carried out. Tasks 8 and 9 are relevant for 10 out of the 20 zones, and task 10 is relevant for 15 of the zones.

A simple calculation combining the data and the percentage represented by each task (3rd column) makes it possible to determine the amount of work completed. For example, the work for task 13 was 50% complete in city Y and totals 0.5, or 5% of the entire operation.

In all, the work completed for cities X, Y, and Z is 100%, 38%, and 24%, respectively.

By weighting each result according to the population, we see that the overall addressing operation was only 41% complete.

Table A.1. Tracking implementation progress

Step	Task	%	Tasks	X 100 000 / 8		Y 200 000 / 12		Z 300 000 / 20	
			City / Population / Number of zones	Data	Results	Data	Results	Data	Results
A	1	1%	Operation launch	100%	1.0	100%	1.0	100%	1.0
	2	2%	Awareness, codification	100%	2.0	100%	2.0	100%	2.0
	3	1%	Addressing unit created	100%	1.0	100%	1.0	100%	1.0
	4	1%	Approval by municipality	100%	1.0	100%	1.0	100%	1.0
B	5	4%	Provisional base map	100%	4.0	100%	4.0	100%	4.0
	6	1%	Preparing documents for operation	100%	1.0	100%	1.0	100%	1.0
	7	2%	Pilot operation	100%	2.0	100%	2.0	100%	2.0
	8	10%	Surveys: streets, doorways	8	10.0	6	5.0	10	5.0
	9	10%	Stenciling doorway numbers	8	10.0	6	5.0	10	5.0
C	10	2%	Base map w/key city features	8	2.0	6	1.0	15	1.5
	11	2%	Signage map	8	2.0	6	1.0		-
	12	2%	Survey forms on spreadsheet	8	2.0	3	0.5		-
	13	1%	Street index	100%	1.0	50%	0.5		-
	14	1%	Acceptance of work	100%	1.0		-		-
	15	3%	RFB for sign supply	100%	3.0	100%	3.0		-
D	16	4%	Order from supplier	100%	4.0	100%	4.0		-
	17	3%	Acceptance by addressing unit	100%	3.0	50%	1.5		-
	18	5%	Delivery of signs to municipality	100%	5.0	50%	2.5		-
	19	2%	RFB sign installation	100%	2.0	100%	2.0		-
E	20	27%	Sign installation	8	27.0		-		-
	21	1%	Acceptance of work	100%	1.0		-		-
F	22	5%	Computerized map finalized	100%	5.0		-		-
	23	2%	Index and map printed	100%	2.0		-		-
	24	8%	Directory on addressing software	100%	8.0		-		-
Total		100%	Results		100%		38%	24%	41%

Annex 5. Purchase of supplies and materials for street addressing

Technical specifications for bid documents

Scope of work
This contract covers the supply of addressing materials needed for street signs in the city of ...., including the tools required to install the signs.

Deadlines, terms and conditions for delivery, and documentation
The deadline for delivery is no longer than five (5) months from the date of notice of award to the supplier. The materials covered under this request for bids will be delivered to and officially received at the following address:

Addressing unit ....
Municipality of ......

Therefore, the supplier's price must include all expenses related to making these materials available to the above address. The supplier shall be solely responsible for all shipping and storage at the port of arrival so that the municipality of .... will not experience any difficulties with shipping or storage.

During shipping, the supplier shall notify the municipality and the insurance company, by cable or telex, of all shipping details including: contract number, description of supplies, the ship, number and date of the bill of lading, port of loading, shipping date, port of discharge, etc. The supplier shall forward the following documents to the municipality of ...., and shall send a copy to the insurance company:

(i)   copies of supplier invoices describing the items supplied, quantities, unit price, and total invoice amount;
(ii)   original and three copies of the clean on board negotiable bill of lading, marked "expenses paid," and three copies of the nonnegotiable bill of lading;
(iii)   three copies of packing lists identifying the contents of each package;
(iv)   insurance certificate;
(v)   manufacturer's or supplier's warranty certificate;
(vi)   certificate of inspection issued by the appointed inspection department and factory inspection report from the supplier; and
(vii)   certificate of origin.

The municipality of .... shall receive the above documents at least one week prior to the arrival of the supplies in port, and if such documentation is not received, the supplier shall be liable for all resulting expenses incurred.

Types of materials

The materials include street signs, mountings, and the tools and equipment needed to install the signs. The municipality of …….. shall send to the winning supplier a complete list of street names and street numbers and the number of signs and signposts to be manufactured. The supplier shall not be responsible for installation.

Materials covered in this contract include:

(a) street name signs to be installed on mountings (bidirectional signposts),
(b) street name signs to be installed on building façades or enclosures,
(c) temporary street number signs to be installed on mountings (bidirectional signposts),
(d) street number signs to be installed on building façades or enclosures,
(e) sign mountings: bidirectional signposts,
(f) mounting hardware,
(g) tools and equipment for attaching signs (kits).

Warranty

All materials and equipment supplied under this contract are warranted against any manufacturing defects and against any risk to users under normal conditions of use of the aforementioned supplies. In particular, the materials shall be guaranteed to be rust- and weather-resistant.

The supplier's obligation under this warranty does not include any guarantee against defects caused after the client has accepted delivery and particularly any defects caused by poor maintenance, deterioration caused by poor installation or acts of vandalism, modifications made to the materials without the builder's written consent, or inappropriate repairs made by the municipality of …………. .

The warranty period shall be in effect for two (2) years starting from the date of delivery.

Certificate of completion

Upon delivery, the materials covered under this contract shall be inspected at the following address : ……………. .

A provisional completion of work certificate will be issued following the inspection.

At the end of the warranty period, the supplier will perform an inspection in order to issue a final certificate of completion. Inspections will be made of the quantity, dimensions, type of materials, quality, performance of tools, and compliance with specifications.

Description of materials

Street signs

Signs will be made of enameled steel, will be at least 12/10° thick, and will have been treated with a vitrification process in an oven heated to over 800°. They will not have turned-down edges. They will be predrilled with holes to attach the signs to the mounting. They will measure approximately 250 x 400 mm, which may vary depending on the complexity of the inscription. The letters, in a sans serif typeface, will be white. The sign will have a white border. The sign will be blue; however, for the basic bid, the supplier will indicate the cost of an option for signs with a blue background and another option where, depending on the district, the street signs would be different colors.

The signs will be installed either on enclosures, building façades, or on mountings (bidirectional signposts). The number street signs will have simple inscriptions. The signs with names will have more complex inscriptions. All of the signs will include a reference to the municipality and the district (see figure).

Mountings: bi-directional signposts

These mountings are placed at intersections where it is not possible to attach signs to building façades or enclosures. The bidirectional mounting is designed to hold two (2) street signs (either two name street signs, two number street signs, or one of each).

The poles themselves will have a section with a surface measuring approximately 60 mm x 60 mm. The poles will be three meters long, including about 50 cm for the foundation. The poles will be made of galvanized steel. The top of the pole will be protected (by a metal or plastic end cap), and the bottom will have a device to prevent the pole from swiveling in its concrete pedestal.

Mounting hardware

The supplier will deliver the necessary hardware for mounting the signs to signposts, building façades, or walls. Under normal conditions of use, the system used to mount signs must not damage the sign or its mounting when the sign is installed or removed. The materials for mounting signs on signposts shall be compatible with the materials used to manufacture the signpost.

The supplier shall also provide the hardware needed to mount the signs on the mountings (bidirectional signposts). The quantity of hardware delivered shall exceed the original amount calculated by 10 percent.

Mounting tools
The supplier shall provide six sets of tools (kits) needed to mount signs on bidirectional signposts and on building façades and enclosures. These tools include, but are not limited to, drills with bits, anchors, and special screws for attaching signs to walls, and possibly small generators.

Number of signposts and signs
The supplier shall bid on the three options for quantities indicated as options A, B, and C, in the bid notice and on the price schedule (table A.2); however, the bid will primarily be evaluated based on the quantities in the *basic bid* (option B).

Option(s)
The supplier may choose to present one or more options for mountings and signs, as long as the supplier submits the basic bid requested and provides all descriptions, technical information, and costs of this (these) option(s), for the quantities as indicated in the three options A, B, and C. The supplier may present options for the inscription design proposed in activity 10. He shall attach information clearly outlining the variations in cost compared to the basic bid.

Prototype provided with bid
The supplier shall present, along with his bid, prototypes of signs and the bidirectional signpost for the basic bid. This shall be an 80 cm model, which will include (a) the top of the signpost with two signs, and (b) the bottom of the signpost with an anti-swiveling device.

The quality of materials delivered by the winning supplier shall not be inferior to the quality of the materials presented in the prototype.

Read and approved on….   The supplier
                     (signature and stamp)

Table A.2. Price schedule

Option A Description of supplies	Number of items	Unit price	Total
1. Signs with street name, to be installed on signposts	700		
2. Signs w/street name, installed on building façades or enclosures	2,600		
3. Signs with street number, to be installed on signposts	700		
4. Signs w/street number, installed on building façades or enclosures	3,000		
5. Mountings (bidirectional signposts)	700		
6. Mounting hardware	QSF[1]		
7. Mounting materials and tools (kits)	6		
Total costs of option A (before taxes)			
Basic bid - Option B Description of supplies	Number of items	Unit price	Total
1. Signs with street name, to be installed on signposts	1,000		
2. Signs w/street name, installed on building façades or enclosures	3,000		
3. Signs with street number, to be installed on signposts	1,000		
4. Signs w/street number, installed on building façades or enclosures	4,000		
5. Mountings (bidirectional signposts)	1,000		
6. Mounting hardware	QSF		
7. Mounting materials and tools (kits)	6		
(a) Total cost for basic bid if all signs have blue background (before taxes)			
(b) Total cost (before taxes) for basic bid if signs have different colors in different municipalities (five colors)			
Option C Description of supplies	Number of items	Unit price	Total
1. Signs with street name, to be installed on signposts	1,200		
2. Signs w/street name, installed on building façades or enclosures	3,600		
3. Signs with street number, to be installed on signposts	1,200		
4. Signs w/street number, installed on building façades or enclosures	6,000		
5. Mountings (bidirectional signposts)	1,200		
6. Mounting hardware	QSF		
7. Mounting materials and tools (kits)	6		
Total cost of option C (before taxes)			

1. QSF: quantity sufficient for

Table A.3. Summary of prices

	Option A	Basic bid Option B	Option C
Price of supplies FOB at port of loading			
Unit price CIF port of destination (indicate port) or CIP destination			
Maritime shipping cost			
Cost of shipping from port of entry to final destination			
Insurance costs (ex works to delivery on site) and other delivery costs			

Annex 6. Preparing the address map: aerial photography

Below are a number of technical specifications for the preparation of various documents that are needed to create an address map. These documents include: aerial photos, orthophoto maps, photographic enlargements, and urban sketch maps. In the interest of simplicity, we have assumed that aerial photographs would be used to produce:

- orthophoto maps for cities on the "A" list and
- photographic enlargements and urban sketch maps for cities on the "B" list.

Technical specifications

Under project _____, a series of aerial photographs and orthophoto maps will be produced for _____ (list of "A" cities), and photo enlargements and urban sketch maps will be produced for _____ (list of "B" cities). The administrative entity responsible for the work is _____. The work to be conducted includes:

1. Aerial photography

The work will be performed with an aircraft especially adapted for taking vertical-axis aerial photographs for use in producing standard aerial surveys. If possible, the shot will include GPS coordinates of the center of the photo. The equipment recommended below is for information only and should be considered a minimum standard of quality for equipment to be used.

1. Territories to be covered. See annex: coordinate table.
2. Photographic scale, emulsion. Format 24 x 24 cm, on panchromatic emulsion at an average scale of 1:15,000.
3. Camera. The photos will be taken with a standard-field photogrammetric camera, of type Wild RC 10, Zeiss RMK TOP15 or similar equipment, or a more recent model equipped with GPS.
4. Flight plans, overlap. The client will submit overflight authorization requests to the appropriate authorities once the consultancy services contract comes into effect.

   Flight plans will be prepared by the winning bidder and submitted to the client for approval at least 10 days before flights begin. If, at the end of that time, no objection has been made, the flight plans may be considered approved.

Without exception, aerial photographing passes will be oriented in an east-west direction. If the flight plan consists of only one pass, the operator will take a photograph centered over the city.

Longitudinal photograph overlaps will be 60% ± 5%. Lateral overlap between adjacent passes will be 20% ± 5%.

5. Indication of the optical axis of the camera. The angular deviation of the optical axis must not exceed three degrees from the vertical.
6. Drift. The drift correction error must not exceed four degrees from the flight axis.
7. Exposure, image movement. The exposure time and aircraft speed must be such that image movement does not exceed five micrometers.
8. Development, presentation of photographs. The density of the original negatives must fall between 0.5 and 1.2. They must be numbered consecutively by city, and must include reference information, namely: year, country, number, and average scale. Photos must be cut and delivered in separate plastic envelopes in carefully numbered and labeled boxes.
9. Contact printing. The photographic medium used for contact prints must be of a stable plastic paper of minimum thickness 0.1 mm and of a grade that allows for the best possible contrast. All information on the margins of the negatives must be clearly visible. Prints must be delivered in carefully numbered and labeled boxes.
10. Index map. An index map will be provided on cardboard (1:50,000 if available, or if not available 1:100,000). In addition to the center position for each photo, the index map must include photo mission references, photo scale, date and time the photos were taken, camera number, type, and focal length.

Deliverables and deadline
Six weeks following the signature of the contract with the client, the winning bidder shall provide:

- original negatives,
- three sets of contact prints on paper,
- three sets of index maps of aerial shots.

2. Orthophoto maps

The winning bidder, using photographs taken of "A" cities, shall produce *orthophoto maps* at a scale of 1:5,000 covering an area _____ km² in size (annex). On the basis of the supplier's proposal and after examining the aerial photographs, the client will decide on the exact delineation of the zones for which orthophoto maps will be produced.

1. Original prints of the aerial photographs will be scanned at 28 *microns* on a high performance photogrammetric film scanner. The requested orthophoto maps are required for *final output pixel resolution of 30 cm on the ground*. It will be georeferenced in the UTM coordinate system.
2. All geometric and radiometric rectifications, along with assembling and cutting the scanned photographs into "tiles," shall be performed using accepted photogrammetric practices that incorporate the notions of geodetic control (stereopreparation, aerial triangulation) and the Digital Terrain Model. The software program(s) used for orthorectification will be documented in the tenderer's bid.
3 In addition to aerial photos, data available or acquired during the project will be used including:
   – Data files and locations of stereopreparation and aerial triangulation points;
   – Ground control points;
   – On-board GPS flight path tracking data simultaneously referenced on the ground, observed during new aerial photography;
   – Digital Terrain Model (DTM).

Deliverables and deadline
The winning bidder shall supply:

1. Digital files: on CD-ROM (TIFF format), one copy. To be delivered 12 weeks after receipt of the photographs by the client;
   – Images: orthophoto map in TIFF format as well as in a compressed MrSID, ECW or JPEG 2000 format.
   – Accompanying georeferencing: DXF format, map showing position of photo pairs and their control points, liaison and control coordinates produced from aerial triangulation. These digital files must be compatible for use with software such as MapInfo.
2. Paper documents: to be delivered 16 weeks following receipt of the original photographs by the client. Produced by an imagesetter onto plasticized photo paper at a scale of 1:5,000, jointed plates of 3 x 3 km^2, three copies including a frame, a title, marginal grid ticks for ground coordinates, plate number, and an index map.

3. Photographic enlargements
For the "B" cities, photographic enlargements at 1:5,000 will be made from the aerial photographs.

• *Selection of photos.* After examining the photos, the client will choose those with the best coverage of the urban area, that is, one photo in two in principle depending on overlap. A single photo may be enough for the geographically smaller centers. The client will be responsible for selection based on proposals from the winning bidder. The client will have a maximum of one week after receipt of the photographs. If the client fails to respond within this period, the winning bidder will refer to his/her own proposals.

- *Enlargements.* The photo or photos selected will be blown up, using a photographic enlarger equipped with an orthoscopic lens. The average scale required is 1:5,000.

Deliverables and deadline
Six weeks after the client receives the photographs, the winning bidder will provide:

- two sets of enlargements to 1:5,000 per city on plasticized paper of format A0 or A1;
- a set of enlargements to 1:5,000 per city on reproducible medium to obtain the highest quality prints possible (using an ammonia solution).
- the digital raster for the selected scanned photos (on high resolution scanner) to be delivered for each city on CD-ROM in DXF format and TAB format for MapInfo.

4. Urban sketch maps
For the "B" cities, urban sketch maps[1] at a scale of 1:5,000 will be prepared from aerial photographs.

Methodology. The photos will be used to prepare digital "urban sketch maps." These sketch maps will be to a scale of roughly 1:5,000. They will be produced, for cases (a) and (b) below, on a digital plotting device as "flat models" that allow the plotting details to be viewed stereoscopically. This may be done in three ways, depending on the number of stereopairs to be processed:

- Six pairs or more: the pairs will be keyed to aerial triangulation points calculated using control points identified and measured on maps or on the ground (at least 4 GPS points) and/or from the flight path recording (if this is available);
- Three to five pairs: the pairs may be mounted without specific control points;
- Two pairs: if the city is contained within the single central photo, the sketch may be made by vectoring the scanned photo directly on the screen.

The surface area covered will be the same as the urban zone selected from the enlarged photos.

Features to be shown. The following objects should be identified:

- major hydrographic features;
- major slopes and escarpments;
- the contours of built-up areas, without showing buildings (except in the case of major facilities);
- communication routes, including those around the urban periphery;
- major facilities, with the principal contours of their buildings (airports, stadiums, large municipal buildings, train and bus stations, major marketplaces, and large industrial buildings);
- schematic contours of large forested areas.

These features will be organized into separate information layers, with a legend to be provided by the supplier.

Deliverables and deadline
In 18 weeks following receipt of the photos by the client, the winning bidder will supply, for each city:

- Two prints per city on paper of format A0 or A1, to a scale of 1:5,000;
- One print per city on reproducible material in format A1, to a scale of 1:5000;
- One CD per city of the urban sketch map in DXF format and in TAB format for MapInfo. The urban sketch map of each city will be furnished in a single computer file rather than split into several smaller files.

5. Samples
The supplier's bid must include samples. The electronic files must be compatible with MapInfo and will be examined when the bids are opened. Samples to be supplied include:

1. Negative of a panchromatic shot of the city to a scale of 1:15,000, and a contact print,
2. Enlargement on paper and on reproducible medium to a scale of 1:5,000, of one part of the previous negative (approximately A3 format),
3. High resolution scan of the corresponding photo, on CD in DXF format and TAB format for MapInfo,
4. Urban sketch map corresponding to the previous enlargement delivered on paper and on CD in DXF format and in TAB format for MapInfo.

Annex: Coordinates of city perimeters

Cities are located within rectangles defined by upper-left-hand (X1, Y1) and lower-right-hand (X2,Y2) axes.

	X1	Y1	X2	Y2
City A1				
City A2				
City B1				
City B2				
City B3				

Note

1. The name "urban sketch map" refers to the fact that any representation of individual buildings is limited to very large structures.

Annex 7. Preparing address and signage maps

Terms of reference

Background

The government of ...... has received credit from .... in the amount of ...... to finance the .... project. Part of this program includes street addressing initiatives that are designed to facilitate: (a) the provision of city services (ambulance, fire, taxi, and police); (b) the location of residences, government buildings, utility concessionaires, businesses, manufacturing facilities, and other services; (c) payment collections, particularly by utility concessionaires.

Street addressing includes several tasks:

- *Codification*: working with local authorities to adopt boundaries for address zones and a system for naming and numbering streets and doorways;
- *Mapping and street index*: establishing an address map, a signage map, a street index directory, and list of necessary supplies;
- *Street sign installation*: installing street identification signs at intersections;
- *Surveys and numbering doorways*: placing numbers on doorways of premises, buildings, or utilities;
- *Data recording*: collecting survey data in an ad hoc software program.

These terms of reference cover the implementation of the first street addressing tasks in the city of . . . . The municipality is the contract manager for the work, and it has established an addressing unit that is in charge of monitoring the work and conducting a media campaign on the operation. However, since the addressing unit's resources are considered insufficient, the municipality has decided to engage a consultant to help implement the project's main tasks. Therefore, the consultant will work closely with the addressing unit throughout the project.

Consultant responsibilities

The consultant's responsibilities will be carried out in two phases during which the consultant will collaborate with the addressing unit as follows:

- The first phase includes performance of tasks A and B: codification, mapping, and creation of a street index.
- The second phase, which includes the performance of tasks C and D, is conditional and may be covered under another consultancy contract.

Phase 1. Task A: Codification
The consultant will collaborate with the addressing unit to:

- Establish address zone boundaries;
- Define a system for street identification and doorway numbering.

Phase 1. Task B: Mapping, street index, list of supplies
The consultant will review:

- The zones to be assigned addresses in order to verify, correct, and complete the street layout found on the map provided by the municipality;
- All intersections in order to determine those intersections where signs can be affixed to building façades and those intersections where bidirectional signposts need to be installed.

The consultant will prepare an *address map* to a scale of 1:10,000 in computerized file format. This map will include the following:

- Address zone boundaries;
- Streets including their numbering and/or their name as well as an indication of where the streets begin and end;
- Identification of main facilities (such as main government buildings, high schools, elementary schools, hospitals, health centers, important religious buildings, markets, large groups of buildings, train and bus stations, military camps, stadiums, racetracks, large factories and warehouses);
- Corresponding toponymy.

The consultant will prepare a *signage map* to a scale of 1:5,000 that shows the location of street signs to be placed on building façades, enclosures, or signposts.

The consultant will prepare a *street index* on a spreadsheet based on the attached model.

The consultant will prepare the *supply list* for ordering supplies (street signs and signposts). This list will be prepared based on three elements:

- The municipality's budget earmarked for this order;
- The unit price of supplies, document to be provided by municipality;
- Signage density: the density should be greater in the city center than on the outskirts. All streets must have at least one street sign. The use of signposts must be limited to major intersections that do not have walls or enclosures that can accommodate signs.

Phase 2. Task C: Surveys and numbering of doorways
The consultant will create survey and numbering teams charged with:

- Marking doorways by stenciling numbers on building façades;
- Distributing to occupants the information sheet prepared by the municipality about the addressing operation,
- Gathering survey data based on the attached model.

Phase 2. Task D: Creating a database
The consultant will transfer data to a spreadsheet and will organize the data based on the attached model.

Consultant's team
For phase 1, the team will include: a *project coordinator* and a senior technician who will both have experience with mapping software.

Project coordinator. Profile: urban planner, surveyor (baccalaureate diploma + 4 years). The *project coordinator* is responsible for:

- Overall coordination of work,
- Update and creation of maps,
- Generation of various reports requested.

Senior technician. Profile: urban planner, surveyor, land developer, civil engineer. The technician assists the *project coordinator* in his various duties and is responsible for supervising, updating, and creating address and signage maps.

For informational purposes, the *project coordinator* could organize each survey and numbering team for phase 2 (conditional) as follows: a team leader, two survey takers, a field surveyor, two painters, and two laborers.

Documents submitted by consultant
The consultant shall submit to the municipality:

Phase 1

(a) A codification report, 15 days after start of study;
(b) Address map and street index (draft version), 45 days after start of study;
(c) A signage map and list of supplies (draft version), 80 days after start of study;
(d) End-of-work report and final version of all documents submitted, 10 days after receipt of comments from municipality.

When each report is submitted, the consultant will present the results of his work to municipality representatives. The municipality will provide comments to the consultant no later than eight days following receipt of documents (a) and (b).

Phase 2

(a) An implementation schedule including the composition of survey teams and their itinerary: before start of surveys;
(b) Survey forms grouped by neighborhood and by street: at end of project;
(c) Survey forms presented in a list on a spreadsheet: at end of project;
(d) An end-of-project report.

Term of work
The term of services is estimated at ..... months (*exact time period will depend on the number of surveys to be performed*).

Documents and materials provided to consultant
The municipality will provide the consultant with the following documents:

- City map on paper and on electronic medium,
- Division into neighborhoods,
- List of neighborhoods to be assigned addresses,
- Models of the address map, signage map, and street index,
- An estimated budget for supply of street signs and signposts; unit prices of supplies.

Annex 8. Printing the address map and street index

Technical specifications

The following clauses define the technical specifications for printing the address map and street index for the city of ……

Documents to be produced
The following documents shall be produced: (a) address map and street index for distribution, (b) address map for posting.

City address maps
Print format 68 x 98 cm. Four-color, one-sided printing. Medium: map paper 115 gr/m². Finishing: fanfolded in 17 x 24.5 cm format. Number of copies: 2,000.

Street index
Print format 17 x 24.5 cm closed. Cover: coated paper 300 gr/m² laminated. Inside: dull-coated paper 115 gr/m². Four-color, two-sided printing. Binding: stitched folios, square back. Number of pages: 50. Number of copies: 2,000.

Address map for posting
Print format 140 x 180 cm. Four-color printing with UV ink on laminated photographic paper. Number of copies: 10.

Documents provided by municipality
The municipality shall provide:

- To the bidder: the entire request for bid file with CD-ROM including a map to be used to produce a sample. This map will be submitted with the proposal in order to determine the bidder's ability to produce this type of document.
- To the winning bidder: electronic files containing address maps and street indexes.

Supplier tasks (winning bidder)

- Verify quality of files provided by municipality;
- Provide a Cromalin proof of address map;
- Provide a model of street index;
- Submit proof and model for "OK for printing" to be signed by municipality;

- Deliver products to following address:
  ....

Time frame

- Period between date files are supplied along with notification of start of work and date of submission of proof and model for OK for printing: 1.5 months.
- Period between date of OK for printing from supplier and date of delivery of products to municipality: 2.5 months.

Supplier qualifications
The supplier's experience will be evaluated based on the following products and references:

- Five samples of maps produced by the supplier;
- One proof in format A3 of the map on CD-ROM attached to the request for bid file;
- Minimum required equipment: minimum 600 DPI plotter; imagesetter of format 70 x 100 cm; color proofing machine (Cromalin or similar); four-color printer, format 70 x 100 cm; folding machine; book sewing machine; laminating machine; square-stuck back binding machine;
- Computer equipment: ability to exchange FTP data; image and map processing equipment; illustration software;
- Human resources: at least two experienced computer graphics designers (attach CVs).

Annex 9. Installing addressing materials

Technical specifications

Background

The government of …….. has received credit from ….. in the amount of … to finance the ……... project. Part of this program includes street addressing operations. The following specifications cover installation of addressing materials in the city of ……….

Purpose of contract

This contract covers the installation of addressing materials in the city of ……. The work to be conducted includes:

• The installation of street signs on building façades or enclosures;
• The installation of signposts at the corner of certain streets;
• The installation of doorway signs on the façades of identified buildings.

Types of materials to be installed

Street and doorway signs shall be made of enameled steel sheet metal about 12/10 thick. Street signs to be affixed to walls or signposts shall be 450 mm long by 250 mm wide. Doorway signs will measure 150 mm by 100 mm.

The signposts are square and measure three meters long. They have a 60 mm square section. The bottom of each pole has a device to prevent the pole from swiveling in its concrete pedestal.

The addressing materials that will be supplied to the contractor also include the materials needed to affix the signs to their mountings.

Delivery of addressing materials

Addressing materials are stored at the following address:

……………………

The municipality, represented by the addressing unit, will deliver the addressing materials to the contractor responsible for installing the materials. A statement drawn up between the addressing unit and the contractor will list the materials. After this list has been drawn up, the contractor can in no way dispute the quantities in the statement.

The contractor handling the installation will be responsible for ensuring the safe storage of the addressing materials in adequate storage facilities furnished or rented by the contractor specifically for these materials such that the facilities guarantee protection against any deterioration. The contractor shall protect the materials from theft, specifically by providing 24-hour security. The contractor will be fully liable for all materials delivered to it.

Documents provided to bidders are as follows:

- City address map (1:10,000): including, among other details, the names and numbering to be used for streets;
- Signage map (1:5,000): showing the location of various signs to be installed on building façades or on signposts;
- List of number signs for doorways and streets;
- These special technical specifications.

Installation work

Before work begins, the contractor shall provide the municipality with an implementation schedule by zone. This schedule will include details about the composition of the installation team, its itinerary, and equipment to be used. The contractor may take this opportunity to make suggestions for improvements to the work of installing addressing materials.

The municipality shall furnish mounting hardware (assembly jigs, screws, nuts, and bolts delivered by the supplier with the rest of the addressing materials [signs and signposts]) to the contractor. To complete the installation work, the contractor shall have available tools (drills, screwdrivers, wrench sets, and small masonry materials) as well as the logistics required to operate the tools (batteries, small generators, and double-sided ladders) and to transport the installation teams throughout the area (vehicles).

Installation of signs on walls will be performed as follows:

- Signs will be placed on the walls of buildings or of permanent façades preferably 2.5 m above the ground and at least 30 cm from the corner of the wall in accordance with the indications on the signage map.
- The doorway signs will preferably be placed above doors and on permanent mountings. If this is not possible, they will be placed to the right or left of the doorway, 2 m above the ground, and on the side opposite from the hinge side, so that the signs are not obscured in any way.

Bidirectional signposts will be installed and street signs affixed as follows:

- The signposts will be placed in the ground according to indications on the signage map. They shall not impede pedestrian or car traffic.
- The signposts shall have a base made of shuttered concrete with a density of 350 kg/m^3, with a 40 cm x 40 cm cross section. The base shall be about 60 cm high, including 10 cm above the natural ground and at least

50 cm buried. The bottoms of the holes for the bases shall be cleared of all debris, organic materials, and any other substances that could interfere with the quality of the work. In addition, the contractor shall be required to show the source of the materials by means of invoices or any other documents signed by suppliers.

Addressing materials installation teams

The contractor shall be required to take all necessary measures to provide a sufficient number of installation teams to complete all work within the contractually required deadline. The contractor is also responsible for assigning at least one senior technician (civil engineer, urban planner, or topographer) to remain on the job site at all times.

Time frame

The time frame for completion of work is set at ...... from the date of signature of this contract.

Guarantee

The contractor shall be solely liable for all risks associated with installation and storage of the materials until acceptance of work. The guarantee period shall be two (2) years starting from the acceptance date.

Quantities

The quantities of addressing materials to be installed are as follows:

- Street signs.   ....
- Signposts.   ....
- Doorway signs.   ....

Cost of services

The contractor is assumed to have full knowledge of the project's limitations and all local conditions that may affect the performance of the work, including but not limited to:

- Travel conditions and access to worksites;
- Difficulties of any kind related to storage, supply, and installation.

The prices proposed must include all charges required for the performance of all work, including: labor costs, travel costs, insurance costs, costs of supplying materials, equipment, and tools, costs incurred due to damages caused to a third party, costs related to poor handling of mountings, street sign maintenance costs during the guarantee period, costs related to limitations and unexpected and unforeseen occurrences.

Generally speaking, all constraints and limitations that the contractor experiences in the course of successfully performing the work are covered under this contract, whether or not they are specifically listed herein. The contractor is assumed to have full knowledge of all such circumstances, having personally completed a field assessment before presenting his bid.

Inspection and monitoring
The municipality or its authorized agent reserves the right to perform field inspections during the work. The contractor shall take all necessary measures to ensure that these inspections are carried out under the most favorable conditions. If inspections reveal mistakes made in the work, the contractor will be responsible for correcting these mistakes to the satisfaction of the municipality or its agent.

Provisional and final certificate of completion
The date for provisional acceptance of work is set for ...... [date]. Provisional and final acceptance will be made in the presence of the contractor and the manager of the addressing unit representing the municipality. A statement of provisional acceptance will be drawn up at the end of the work for each lot. Final acceptance shall take place two years following provisional acceptance and will be announced under the same conditions as for provisional acceptance. Contract-related inspections will specifically cover: quantity of addressing materials installed, quality of installation, and compliance of installation.

Read and accepted,   The contractor

Glossary

(Addr.): Terminology used specifically for street addressing; (Fr.): Terminology used in France

Address directory	List of all buildings and urban fixtures surveyed during street addressing surveys including information such as: type of building, number of households per building, level of services, condition of facilities, cadastral references, water and electric meter numbers. *(Addr.)*
Address map	A map that specifically indicates street names and numbers, the beginning and end of each street, and the main facilities. This map is accompanied by a street index.
Arc	Ordered series of vertices (x, y coordinates) in Arc/Info. Points at the beginning and end of an arc are called "nodes." Arcs make up line features, "lines," and contours of area features, "polygons."
Arterial system	System of interconnecting lines that represent public roadways (street system).
Assessment	Method of calculating taxes by applying a particular rate to the taxable base.
Assets	All of the property held by an individual or legal entity.
Attribute	Characteristic of a map feature. Street attributes may include its name, length, width, etc.
Base map	Map used for positioning elements (locations and boundaries) on a new map.
BDU	Urban data bank. Related files that are organized for efficient retrieval of urban data.
Block plan	A graphic document showing developed land or land to be developed, at a scale of 1:100 to 1:1,000; it includes the perimeter dimensions, the access road(s), and the location of any existing buildings.

Boundary survey	Marking out the boundaries between two adjoining private properties.
Cadastral conservation	The general process of keeping documentation updated to reflect any changes in the status of property and ownership.
Cadastral excerpt	Document to be produced in support of any registered deed of instrument filed with the Mortgage Registry for publication in the real property directory. Issued from the master cadastre, it includes the owner's name, cadastral references of the plots for which there is a change of ownership, and the plot contents.
Cadastral map	A graphic representation drawn to scale showing all of the municipal territory with complete details about its division into smaller properties.
Cadastral modification	Method of cadastral map renewal: either by simply "updating" the Napoleonic map or by a "renewal" consisting of an entirely new plot survey based on cadastral triangulation.
Cadastral reference	Number assigned to each plot in a municipal territory in order to positively identify the plot. For any given municipality, cadastral references of a plot are comprised of the letter(s) indicating the section in which the plot is located followed by the plot number (Ex.: A 212, AB 32, etc.).
Cadastral reform	Method of renewing the cadastre introduced in France in 1955 that gave rise to an entirely new plot survey accompanied by mandatory delimitation between public and private property headed by a property delimitation commission. *(Fr.)*
Cadastral renewal	Undertaken in France (1930) to replace the Napoleonic cadastre with new, updated cadastral documentation designed to be kept continually up-to-date. *(Fr.)*
Cadastral revenue	Revenue assigned to each plot, tax subdivision, or local subdivision, to compute the amount of tax potentially generated from local direct taxation (property taxes on undeveloped and developed properties and, partially, occupancy tax).
Cadastral revision	Launched in France (1974) for cadastral renewal in order to improve the quality of the cadastral map when it became impossible to correctly identify and physically locate buildings. The

	revision was performed using the cadastral reform procedure. *(Fr.)*
Cadastre	A comprehensive and ongoing inventory that describes and evaluates landholdings (plots of land or built structures). "Civil status of landholding." Another definition: "general inventory of built structures and undeveloped land in a municipal territory, with an individual listing of their physical composition, using a planimetric plot representation, their economic use (return), and their ownership, to provide the government with a sufficiently precise estimate to equitably divide taxes on the landholding." This inventory is most often found in the form of graphic documentation (cadastral maps) and literal documentation (registers and files).
Civic addressing	Matching a telephone number with an address in an "Emergency Response System," so that fire, ambulance, and police services can quickly respond to a request. *(Canada).*
Codification	The process of identifying streets by a name or number and assigning a number to doorways. *(Addr.)*
Compulsory acquisition	Procedure in which a public body requires that an individual transfer all or part of privately owned property for public use in exchange for financial consideration.
Coordinates	Numbers associated with points on a map.
Designation	Specific term, common name, and not a toponym, printed on a map that designates a geographic object by its properties: Examples: cemetery, water tower, etc.
Digitizing	Process that involves encoding the geometric description of geographic objects (points, lines, polygons, etc.) in digital form (x, y coordinates).
DTM	Digital Terrain Model. A digital 3-D representation of a geographic area. It may include spot elevations, contour lines, facets, or, in raster mode, cells.
Easement	Encumbrance imposed upon property for the use or benefit of another property belonging to another owner. *Public easement*: right of enjoyment

	is vested in the public rather than the individuals who are owners of the property subject to an encumbrance. *Private easement:* established by law, created on a property known as the servient property, for the use and enjoyment of another property, the dominant property. For example: joint ownership, views, right of way, etc.
FANTOIR	*Fichier Annuaire Topographique Initialisé Réduit (Fr.)* Computerized directory of streets and placenames in France.
Field surveyor	In street addressing, the person who measures distances to assign numbers. *(Addr.)*
Frontage	The boundary between private property and a recognized, classified public street. The boundary is determined unilaterally by the administrative authority that establishes boundaries between public streets and private property.
Frontage map	A map that determines, after a public survey, the boundary between the public roadway and private property. *(Addr.)*
Geocodification	Assigning identifiers to geographic objects. *(Addr.)*
Geocoding	Positioning on a map using x, y coordinates. *(Addr.) Geocoding by postal address*: process that assigns geographic coordinates (x, y) to postal addresses to represent them as points on a map. Geocoding by postal address requires a street map. *(Addr.)*
Geodetic network	All points physically linked to the Earth's crust. The position of these points is defined by estimated coordinates and their variations.
Geographic coordinates	Measurement of a position on the Earth's surface expressed in degrees of latitude and longitude.
Geomatics	All of the techniques used to gather, store, process, and disseminate geographic information. *(Addr.)*
Georeferenced data	Form of computerized cartography that matches data to geographical positions and locates addresses on a map using point features.
Georeferencing	Process that establishes a (mathematical) relationship between paper coordinates (example: centimeters or millimeters) on a planar

	map and actual (geographic) coordinates. The coordinates of a certain number of points (registration points or ticks) must be known in both systems for georeferencing.
Georoute	Database (National Geographic Institute *Fr.*) that describes the street network of population clusters of more than 10,000 inhabitants.
GIS	Geographic Information System. An organized system that combines hardware, software, and the geographic data needed to enter, store, update, process, analyze, and display all sorts of georeferenced information.
GPS	"Global Positioning System": A global satellite positioning system that locates and calculates, using Lambert coordinates, datum points on a map with the help of satellites that orbit the earth. Initially designed by the United States for military purposes, it is now being used for civil applications as well, particularly for geodetics.
Index map	Schematic diagram of the municipal territory, generally at scale of 1:10,000 or 1:20,000, on which various plot sheets and the main topographic details are represented.
Land delimitation	Recognizing and defining the property boundaries of real estate, officially recorded in a "boundary survey."
Land register	All of the written and graphical documentation that provides a precise and complete definition of real property and rights in rem associated with the property.
Land use plan	Document that regulates the use of land according to master plans or that is established according to national urban planning regulations.
Literal information	Information contained in the cadastre's literal documentation (such as owners' names, contents of plots, type of crop, cadastral revenue, description of premises, etc.).
Local placename	Group of plots in the municipal territory, which local citizens call by a particular name. *(Addr.)*
MAJIC	"Cadastral Information Updating System." A computer system that automatically processes and edits literal data contained in magnetic real estate files. *(Fr.)*

Master cadastre	A summary register that lists each owner's property and its assessment.
Media campaign	General publicity campaign regarding a street addressing project that presents the changes and benefits of the operation.
Number assignment	Assigning a number, a classification, to something. *(Addr.)*
Numbering system	System for assigning a sequential number or classification to something; classification order. *Metric numbering system* (street addressing): assigning a number based on the building's distance from the beginning of the street. *(Addr.)*
Odometer	Device used to measure distances, generally comprising a wheel and a counter. Used in street addressing for metric numbering of buildings. *(Addr.)*
Odonym	The proper name of a traffic route feature: way, route, street, etc.
Oronym	Name applied to a feature of topographic elevation such as a mountain, hill, or ravine.
Pilot operation	With regard to street addressing: trial run before the project begins, to test the project's organization, the know-how of surveyors, and the method for installing signs. Space is limited to a few streets used to test the signs and codification system chosen. *(Addr.)*
Plat	Representation of plots that takes into account property boundaries, rights, and easements of the properties after a survey and delineation performed on the land by a certified surveyor in the presence of all parties.
Plat report	A list containing the property description and owner names for a group of plots. Prepared when a project requires a public interest statement (acquisition, frontage map, etc.).
Plot number	A number assigned to a plot within a section, and, when listed with the name of the section, constitutes the cadastral reference for that plot.
Plot sheet	Sub-part of the Section.
Point zero	Point marking the beginning of a street. Numbering of buildings begins at this point.
Property	Piece of land. Land on which a building is built.

Property appraisal	Value of a property according to various methods such as market value, rental value, assessed value, contribution value, building value for a built-up structure, productive value for a rural property.
Publication of rights	All of the rules, techniques, and methods of implementation that ensure the collection, preservation, and issuance of legal information about property for general legal purposes.
Real property	Having to do with real estate.
Real property directory	General documentation, which includes, in the form of verbatim excerpts, formalities subject to the "publication of rights" system: deed registrations and court decisions regarding real property rights.
Real property report	A certified surveyor, at the request of one of the parties or of a court, is responsible for performing a technical evaluation of both built structures and undeveloped land, and to disclose the results in a report. These reports may be generated for estimates, valuations, division of property, or compulsory purchases.
REPLIC	Inventory of Infracommunal Location: address-block table *(Fr.)*
RFU	Urban Land Register (Benin): real estate information system with multiple uses, based on plot cartography, an address system, and an urban database.
RGE	Large-scale referential system: a coherent collection of large-scale objective information describing the territory (with at least metric accuracy). *(Fr.)*
RIVOLI	"Computerized Directory of Streets and Placenames." A computerized directory of streets (in France) that codifies, by municipality, streets, local placenames, and groups of buildings. It is composed of files that include the code number and name of the street, placename, or group of buildings; a list in ascending order of street codes. *(Addr.) (Fr.)*
Section	Portion of the municipal territory including a complete accounting of local placenames the

	perimeter of which, when possible, is made up of natural or sufficiently permanent boundaries.
Sign installation	Installing street sign panels and plates at intersections. *(Addr.)*
Signage map	A map that shows where street sign panels and plates should be placed (on posts or on building façades). *(Addr.)*
Stencil	A thin sheet of cardboard, plastic, or metal that makes it easy to paint cut-out shapes. *(Addr.)*
Stenciling	In street addressing, this method is used to paint street numbers or names with a stencil. *(Addr.)*
Street Addressing	*Within the context of this document*: A system used to locate a building or plot, using the street name and a doorway number. Involves sign installation, numbering building doorways, mapping, and recording these data. *(Addr.)*
	(Internet). Domain name system: A database and server system that ensures that domain and site names used by Internet users correspond to digital addresses used by computers.
	(Information systems - spreadsheets). "Relative" addressing: the cell address changes when a formula is copied. "Absolute" addressing: the address remains the same when a calculation refers to a specific cell.
Street index	A table that lists streets in alphabetical order or by neighborhood so that they can be located on a map using an alphanumeric grid. *(Addr.)*
Street sign panel	A sign that designates a street and is placed at intersections during a street addressing project. It is distinguished from a street sign plate by its turned-down edges that make it look like a small box. *(Addr.)*
Street sign plate	A sign that designates a street and is placed at intersections during a street addressing project. It is distinguished from a street sign panel, which has a more elaborate design (turned-down edges). *(Addr.)*
Subdivision	Division of real property in order to put buildings on the property. Subdivision more than doubles (or more than quadruples, in the case of partition of an estate) the number of plots created from said property.

Tax base	All of the rules and transactions that help determine the items (profits, sales volume) subject to taxation.
Tax roll	List of taxpayers indicating amount of taxes they owe.
Taxpayer	Person who pays taxes.
Topographic map	A graphic representation of natural and man-made features indicating their relative position and altitude.
Topographic plat	Representation, using cadastral data, of the plot boundaries; generally accompanies a topographic plan.
Topometer	See "odometer. *(Addr.)*
Toponymy	Science that studies the formation and evolution of place names or toponyms. All of the names of places in a country or region, on a map or a list.
Voluntary boundary survey	Customary process of a boundary survey, but if one of the parties refuses or does not agree with the survey, the other party may resort to a "court-mandated" boundary survey. The boundary between private and public property is not established by a boundary survey. Rather, the government establishes a delimitation known as frontage.

Bibliography

ADC The Map People, Metro Washington, DC. Street system of the District of Columbia (p. 32).

Alexandre-Debray, J. 1963. *Questions…à M. le Préfet de la Seine sur les moyens d'améliorer les systèmes traditionnels de signalisation de la voirie… (abaisser les plaques de numéros, indiquer le sens montant et descendant des séries, développer les signalisations lumineuses.*(p. 261). *Bull. municipal de Paris.*

Almanach parisien. 1827. *Liste générale des habitants de Paris, classés par rues et par numéros des maisons. Ed. Marais-du-Temple*, 14.

Association canadienne des sciences géodésiques. 1985. La rénovation cadastrale et la gestion foncière au Québec. PUF, Collection Que sais-je ?, No 3174.

Balima, A. S. 1996. *Légendes et Histoire des peuples du Burkina Faso.*

Bellan, L. 1922. *Proposition relative au numérotage des maisons dans le Ville de Paris. Impr. Municipale.*

Bertrand M. 1998. "*Ville en traverse, mobilité populaire, repérage urbain (Bamako, Mali)*" in Parole, n°5-6, p.81-110.

Billot, P. and Pinchon, C. 2001. *Adressage et géocodification à Paris.* APUR Note.

Biver, M.L. 1963. *Le Paris de Napoléon : aperçu du système de numérotation de Frochot (1800 1804) et du système finalement adopté en 1805.* (p. 53). *Plon.*

Boissin. 1961. *La signalisation lumineuse des noms des rues et des numéros d'immeubles à Paris. Techniques et sciences municipals.*

Bourson, F. 1878. *Le numérotage des maisons de Paris au Moyen Age. Bull. de la Sté de l'histoire de Paris.*

Bouvier J.C., and Guillon, J.M. (dir.) (2001) *La toponymie urbaine : significations et enjeux, actes du colloque tenu à Aix-en-Provence.* December, 1998.

Brandenberger, A.J. 1976. "Status of world mapping" World Cartography, Volume XIV, Part One. ST/ESA/SER.L/14. New York: United Nations, pp. 3-71.

Brandenberger, A.J. and Ghosh, S.K. 1983. "World topographic mapping, 1980; Analysis of the status of world topographic mapping; World cadastral surveying and mapping, 1980; Annexes." World Cartography, Volume XVII, Part one. ST/ESA/SER.L/17. New York: United Nations, pp. 1-33 and 45-65.

⸻. 1990. "Status of world topographic and cadastral mapping." World Cartography, Volume XX, Chapter I. ST/TCD/14. New York: United Nations, pp. 1-116.

Brongniart, A. *Traité des arts céramiques (renseignements sur la réalisation des plaques de numéros de 1847)*.

Calvet, L.J. 1994. *Les voix de la ville. Introduction à la sociolinguistique urbaine.* Paris, Payot.

Canut C., and Dumestre G. 1993. *"Le relevé des noms de lieux-dits, problèmes et méthodes,"* Revue Internationale d'Onomastique, Volume VI.

Champion, E. 1910. *Un projet de Choderlos de Laclos sur la numérotation des rues de Paris.*

Cherioux, A. 1930. *Proposition relative aux plaques indicatrices des noms de rues et aux numéros des immeubles. (Paris impr. municipale).*

Choderlos de Laclos, P.A.F. 1787. *Projet de numérotage des rues et des maisons de Paris. Journal de Paris* June 17.

Chomentowki, V. 1987. *"Financer les équipements communaux." Editions du Moniteur.* Paris.

⸻. 1994. *"L'analyse financière des collectivités locales françaises." Etudes techniques-Juris-Classeurs.* Paris.

Comby, J. 1995. Russia, urban development and emerging property markets. Cadastre versus ownership. ADEF.

⸻. *Quel cadastre pour quoi faire ? l'exemple du Gabon. Etude.*

Dale, P. 1976. Cadastral Surveys within the Commonwealth. HMSO, London.

Dale, P., and McLaughlin, J. 1988. Land Information Management. Oxford : Oxford University Press.

Defrance, Mareuse, E and Gosselin-Lenotre. 1899. *Communication au sujet du numérotage des maisons.*

Départ, Suisse Justice et Police/mensurations cadastrales. 1987. *L'avenir de notre sol. Une contribution à l'amélioration de l'information sur le sol et de l'utilisation du sol.*

Derycke, P. H. 1983. *"Les enjeux de la fiscalité foncière."* ADEF. Paris: Economica.

Dia, M. 1996. "Africa's Management in the 1990s and Beyond: Reconciling Indigenous and Transplanted Institutions." Washington, DC: World Bank.

Durussel, R. 1980. *Constitution du cadastre numérique à l'aide des mensurations existantes.* Lausanne: Imprivite SA.

E.M. 1875. *Le Numérotage. en rouge et en noir des maisons de Paris, d'après le décret du 4 février 1805. Gazette des architectes et du bâtiment.*

Fanet, V. 1907. *Le Numérotage des maisons à Paris avant et pendant la revolution. Le Mois littéraire*, no. 107 (p. 524), November.

Farvacque, C. 1983. *Crest en Dauphiné 1650-1789. La ville et son évolution. Imp. Le Crestois.*

Farvacque-Vitkovic, C., and McAuslan, P. 1993. *Politiques foncières des villes en développement. Etudes foncières.* Paris: ADEF.

Farvacque-Vitkovic, C., and Godin L. 1997. The future of African cities. Challenges and priorities of urban development. Washington, DC: World Bank.

Feder, G. 1987. Land Registration and Titling from an Economist's Perspective: A Case Study in Rural Thailand.

FIG. 1995. The FIG Statement on the Cadastre. (Public.11 1995 of the International Federation of Surveyors on the place and role of the surveyor around the world).

———. 1998. Kaufmann Commission, J, Steudler, D. (The cadastre in 2014).

———. 1999. The Bathurst Declaration on Land Administration for substantial Development.

FIG, UN, et al . 1996. The Bogor Declaration. Land Information Center of New South Wales, Australia.

Fleuriau de Bellemare. 1821. *Projet adressé au Roi ... pour l'entreprise du balayage et du nettoyage des rues de Paris... Indication des rues et des numéros des maisons : pour remédier à la mauvaise visibilité des numéros pendant la nuit, la Société propose d'inscrire, devant chaque réverbère, le nom de la rue et le numéro de la maison.* (p. 16. chap. XI). *Impr. d'Everat.*

Franklin, A. 1873. *Estat, noms et nombre de toutes les rues de Paris en 1636 et nombre de toutes les rues de Paris en 1636,* L. Willein.

Ganay, S. (de). 1948. *"Toponymie et anthroponymie de l'Afrique Noire,"* in *Onomastica* , n°2.

Garros. 1795. *Lettre écrite aux administrateurs du Bureau central du canton de Paris (sur la manière de numéroter les maisons). Journal de Paris* 16 thermidor [T.N.: month of the French Republican calendar] year VII.

Godin, L. 1987. "Preparation of land development projects in urban areas." World Bank technical paper. No. 66 F.

Godin, L., Sinet, A., and Bouchaud, C., Groupe Huit. 1995. *"Préparer un projet municipal."* Economic Development Institute. Washington, DC: World Bank.

Hautecœur, L. *Histoire de l'architecture classique en France..., Numérotage royal–Numérotages sectionnaire et impérial.* (Volumes IV and V).

Hegg, L. 1949. *Le cadastre vaudois. Editions ERL–E.* Ruckstuhl SA, Lausanne.

Henard, R. *La rue St. Honoré. Numérotage de 1726, numérotage royal officieux de la rue à la veille de la révolution.* (XXIV. p. 417).

Henrion, Ch. *Encore un tableau de Paris : Numéros des rues (sur l'incohérence du système sectionnaire).*

Henssen, J., 1990. Cadastre, Indispensable for Development. Enschede: International Institute for Aerospace Survey and Earth Sciences (ITC).

Henssen, J. and Williamson, I. P. 1990. *Registro Territorial, Catastro y Su Interacción una Perspectiva Mundial. Topografia y Cartografia,* Vol VII, No. 40.

Hirschowitz, M. 1936. *Proposition tendant à doter les immeubles parisiens d'un dispositif pour indiquer la rue et le numéro de chaque maison,* Paris, Impr. municipale.

Huard, Cdt A. *Numérotage des rues de Paris,* in the *Fureteur médical.*

Hurtaux, P.T.N., and Magny, P. 1779. *Dictionnaire historique de la ville de Paris. Note sur les plaques d'inscription des noms des rues, posées en 1728.* (p. 259. Volume IV). Moutard.

Husson, A. 1851. *Traité de la législation des travaux publics et de la voirie en France, renouvellement du numérotage de 1847-1853.* (p. 883).

Huvé, J.J. 1798. *Numérotage des rues de Paris, Journal des bâtiments civils, des monuments et des arts,* 9 nivôse year X, (p. 37) : *placer les chiffres indicatifs à distance égale, comme de dix en dix mètres... [ce qui] donnerait en même temps la longueur des rues" ; à rapprocher du "système métrique" du citoyen Leblond.* Official Gazette of the French Republic.

——. *Décret de 9 juin 1938 portant "réglementation des droits et obligations de l'administration municipale et des propriétaires riverains des rues de Paris en ce qui concerne l'indication des noms de rues et le numérotage des maisons."*

——. 1827-1828. *Almanach parisien ou liste générale des habitants de Paris, classés par rues et par numéros de maisons, contenant plus de 55 000 adresses.*

——. 1768. *Ordonnance du Roi pour régler le service dans les places et dans les quartiers... numérotation des maisons "dans toutes les villes… bourgs et villages sujets au logement des troupes"* (art. 3 Title V).

——. *1938 Décret portant "réglementation des droits et obligations de l'administration municipale et des propriétaires riverains des rues de Paris en ce qui concerne l'indication des noms de rues et le numérotage des maisons."*

Kessides, C. 1993. The Contributions of Infrastructure to Economic Development: A Review of Experience and Policy Implications. World Bank Discussion Paper 213. Washington, DC: World Bank.

Kreenfelt de Storcks, M. 1899. *Numérotage des rues de Paris, 7 avril 1791 (mémoire contre le numérotage des sections)* in L. Lazard, *Inventaire sommaire.*

Kriegel, O., and Herzfeld, G. 1993. *Katasterlkunde in Einseldarstellungen. Loseblattsammlung,* Herbert Wichmann Verlag, Karistuhe, ISBN 3-87907-236-1.

Lanzac de Laborie, L. 1905. *Paris sous Napoléon (T.II : le numérotage de Paris: anarchie du système révolutionnaire.* p. 108).

Larsson, G. 1991. Land Registration and Cadastral Systems. New York: Longman Scientific and Technical.

Lavedan, P. 1952. *Histoire de l'urbanisme. Epoque contemporaine : projet de numérotage "métrique" de l'architecte Huvé (an X) ; institution du système actuel* (Decree of 1805.) H. Laurens.

Lazare, F & L. 1855. *Dictionnaire administratif et historique des rues et monuments. Numérotage impérial et opération de régularisation prescrite par Rambuteau* (p. 126). Paris. *Revue municipale.*

Leblond, A.S. 1797. *25 brumaire year IX. Numérotage des rues de Paris. Projet de "numérotage métrique," consistant à placer, de dix en dix mètres, des plaques indicatives de ces longueurs, qui identifieraient en même temps les emplacements des maisons. Journal des bâtiments et des arts,* n°142.

Lelarge, A. 1920. *Le numérotage des maisons de Paris sous Louis XVI et pendant la Révolution. Bull. de la Sté de l'histoire de Paris.*

———. 1933. *Le numérotage des maisons de Paris sous Louis XVI. privilège du 2 juin 1779 accordé à Kreenfelt de Storks.*

Léry, E. 1918. *Les Anciens numérotages de Paris et de Versailles. Bull. Ville de Paris.* January 59, p. 162.

Levallois, J.J et al. 1988. *Mesurer la terre. 300 ans de géodésie française ; de la toise du Châtelet au satellite. Ecole nationale des Ponts et chaussées. Association Française de Topographie.*

Ljung, P., and Farvacque-Vitkovic , C. 1988. "Addressing the Urban Challenge: A Review of World Bank FY87 Water Supply and Urban Development Operations." Infrastructure and Urban Development Department Report INU 13. Washington, DC: World Bank.

Massard, A. 1959. *Question écrite …. pour obtenir l'abaissement systématique des plaques de numéros.*

Merruau, Ch. 1862. *Rapport sur la nomenclature des rues et le numérotage des maisons de Paris.* De Mourgues.

Michaux, L. 1901. *Communication relative au numérotage des rues. Comm. municipale du Vieux Paris;* 1901 p. 183.

Milenkovic, B.C. 1998. Belgrade, People and Streets (Beograd, Ljudi i Ulice). Beostar Beograd.

Morris, A.E.J. 1979. *History of Urban Form.* George Godwin Limited.

Nichols, S. 1993. Land Registration: Managing Information for Land Administration. Technical Report 168. University of New Brunswick, Canada.

Ordonnance du Roi. 1768. *Ord. pour régler le service dans les places et dans les quartiers (numérotation dans toutes les villes, bourgs et villages sujets au logement des troupes). Archives Nationales* Fr. AD+978.

Organization of Surveying and Mapping in the Federal Republic of Germany. *Schriftenreihe 1993 des Deutschen Vereins für Vermessungswesen*, ISSN 0940-4260.

Poisson, G. 1964. *Napoléon et Paris. Aperçu du système de numérotage élaboré sous l'Empire* (p. 96). Berger-Levrault.

Pronteau, J. 1965. *Construction et aménagement des nouveaux quartiers de Paris.*

———. 1965. *Note sur les maisons parisiennes habitées ou possédées.*

———. 1966. *Les numérotages des maisons de Paris du XVe siècle à nos jours. Ville de Paris.*

Rambuteau. 1847. *Rapport de pour le renouvellement du numérotage des maisons de Paris* (Arch. Nat. F2 II Seine 22, *Voirie Urbaine*).

Renard, V. 2002. *L'improbable convergence des systèmes fonciers. Etudes foncières* – n°100.

Riviere d'Arc, H. 2001. *Nommer les nouveaux territoires urbains*, Paris. Unesco - *Maison des sciences de l'homme.*

Schenk, E. 1990. *Das Liegenschaftskataster in der Bundesrepublik Deutschland - Stand und weitere Entwicklung.* FIG-Kongreß 1990 Helsinki, ISBN 951-96097-0-9.

Sellier, L. 1917. *Vœu en vue d'obtenir de l'Administration des mesures propres à placer à une hauteur maximum de deux mètres les indications du nom des rues et des numéros des immeubles… Paris, Impr. Municipale.*

Simpson, S., and Rowton. 1976. Land Law and Registration. London: Surveyors Publications.

Taxil, L. 1904. *Ancien numérotage des maisons, Commission municipale du Vieux Paris*, 1904.

Thiam, N. 1998. "*Repérages sociolinguistiques dans les désignations de la ville de Dakar (Sénégal)" Parole*, no. 5-6.

Tribillon, J.F. 1994. "*Nouveau manuel d'aménagement.*" ADEF. *Etudes foncières.* Paris.

United Nations. 1973. Report of the Ad Hoc Group of Experts on Cadastral Surveying and Mapping. New York.

United Nations. 1985. Conventional and Digital Cadastral Mapping. Report of the Meeting of the Ad Hoc Group of experts on Cadastral Surveying and Land Information Systems. Economic and Social Council E/CONF.77/L.1.

Various. 1980. *Le Cadastre Sarde de 1730 en Savoie. Musée Savoisien*, Chambéry.

Vauthier, G. 1925. *Le numérotage des rues de Paris. Bull. de la Sté de l'histoire de Paris et de l'Ile de France.*

Vénard, J.L. 1986. "*25 ans d'intervention française dans le secteur urbain en Afrique noire francophone" DAEI.* Paris: Economica.

Vimont, M. 1931. *Essai sur les différents numérotages des maisons de la rue St. Denis Paris. Impr. des Orpbelins-apprentis d'Auteuil.*

Vincent, P. 2002. *Le Japon sac au dos* (on addressing in Japan).

Williamson, I. 1986. Cadastral and Land Information Systems in Developing Countries. The Australian Surveyor, Vol. 33.

World Bank. 1972. "Urbanization." Sector Policy Paper. Washington, DC: World Bank.

———. 1974. "Sites and Services Projects." Sector Policy Paper. Washington, DC: World Bank.

———. 1975. "Housing." Sector Policy Paper. Washington, DC: World Bank.

———. 1979. *World Development Report.* "Urbanization: practices and policies." Oxford University Press.

———. 1983. "Learning and Doing." Washington, DC: World Bank.

———. 1988. "Seminar on local development banks in the countries of Maghreb." Economic Development Institute (Infrastructure Division) and EM2IN and EMTIN Divisions of the Regional Bureau of the Orient and North Africa. Seminar notes.

———. 1990. *World Development Report.* "Poverty." Washington, DC: World Bank; New York: Oxford University Press.

———. 1991 "Urban Policy and Economic Development: An Agenda for the 1990s." World Bank Policy Paper. Washington, DC: World Bank.

———. 1992. *World Development Report.* "Development and the environment." Washington, DC: World Bank; New York: Oxford University Press.

———. 1994a. "Housing. Enabling Markets to Work." General Policy Document of the World Bank. Washington, DC: World Bank.

———. 1994b "Municipal Development." Sector Review. Urban Development Division. Washington, DC: World Bank.

———. 1994c. "Twenty Years of Lending in Urban Development, 1972-92: An OED Review." Operation Evaluation Department, Washington, DC: World Bank.

———. 1995a. "A Continent in Transition: Sub-Saharan Africa in the Mid 1990s." Africa region.

———. 1995b. *World Development Report, 1995.* "Infrastructure and Development." Washington, DC: World Bank; New York: Oxford University Press.

———. 1995c. "Round table on the financing of municipal investments in the countries of Maghreb." Economic Development Institute and Division MN1P1 of the Regional Bureau of the Orient and North Africa. Seminar notes.

Index